ST. MARY'S COLLEGE OF MARYLAND
ST. MARY'S CITY, MARYLAND
W9-BBC-175

GREAT LIVES OBSERVED

Gerald Emanuel Stearn, *General Editor*

EACH VOLUME IN THE SERIES VIEWS THE CHARACTER AND ACHIEVEMENT OF A GREAT WORLD FIGURE IN THREE PERSPECTIVES—THROUGH HIS OWN WORDS, THROUGH THE OPINIONS OF HIS CONTEMPORARIES, AND THROUGH RETROSPECTIVE JUDGMENTS—THUS COMBINING THE INTIMACY OF AUTOBIOGRAPHY, THE IMMEDIACY OF EYEWITNESS OBSERVATION, AND THE OBJECTIVITY OF MODERN SCHOLARSHIP.

LOUIS L. SNYDER *is Professor of History at the City College of the City University of New York. He has written numerous books on German history and on the meaning, characteristics, and development of modern nationalism.*

42394

GREAT LIVES OBSERVED

Frederick the Great

Edited by LOUIS L. SNYDER

The ox must plough the furrow, the nightingale must sing, and I—I must make war.

—FREDERICK II, KING OF PRUSSIA

PRENTICE-HALL, INC., ENGLEWOOD CLIFFS, N.J.

To James Royal Roseberry, Jr.

—Gentleman, philosopher, and cherished friend

Copyright © 1971 by Prentice-Hall, Inc.,
Englewood Cliffs, New Jersey.

A SPECTRUM BOOK

All rights reserved.
No part of this book may be reproduced
in any form or by any means
without permission in writing from the publisher.

Current printing (last number): 10 9 8 7 6 5 4 3 2 1

C–13-330605-4

P–13-330597-X

Library of Congress Catalog Card Number: 79-133053

Printed in the United States of America

Prentice-Hall International, Inc. (*London*)
Prentice-Hall of Australia, Pty. Ltd. (*Sydney*)
Prentice-Hall of Canada, Ltd. (*Toronto*)
Prentice-Hall of India Private Limited (*New Delhi*)
Prentice-Hall of Japan, Inc. (*Tokyo*)

Contents

Introduction 1

Chronology of the Life of Frederick the Great 8

PART ONE
FREDERICK THE GREAT LOOKS AT THE WORLD

1
Frederick on the Art of War 11

Military Instructions for the Generals, *11* Call to Arms: Frederick to His Troops before Battle, *17* Battle of Rossbach, 1757, *17* Battle of Leuthen, 1757, *18* Siege of Olmütz, 1758, *19* Explaining Defeat at the Battle of Kunersdorf, 1759, *20* War of the Bavarian Succession, 1778, *21*

2
Frederick as Ruler and Autocrat 23

On the Philosophy of Government and the Duties of Sovereigns, 1781, *23* Regulation on Using Simple Prose, 1740, *28* Order to Speed Up Lawsuits, 1745, *29* Refusal to Promote a Field Marshal's Son, 1748, *30* Reward for a Peasant Woman, 1748, *31* Conversation with a Soldier, 1760, *32* A General's Refusal of the King's Command, 1761, *33* Quicker Justice for the Citizens of Frankfurt, 1767, *34* Reminder to a Lady to Pay Her Debts, 1772, *35* Commutation of Two Death Sentences, 1776, *36* An Order for Economy, 1777, *37* Recommendation for More Humane Treatment for a Musketeer, 1781, *37* Response to a Petition by a Catholic Priest, 1785, *38* Protection for a Colonel's Widow, 1786, *39*

3

Frederick as Letter Writer **41**

The Sixteen-Year-Old Frederick to His Father, 1728, *41* Frederick's First Fan Letter to Voltaire, 1736, *42* An Acrimonious Exchange with Louis XV, 1745, *45* A "Victory Letter" to the Queen Dowager, 1757, *48* A Despairing Communication to Wilhelmina, 1757, *49* Frederick and Voltaire Correspond on the Virtues of Peace, 1759, *51* A Thank-You Letter to the Ex-King of Poland, 1760, *53* A Letter of Complaint, 1760, *54* A Soothing Letter to Voltaire, 1777, *55* A Final Message to the Duchess of Brunswick, 1786, *57*

4

Ideas and Ideology: Frederick as Advocate **59**

A Manifesto Defending Aggression, 1740, *59* Justification for the Silesian War, 1740, *61* A Celebrated Interview with Herr Professor Gellert, 1760, *63* Panegyric of Voltaire, 1778, *65* Contempt for German Language and Literature, 1780, *67*

5

Frederick's Will, 1769 **69**

PART TWO
THE WORLD LOOKS AT FREDERICK THE GREAT

6

The Early Days **74**

Frederick William's Instructions, 1719, *74* Attempt to Run Away, 1730, *76* The Hanging of Lieutenant Katte, 1730, *78* Frederick at the Wedding of Wilhelmina, 1731, *81*

7

Personality and Character as Observed by his Contemporaries **84**

Courage: The Prince Royal before His Baptism of Fire, 1734, *84* Impatience: Frederick Ready to Mount the Throne, 1734, *86* Dissimulation: Patron for Ballet Dancer La Barberina, 1744, *88* Military Genius: Battle of Hohenfriedberg, June 4, 1745, *89* Grief: Reaction on Death of His Brother, 1758, *92* Depression: Defeated at the Battle of Hochkirch, Frederick Contemplates Suicide, 1758, *94* Curiosity: A French Scholar's Account of Frederick's Personality, 1765, *96* Distress: Death of Prince Charles of Lorraine, 1779, *100*

8

Eyewitnesses on Life at Potsdam **101**

A British Visitor, 1740, *101* A Day at Potsdam, 1759, *102* A British General at Potsdam, 1774, *105* A British Visitor on Frederick at the Age of Sixty-Seven, 1779, *107*

9

Frederick in the Eyes of the Great Voltaire **109**

The First Meeting, 1740, *109* Voltaire's Sojourn in Berlin, 1750, *112* Beginning of the Maupertuis Affair, 1752, *114* The Publication of *Doctor Akakia* and a Broken Friendship, 1752, *117* Voltaire's Request for Sick Leave, 1753, *120* Voltaire's Declaration from a Prison Cell, 1753, *123*

10

Dr. Zimmermann on the Case of the Miller Arnold, 1779–1780 **125**

11

Contemporary Views on the Medical History of Frederick the Great **129**

Reader Catt on the Illnesses of Frederick during His Campaigns, 1758, *129* Dr. Zimmermann's Defense of Frederick against Accusations of Homosexuality, *132* Frederick's Desperate Call for Medical Help, 1786, *136* Dr. Zimmermann's Account of the Final Illness, 1786, *139* Count Mirabeau on Frederick's Last Days, 1786, *144*

PART THREE

FREDERICK THE GREAT IN HISTORY

12

Obituary from the *Annual Register*, 1786: "One of the greatest captains and masters of the art of war that ever lived." **146**

13

Macaulay's Unfavorable Estimate, 1842: "A tyrant of extraordinary military and political talents. . . ." 151

14

Thomas Carlyle's Romanticized Portrait, 1852–1865: "He is a King every inch of him." 155

15

W. F. Reddaway on Frederick and Three Great Phenomena of History, 1904: "By his single will he shaped the course of history." 158

16

Pierre Gaxotte on Frederick's Personality and Character, 1942: "He had extraordinary vivacity, exuberance of speech, transports of anger, and fits of violence." 161

17

George Peabody Gooch on Frederick as Benevolent Despot, 1947: "Without him there might have been no Bismarck. . . ." 165

18

D. B. Horn on the Transfiguration of Frederick, 1964: From "enlightened Prussian king . . . into the 'patron saint of Germany.'" 168

Afterword: Dazzling Success or Tainted National Hero? 173

Bibliographical Note 176

Index 179

Preface

The story of the Prussian Frederick II is of fascinating interest to those who take pleasure in the observation of great lives. This present contribution owes much to two institutions of personal import—the British Museum and my wife. The magnificent Reading Room of the British Museum yielded such gems over the years as Dr. Zimmermann's report on the king's "small mutilation" and Frederick's last will, both included here among other finds of the eighteenth century. To my wife, again and as usual, I express my thanks for her critical acumen and her delicate sense of style.

LOUIS L. SNYDER

Introduction

The subject of this "Great Life Observed" is inextricably linked with the history of Prussia. There was no "growth" of Prussia in the usual sense, for she represented no popular force, and she scarcely belonged to Germany either geographically or culturally. Her lone asset was a sense of ruthless power acquired in the process of dominating the Slavs. Yet, it was Prussia that impressed upon the remainder of what today is Germany a pattern of traditions that came to be recognized as universally German.

Of decisive import in the story of Prussia was the royal house of Hohenzollern. The ancestral home of the dynasty was a Swabian castle in the upper Nechar region, just north of Switzerland. In 1170, Conrad of Hohenzollern left home to seek his fortune with Frederick Barbarossa (Redbeard), head of that Hohenstaufen family dubbed by an unfriendly pope "the viper brood." Two centuries later, one of Conrad's descendants was awarded Brandenburg in the northeastern corner of the Germanies. Displaying its emblem, "From the Mountains to the Sea," the Hohenzollerns began to play a role in North Germany similar to that of the Habsburgs in the South. To consolidate and increase its territories by acquiring additional land became the dominating passion of this ambitious family.

Frederick William, the Great Elector (reigned from 1640 to 1688), was responsible for bringing efficiency and order to Brandenburg. He showed remarkable skill as an administrator while at the same time increasing the area of his dominions. As a youth he had spent four years at the University of Leyden in the Netherlands, where he became familiar with Western ideas. He centralized the administration of Brandenburg, organized a Council of State, established a new financial system, and encouraged commerce, industry, and agriculture. He built the Frederick William Canal joining the Oder to a branch of the Elbe and thereby created an outlet to the North Sea. Most important for the future of his state, he replaced his once undisciplined troops with an efficient national force. After Louis XIV's revocation of the Edict of Nantes in 1685, the Great Elector welcomed to his country more than 20,000 French Huguenots, whose skill and industry contributed much to the prosperity of his realm. He excused his absolute rule by saying that it brought unity, strength, and order. At his accession he had found a country with deserted villages, weakened agriculture, impoverished people, and demoralized commerce and industry. At his death Brandenburg was a prosperous state.

The son of the Great Elector, Frederick III (reigned from 1688 to 1713), lacked the qualities of his father. "Great in small things and small in great things," he allowed many reforms to lapse. He was dissatisfied with his title, Elector of Brandenburg and Duke of Prussia. He was said to have felt humiliated when, in an interview with King William III of England, he was obliged to sit in a chair without arms while the British monarch was comfortably seated in a magnificent armchair. By tradition it was necessary to obtain the consent of his liege lord, the Holy Roman Emperor, Leopold I, for a royal title.

An opportunity came in 1700, just preceding the War of the Spanish Succession, at a time when the emperor needed Frederick's support. In 1701, Leopold granted him the coveted dignity, but made the title read Frederick I, King *in* Prussia, thus sparing the feelings of the King of Poland, who still ruled West Prussia. At the same time, the bargain made it clear that Prussia remained outside the boundaries of the Holy Roman Empire. Later Prussian monarchs changed the title to King *of* Prussia.

The next Hohenzollern, Frederick William I (reigned from 1713 to 1740), began to build a large army and a subservient bureaucracy. A man of violent temper but phenomenal energy, Frederick William consolidated his government, practiced rigid economy, and encouraged commerce and industry. Miserly in other respects, he never hesitated to spend state funds lavishly for military purposes. His one great extravagance was his regiment of tall soldiers, for whom he was willing to pay high prices. He did not use his army for conquest, but he gave his son the means for making Prussia one of the first states of Europe.

The successor to Frederick William's throne is the subject of this "Great Life Observed." An effeminate young man, Frederick detested the monotonous drills that his hard-bitten father liked. Frederick William imposed a harsh discipline on his son. From this education, which included witnessing the execution of his best friend, royal Prince Frederick emerged sobered but embittered and skeptical. The young man who hated toy soldiers was destined to become one of the great warlords of history.

Frederick II (reigned from 1740 to 1786) enabled Prussia to compete with the Great Powers even though she lacked the size, population, and wealth to become one of them. He asserted his equality with the Austrian Holy Roman emperor, and he made Prussia the main rival of Austria in the Germanies. Some historians say that the cult of military force that he instilled in Prussia, and indirectly in Germany, set a standard that guided both Bismarck and Hitler and led Prussia-Germany to both the pinnacle of power and the nadir of defeat.

Frederick ascended the throne at the age of twenty-eight. Making shrewd use of his army, he insisted that the Austrian empress return the four Silesian duchies that Prussia had lost during the Thirty Years' War. When his demand was refused, Frederick invaded and annexed Silesia. He was not deterred by any moral or legal justification for his action.

Emboldened by Frederick's coup, Bavaria, supported by France, Spain, and Saxony, began the War of the Austrian Succession (1740–1748). Frederick entered and withdrew from the contest several times. By 1748, all parties were weary of the inconclusive struggle. The Peace of Aix-la-Chapelle recognized Maria Theresa as ruler of nearly all the Habsburg lands. But Frederick retained Silesia.

The Peace of Aix-la-Chapelle proved to be impermanent, for it was satisfactory neither to the French nor to the Austrians. Maria Theresa resented the agreement leaving Silesia to Frederick. The French, alarmed by Frederick's rapid rise, felt that their efforts in the war had not been rewarded. A renewal of the war seemed inevitable, but hostilities did not begin for another eight years. During this period, a rearrangement of political alliances occurred that amounted to a diplomatic revolution. Austria and France, convinced now that Frederick was a real menace, buried their long-standing differences, reversed their relations, and formed an alliance directed against Prussia; Russia and Sweden quickly joined the coalition. At the same time, England, whose interests in North America and India were threatened by French trade and colonization, entered into a treaty of alliance with Frederick. Thus England and France, both desiring to obtain maritime and colonial supremacy, changed sides in the alignment of European powers.

While the diplomatic maneuvers were being completed in Europe, the French and English began hostilities in India in 1751 and in North America in 1754. In Europe the war opened in 1756 with a sudden invasion of Saxony by Frederick II. Believing that Austria, Russia, France, Sweden, and Saxony were planning to attack Prussia from different directions, Frederick had requested Maria Theresa to give him an assurance that no such assault would be made. Receiving an evasive answer, he became convinced that the best defense lay in striking swiftly.

Frederick began the Seven Years' War in 1756, winning two brilliant victories at Rossbach and Leuthen (1757). It was an astonishing performance. Frederick was hailed as one of the great military geniuses of history. London was illuminated in his honor, and the English Parliament voted him a large monetary prize.

Then followed a long series of disasters. With inferior forces, Frederick tried desperately to exhaust and separate his opponents. In 1759, he suffered a defeat by the Russians and Austrians at Kunersdorf. By this time he was on the verge of ruin with 200,000 bayonets directed at him from all sides. From this predicament he was rescued by what he believed to be a miracle—the death of Czarina Elizabeth in 1762. Her successor, Peter III, was an admirer of Frederick. Not only did Peter make peace, but he also sent an army to help the Prussians. The coalition against Frederick evaporated. The Peace of Hubertusburg (1763) required Frederick to evacuate occupied Saxony, but he was allowed to retain Silesia.

The secret of Frederick's success as a military commander was his willingness to commit himself to battle. In this he presupposed Napoleon. Both were ready to take risks that others would have regarded as suicidal. To Frederick there were two essentials for success in war. The first essential was mobility. He drilled his troops to march fast and move speedily from column to line. He never hesitated to push them to the utmost. At Rossbach he had them march 150 miles in two weeks, a feat far beyond the capacity of the baggage-laden French army. Within another month he retraced his steps and smashed the Austrians at Leuthen.

The second necessity in Frederick's book for war was superior firepower. His Austrian enemies relied on old wooden ramrods which soon warped after use. Frederick saw to it that his men had iron ramrods for their guns. He ordered that they be trained relentlessly in loading and firing.

Added to his understanding of basic strategy was Frederick's ability as a tactician. He mastered the device of oblique order. After attaining local superiority at one point, he would shuttle from one spot to another, always taking care to see that the enemy could not concentrate his forces in overwhelming strength. He would strike, withdraw, move fast, hit again—always avoiding the big battle. These tactics brought him success against odds—and the reputation of a military genius. Actually, the key to Frederick's success was his full use of available military methods. He really added little to the art of war, but he was able to defeat his enemies by exploiting fully the conventional military means of the day.

Frederick returned from the Seven Years' War aged and weakened. He now set about the task of repairing the enormous damage of the war years. The great military tactician became the Great Administrator. Because many of his best soldiers had fallen in his campaigns, he induced thousands of colonists to settle in Prussia. He allowed the nobles to retain their large holdings, but he insisted that they rebuild the ruined farmhouses. He reduced taxes on free farmers but did not abolish serfdom. He reclaimed vast areas by draining swamps and introduced the cultivation of the potato as a cheap article of food. He gave assistance to commerce and industry and prevented the flow of money from Prussia. He built roads and waterways, including a canal connecting a tributary of the Oder with the Vistula River.

"The people," Frederick said, "are not here for the sake of the rulers, but the rulers for the sake of the people." An enlightened despot, he regarded himself as the first servant of the state. He regulated every detail of government and administration. He promoted elementary education, remodeled the judiciary system, and granted toleration to all religions. To eighteenth-century rationalists he was a kind of successful demigod—first in war, first in peace, and first in the hearts of his countrymen.

Frederick's weak health became worse in late 1775, when he was in his sixty-third year. The first of the new gout attacks came at the end of September and lasted about a month, after which the illness abated. When Frederick wrote to Voltaire on October 22, 1775, he added a few words about his illness: "Gout held me tied and garroted for four weeks—gout in both feet and both hands; and, such is its extreme liberality, in both elbows, too; at present the pains and the fever have abated, and I feel only a great exhaustion." By May 1776, the newspapers counted eighteen such attacks. Frederick's strength was much reduced and his health was a matter of concern to his friends.

On May 23, 1785, a young lad was standing by the Halle Gate in Berlin waiting to see Frederick as he returned from reviewing his troops. A large crowd awaited the monarch. Years later, in recording the scene, the eyewitness attributed the silence of the crowd to reverence. That may or may not have been true. As for Frederick himself, the old man was not attracted by either the plaudits or the silence of his fellow citizens. When told that the people were flocking to see their ruler, he replied: "Put an old monkey on a horse and send it through the streets and they would do just the same." Suffering from a catalog of illnesses as his life was drawing to a close, Frederick looked more and more to his dogs for comfort and companionship.

While there was life, Frederick neglected nothing, great or small. Impelled by decades of habit, he tried to carry on his normal routine as much as possible. He still worked many hours each day at affairs of state. He reread, revised, and annotated the literary works that he hoped would keep his name alive. Visitors came to Potsdam to observe him and to write glowing accounts of the great philosopher-king. But by mid-August 1786 the life cycle was near its end.

On August 16, 1786, Frederick lost his power of speech and fell into a coma. Surrounded by doctors, courtiers, and ministers, he slumbered fitfully. At midnight he woke and managed to ask his valet to place a quilt over his favorite dog. At 2 the next morning he gasped: "We are now over the hill. We are better now." A few minutes later he was dead.

Any judgment of Frederick depends on the attitude and prejudices of the individual. To his enemies he was the *Praeceptor Germaniae* in power politics, meant not as a compliment but to denote the father of that militarism that led Germany into two world wars in the twentieth century. Lord Roesbery compared Prussia to a pike in a pond, armed with sharp teeth and endless voracity, poised for a dart when proper prey should appear. Frederick, the greatest of the Hohenzollerns, was, in the view of his detractors, the founder of that aggressiveness that contributed to the tragedy of German history.

According to his critics, Frederick was a tyrant, a man of extraordinary military and political talents, conscientious and able, but nevertheless a despot. They condemned him as a dishonest man who did not hesitate to violate his plighted faith and to plunge all Europe into bloody, ruinous war. They excoriated him for his "rape" of Silesia, the partition of Poland, and other "unscrupulous" acts.

Other critics attacked Frederick for his supreme indifference to the German language, literature, and culture, all of which he underrated and failed to encourage. No national hero, it was said, should despise the language of his fatherland. Moreover, Frederick was censured because of his contempt for religion. Like Voltaire, he believed in a Supreme Being, who had created the world and then left it alone, but he had little use for organized religion. Such cynicism devalued Frederick in the eyes of his critics.

Most of Frederick's countrymen, on the other hand, accepted the title of *Praeceptor Germaniae,* but in a different context. They place him in the Valhalla of German heroes alongside Luther, Goethe, Beethoven, and Bismarck. "Old Fritz" was glorified in textbooks—all new German generations were taught to regard him as the father of his country. Heinrich von Treitschke, Germany's professor-patriot of the late nineteenth century, saluted Frederick as a great figure in German history. Frederick's conception of the state and fatherland imbedded itself in millions of German hearts. "The twelve campaigns of the Frederician epoch have impressed their stamp forever upon the warlike spirit of the Prussians and the Prussian army. A happy understanding existed between the King and the people, which was moved to the depths by the contemplation of true human greatness. . . . Gradually even the masses began to feel that he was fighting for Germany." Treitschke further reminded his readers that the great Goethe had called himself and his friends "Fritz-possessed." Frederick was truly, said Treitschke, the man of his century.

Between these two extreme views is the more moderate conclusion that Frederick was, indeed, a military genius and a great eighteenth-century administrator, representing both the potentialities and contradictions of his time. He made Prussia a model state of enlightened despotism, with all the strengths and weaknesses of that description.

Certainly Frederick regarded his personal power as a trust rather than a source of personal advantage. His achievement was important: at a time when there was little sense of unity among the diverse German states, he aroused in them a sense of common enthusiasm. In molding the greatness of Prussia, he laid the foundation for the later unification of Germany, even though Prussia was to collapse during the Napoleonic wars. Throughout his life he was bothered by his failure to reconcile his ethical and moral ideas as a philosopher with the harsh aggressiveness he found necessary as a military leader, between idealism on the one hand and realism on the other. He was not the only leader in history afflicted by this sort of tension.

Early in his career Frederick was called "the Great" by his subjects. In his case the term "historical greatness" is fair and reasonable: it was applied by his contemporaries as a reward for his military genius, his intensity of purpose, his devotion to duty, his self-discipline, and his love of his country.

This is the story of a strange and gifted man, the offspring of an overstuffed bully and a sensitive mother, a delicate prince who became one of the great military commanders and administrators of history. Frederick is presented here in three dimensions—through his own words, through the observations of his contemporaries, and through the judgment of historians. Within the framework of this special kind of treatment, the text is as chronological as possible.

For lovers of biography and for the curious history buff—good hunting!

Chronology of the Life of Frederick the Great

1712	(January 24) Birth of Frederick.
1713	Frederick's father becomes Frederick William I.
1730	Frederick tries to escape from his father; is imprisoned at Küstrin. Frederick William executes Lieutenant Hans Hermann von Katte. (November 19) Frederick released from prison.
1733	(June 12) Frederick marries Elizabeth Christina of Brunswick-Bevern. Retires to estate at Rheinsberg.
1739	Frederick writes *Anti-Machiavel*.
1740	(May 31) Frederick William I dies. Frederick II becomes king of the Prussians. First Silesian War begins; Prussia and Austria battle over Silesia. Start of War of the Austrian Succession.
1741	(April 10) Prussia defeats Austria at Mollwitz. (June 4) Prussia and France form secret alliance.
1742	(May 17) Prussia victorious at Chotusitz. Maria Theresa signs treaties of Breslau and Berlin. Frederick acquires Silesia and Glatz.
1743	(June 27) Britain's "Pragmatic Army" defeats France at Dettingen.
1744	(May 22) Frederick forms Union of Frankfurt. (July 15) Second Silesian War begins.
1745	(January 8) Maria Theresa forms Union of Warsaw. (May 11) France defeats "Pragmatic Army" at Fontenoy. (June 4) Frederick victorious at Hohenfriedberg. (September 30) Frederick victorious at Soor. Builds castle at Sans Souci. (December 25) Signs Treaty of Dresden with Austria.
1746	Frederick begins legal reforms.
1748	Treaty of Aix-la-Chapelle marks end of War of the Austrian Succession.
1750	Voltaire comes to Frederick's court.
1755	Austro-British alliance breaks down.
1756	(January) Frederick signs Convention of Westminster with Britain. Austria and France sign First Treaty of Versailles. Frederick invades Saxony. Third Silesian (Seven Years') War begins.

1757	(May 1) Austria and France sign Second Treaty of Versailles. (November 5) Frederick victorious at Rossbach. (December 5) Frederick victorious at Leuthen.
1758	(August 25) Frederick defeats Russians at Battle of Zorndorf. Sister Wilhelmina dies.
1759	Prussia defeated at Kunersdorf.
1760	Prussia victorious at Liegnitz and Torgau.
1762	(January 5) Elizabeth of Russia dies. (July 9) Frederick forms alliance with Peter III, who is deposed.
1763	(February 15) Treaty of Hubertusburg ends Seven Years' War. Prussia finally obtains Silesia.
1764	Frederick allies himself with Catherine II.
1769–70	Frederick meets Joseph II at Neisse and Neustadt.
1772–75	Prussia is equal partner in First Partition of Poland.
1778	Frederick fights his last campaign.
1780–81	Frederick loses the Russian alliance.
1785	Frederick sets up the League of German Princes.
1786	(August 17) Death of Frederick.

PART ONE

FREDERICK THE GREAT LOOKS AT THE WORLD

1 Frederick on the Art of War

You are to take care that they are not voluntary slips designed to lead you into a snare.

MILITARY INSTRUCTIONS FOR THE GENERALS

Frederick's chief trust was in his army. He was always willing to commit himself to battle—a characteristic which set him off from other commanders of his day. "War," he said, "is decided only by battles and it is not decided except by them." Placing primary emphasis upon mobility and firepower, he drilled his troops to march fast and swing quickly. Often he fought on several fronts simultaneously. Skilled in basic strategy, he was also an able tactician, invariably seeking to obtain superiority at one point and then moving to another.

Another secret of Frederick's military success was his attention to detail, indicated by this set of military instructions in his own words issued to his generals.[1] *Nothing of importance escaped his critical eye.*

Article XXIII: Why, and in What Manner, to Give Battle

A battle often decides the fate of kingdoms; and in the course of a war it may be necessary to bring on a decisive action, either to extricate yourself out of some difficulty, or to put an end to a quarrel which might otherwise terminate in the ruin of both parties.

A wise general will not give battle without having some important end in view; and if ever he is forced to it by the enemy, it is certainly

[1] From *Military Instructions Written by the King of Prussia for the Generals of his Army,* "translated by an officer" (London, 1763), pp. 146–75.

in consequence of some fault which he has committed, and which has rendered him no longer master of his own actions.

In this observation, it is obvious that I have not spared myself. In five capital battles which I have fought, three of them only were premeditated. At Mollwitz I was obliged to fight, because the Austrians had got between me and Wohlau, which contained my artillery and my subsistence. At Soar, they had cut off my communication with Trautenau, so that it was impossible for me to avoid a battle, without risking the entire ruin of my army. But the difference between such forced battles and those which are premeditated, is very apparent. How different were the consequences of that of Hohenfriedberg, of Kesseldorf, and Czaslau; the last of which procured us a peace.

While I am giving rules for fighting battles, I am not unmindful that I myself have often failed through inadvertence; but I would have my officers profit from my mistakes, and to know that I have endeavored to correct my errors.

It sometimes happens that both armies wish to engage; in that case every obstacle is speedily removed.

The most advantageous battles are those which you oblige the enemy to fight against his inclination; for it is a known maxim in the art of war, that you are constantly to endeavor to force the enemy to act contrary to his inclination, because, your interest being diametrically opposite to his, you are naturally to seek that which he wishes to avoid.

The principal reasons for giving battle are, either to oblige the enemy to raise the siege of a town, to drive him from the possession of a country, to penetrate into some province, to invest a fortress, or to oblige him to lessen the terms of accommodation in case he should be obstinate.

The means of forcing the enemy to fight are either by forced marches to get into his rear, to cut off his communications, or to threaten some town of importance. But in making these attempts, you are to be very careful, lest you expose yourself to those very inconveniences with which you endeavor to distress your enemy, lest you put it in his power to cut you off from your own magazines.

When you have formed a design to attack your enemy's rear-guard, you must encamp as near to him as possible, and as soon as he retires and attempts to pass a defile in your presence, you fall upon his rear with impetuosity. Such attacks are never attended with much loss, and are frequently very advantageous.

It is often the practice of generals to harass their armies to prevent the junction of two corps, when it is in the power of the enemy, by a single forced march, to frustrate all their labor. Nothing can be more unpardonable than to harass your people to no purpose.

In the course of a campaign it will sometimes happen, that the faults of your enemy may invite you to engage contrary to your intention; but you are to take care, that they are not voluntary slips designed to lead you into a snare.

To these reflections I will add, that it is our interest to carry on our wars with great spirit and alacrity, to prevent their continuing too long; because a tedious war must relax our excellent discipline, depopulate our country, and exhaust our finances: therefore it is the duty of every Prussian general to endeavor to the utmost of his abilities to bring matters to a speedy issue. He must not follow the example of Marshal Luxembourg, who when his son was for taking another town, answered him in these words: "What, would you have us return home and plant cabbages?" Let them rather recollect the words of Sannerib the Hebrew: "It is better that one man perish than a whole people."

In the account of the battle of Senef, you will find a striking instance of taking the advantage of an enemy's misconduct, where the Prince of Condé fell upon the Prince of Orange's rear, in consequence of the Prince of Waldeck's having neglected to occupy a defile, which would have secured his rear in their retreat. The battle of Raucouz affords another example of this kind.

Article XXIV: Of Accidents, and Unexpected Events in War

This would be a very long article, if I were to treat of all the accidents that may possibly happen to thwart a general of an army. Great abilities, with a little good fortune, will sometimes remove all difficulties.

The commander of an army is, in one respect, very disagreeably situated. He is very often condemned without being heard. Every gazette takes the liberty to expose his actions to the judgment of the meanest vulgar; and among the thousands who condemn him, there is hardly one man capable of conducting the smallest detachment.

I do not mean to justify those generals who have made flagrant mistakes; I will not vindicate my own campaign in 1744: yet among many faults, the Siege of Prague, my retreat and defence of Kolin, and also my retreat into Silesia were tolerably conducted. But there are many unfortunate events, which no human skill or foresight can possibly prevent. . . .

If sickness should invade your camp during your operations, you will soon be reduced to act defensively, as was my case in Bohemia in 1741, owing to the bad provisions with which the army had been supplied.

At the battle of Hohenfriedberg I sent one of my aide-de-camps with orders to the Margrave Charles, who was the oldest general, to put himself at the head of the second line, General Kalckstein having been detached to the right wing against the Saxons. This aide-de-camp mistaking my orders, told the Margrave to form a second line of the first.

Happily I perceived the blunder in time enough to prevent its consequences.

Hence it is of the utmost importance for the commander of an army, not only to give proper directions, but also to have an eye to their execution. If a general commanding a detachment should be taken ill or be killed, your project may be entirely disconcerted. An army acting offensively requires brave and able generals. The number of these is very small. I have many brave officers; but few generals of great abilities. . . .

Treason in an army is certainly the greatest misfortune that can befall it. Prince Eugene, in the year 1733, was betrayed by General St——, who suffered himself to be corrupted by the French. I myself lost Cosel by the treachery of an officer of the garrison, who deserted to the enemy, and conducted them to the place.

From these considerations it follows, that we ought not to presume too much upon our good fortune, even in the midst of success, since all our foresight and knowledge may be rendered ineffectual by chance and accident, which, by I know not what destiny, so frequently interferes, possibly with a design to correct the presumption of mankind.

Article XXV: Whether It Be Absolutely Necessary for the General of an Army to Call Councils of War

Prince Eugene used to say, that a general who had no mind to fight, need only call a council of war; and it is very certain, that in these meetings the question is generally carried in the negative: even secrecy, which is the very soul of war, is but seldom strictly observed.

A general, whom his sovereign has entrusted with the command of an army, ought to act in consequence of his own opinion, in which he is sufficiently authorized by the confidence which is reposed in him. Nevertheless I am of opinion, that he ought not entirely to reject the advice even of a subaltern, provided, after mature deliberation, it seems reasonable. In that case, he ought to forget the rank of him who started the hint, and act as if it had been his own.

Article XXVI: Maneuvers of an Army

It will appear from the maxims which I have laid down in this work, upon what system are built the evolutions which I have introduced in my army. The principal object of these maneuvers, is to gain time on every occasion, and to bring every engagement to a more speedy decision than was formerly the case; but particularly to bear down the enemy by the impetuosity of our cavalry: for thus even the coward, swept along by the violence of the brave, is compelled to do his duty, and every individual becomes useful.

I flatter myself, therefore, that all my generals, being convinced of the necessity and advantage of discipline, will do their utmost to preserve it, by keeping our troops in constant exercise, as well in time of war as in time of peace.

I shall never forget the words of Vegecius, who with a true military enthusiasm says: *"And at length, the discipline of the Romans triumphed over the strength, cunning, and numbers of barbarous nations, and subdued all the known world."* The entire prosperity of every state rests upon the discipline of its army.

Article XXVII: Of Winter Quarters

The campaign being finished, we are to think of winter quarters, the arrangements of which are to depend upon various circumstances.

Our first business is to form the chain of troops which is to cover our quarters. This is done, either behind a river, under cover of a range of strong posts, or under protection of fortified towns.

In the winter of 1741 and 1742, that body of my troops which quartered in Bohemia, had the Elbe in front. The chain which covered them began at Brandeis, and passing by Nienbourg, Kolin, Podjebrod and Pardubitz, terminated at Königgrätz.

But it must be remembered that rivers may be frozen over, and therefore are not to be depended on. You will have the precaution to intersperse along the chain a number of Hussars, who are to be constantly attentive to the motions of the enemy, and to make frequent excursions in order to observe whether he is assembling troops or continues quiet in his quarters: But besides the chain of infantry, it is also necessary that you should post at proper distances several brigades of cavalry and infantry, to be ready to support any part that may be attacked. . . .

With regard to subsistence of the troops in winter quarters, observe the following:

If circumstances are such, that you are obliged to winter in our own country, the officers are to be allowed a gratuity proportioned to their usual *douceurs,* and the private men are to receive their meat and bread gratis.

Your winter quarters being in an enemy's country, the commander-in-chief shall receive 15,000 florins; the generals of horse and foot, each 10,000; lieutenant-generals 7,000; and major-generals 5,000; the captains of horse, each 2,000; those of foot, 1,800; and the subalterns 100 ducats. The men are to receive meat, bread, and beer, which are furnished by the country, but no money, for that encourages desertion.

The commander-in-chief will take care, that these orders are regularly complied with, and that no pillaging be suffered; but there is no necessity for being too strict, with regard to any trifling profit which the officers may make.

If the army is quartered in an enemy's country, the commander-in-chief is to take care that he is supplied with the necessary number of recruits. He will divide the province into a certain number of circles, allotting so many regiments to each, in proportion to the number of people, in the same manner as we enroll our recruits in our own dominions.

If the states of the country are willing to furnish recruits, so much the better; but if they refuse, you must have recourse to violence. You must insist on their being delivered early in the winter, that you may have time to make soldiers of them before the spring. But this need not hinder the captains from sending out recruiting parties.

As the commander-in-chief ought to inspect the whole economy of his whole army, he must not forget to see that the horses for the artillery and provisions which are the tribute of the country are regularly furnished, either in kind or ready money. He will not fail likewise to see that the contributions are punctually paid into the military chest. It is the custom also, to make the country repair your wagons, and every other part of the apparatus of your army.

Moreover, it is expected, that the general should carry his attention so far, as to be assured that the officers of cavalry have caused their saddles, bridles, boots, etc. to be examined and repaired; and that those of the infantry are sufficiently supplied with shoes, stockings, shirts, and garters, for the campaign. The tents and blankets of the soldiers are likewise to be repaired. The cavalry are to furbish their swords, the infantry to examine and mend their arms, and the artillery to provide them with a sufficient number of cartridges.

The general will also take care, that the infantry, which forms the chain, are in no want of powder and ball, and in short, that nothing is wanting through the whole army.

If time will permit, the general would do well to visit his outquarters, and examine the situation and condition of each, that he may be assured, that the officers do not neglect their duty. It is not only expected that they should exercise the recruits, but all the troops under their command. There is nothing so destructive to an army as idleness.

Before the opening of the campaign, you will change quarters, so as to cantoon your troops in order of battle; viz. infantry in the center and cavalry on each wing. These quarters of cantoonment are to extend about nine or ten leagues in front, and about four in depth. But immediately before you take the field, you will contract them a little.

In quarters of cantoonment, the army should be divided and disposed under the immediate command of the six oldest generals. For instance, one commands the cavalry of the right wing, another that of the left, and so on. By this means, all orders from the chief will be more expeditiously conveyed, and the troops will more easily form their columns, when they are to take the field.

Before I quit this subject, it is necessary to warn you against precipitately establishing your winter quarters, before you are quite certain that the enemy's troops are entirely separated. I would have you often to recollect what happened to the Elector Frederick William, when he was surprised by Turenne, in his quarters in Alsace.

CALL TO ARMS: FREDERICK TO HIS TROOPS BEFORE BATTLE

If the main secret of Frederick's success as a military leader was his willingness to accept battle, another was his concern for the morale of his officers and men. Like other conquerors in history, he reserved his most eloquent words for addresses to officers and troops before battle.

Battle of Rossbach, 1757

Now fight like brave men, and trust for success in God.

The Seven Years' War commenced with a bold coup for Frederick in 1756, but by the next year the weight of enemy resources began to be felt. The campaign of 1757 began badly, but by the end of the year, Frederick was to win two important victories, defeating the French and Imperial armies at Rossbach and the Austrians at Leuthen. At Rossbach, the French army was commanded by Prince Rohan de Soubise, the same Soubise who had conquered Alsace and ravaged the Palatinate. Allied with him was the commander of the Imperial armies, Joseph Frederick William, Duke of Hildburghausen. The Allies joined in Thuringia with the goal of liberating Saxony.

With only one part of his army of 22,000 men, Frederick advanced on the enemy. There are some differences among historians as to the size of the Allied forces: estimates vary from 41,000 to 60,000, but the enemy Imperial army had an advantage of at least two-to-one. Before the battle Frederick addressed his troops with the following words.[2]

The hour is now come, my friends, in which every thing that is, or ought to be dear to us depends upon our arms and our conduct. Time allows me to say but little, and many words are unnecessary.

[2] B. H. Latrobe, *Characteristics, Anecdotes, and Miscellaneous Papers Tending to Illustrate the Character of Frederic II, Late King of Prussia* (London, 1788), pp. 221–22. Hereafter cited as *Miscellaneous Papers.*

You all know that you have suffered no fatigue, no hunger, no cold, no watching, no danger that I have not shared with you, and you now see me ready to sacrifice my life with you and for you. All I desire of you, is the return of that affection and fidelity, which you may be assured of, on my side. I will now only add, not as an encouragement to you, but as a proof of my gratitude for your past services, that from this hour, to the day you get into winter quarters, your pay shall be doubled.—Now! fight like brave men, and trust for success in God.

Battle of Leuthen, 1757

Always remember that you are Prussians.

After Rossbach came the turn of the Austrians. Here again Frederick showed his talent for leadership. He knew that he could depend on his enthusiastic troops and loyal generals. The final words to his officers before the battle of Leuthen show him at his propagandistic best.[3] *In precise phrases he outlined the seriousness of the situation. He urged any general who was unwilling to share the danger with him to depart without any reproaches. The enemy would be defeated "or we shall all lie buried under his batteries."*

Gentlemen,

You are aware that Prince Karl of Lorraine has succeeded in taking Schweidnitz, defeating the Duke of Bevern and making himself master of Breslau. This was done while I was engaged in halting the advance of the French and the Imperial forces. A part of Schleswig, my capital, and all the military supplies it contained, are lost. I should feel myself in a most difficult position, indeed, were it not for my unlimited confidence in your courage, your constancy, and your love for the Fatherland, all of which you have proved to me on many occasions in the past. Your services to me and to the Fatherland have touched the deepest fibers of my heart. There is hardly one of you who has not distinguished himself by some outstanding deed of courage; hence, I flatter myself that in the approaching opportunity you will not fail in any sacrifice that your country may demand of you.

This opportunity is now close at hand. I feel that I have accomplished nothing if Austria retains Schleswig. I tell you now that I propose to attack wherever I find the army of Prince Karl, three times as large as ours, in defiance of all the rules of the art of war. There is no question of the numerical superiority of the enemy or the impor-

[3] Adapted from M. Schilling, *Quellenbach zur Geschichte der Neuzeit*, 2nd ed. (Berlin, 1890), p. 274.

tance of the positions they have gained. I hope to overcome all this by the devotion of my troops and by the careful implementation of my plans. I must take this step, else all will be lost. We must defeat the enemy, or we shall all lie buried under his batteries. This I believe. So shall I act.

Pass on my decision to all officers of the army. Prepare the troops for the trials that are to come. Tell them that I expect blind obedience. Always remember that you are Prussians and that you cannot fail to show yourselves worthy of that distinction. If there be any one among you who fears to share with me any and all danger, he shall be given his discharge immediately without any reproaches from me.

[*Pauses.*]

I was convinced that no one of you would desire to leave me. I count, then, absolutely, on your faithful assistance and on certain victory. If I do not return to reward you for your devotion, the Fatherland itself must do it. Return now and repeat to your troops what you have heard from me. . . .

If any regiment of cavalry does not attack the enemy immediately upon given orders, it will be unmounted at once after the battle and made a garrison regiment. Any infantry battalion that hesitates, no matter what the danger may be, shall lose its colors and swords and shall have the gold lace stripped from its uniforms.

And now, gentlemen, farewell. Before long we shall either have defeated the enemy or we shall see each other no more.

Siege of Olmütz, 1758

I shall march towards the enemy.

After defeating the Austrians at Leuthen, Frederick campaigned in Moravia, but was not successful in his goal of seizing Olmütz. During the siege of Olmütz in early 1758, the enemy surprised his forces and at Domstädtel captured a supply of ammunition and artillery being sent from Silesia. When he got news of this unexpected coup, Frederick ordered all his commanding officers to attend him in his headquarters at Schmirsiz. When they were assembled, Frederick talked to them with these biting words.[4]

Gentlemen! The enemy has found an opportunity of taking away the supplies I expected from Silesia. This unfortunate accident obliges me to raise the siege of Olmütz. But my officers are not, on this

[4] *Miscellaneous Papers*, pp. 214–15.

account to suppose, that everything is lost. No! they may be assured, that I will repair this loss in such a manner, that our enemies will not easily forget it. I therefore now desire of all my officers, that they encourage their men, and not suffer any of them to murmur. I hope that none of my officers will show the least discontent: for should I perceive the least symptom of dissatisfaction in any one of them, I shall punish it severely. I now intend to break up, and put my troops into motion: I shall march towards the enemy; and wherever I find him, I will fight and beat him, let him be posted as he will, let him be covered by one or more batteries.—But, (*continued he, rubbing his forehead with the head of his cane*) I will, however, never act without consideration and prudence. I am likewise convinced that all my officers, as well as private soldiers, will do their duty, as men of courage and skill, as they hitherto have done.

Explaining Defeat at the Battle of Kunersdorf, 1759

You can imagine, my dear sir, the confusion and consternation of my troops.

During the first three years of the Seven Years' War, Frederick successfully utilized fast-breaking tactics, but in 1759 he found his army too weak to move to the offensive. It was necessary, he felt, for the other side to attack first. He did not have to wait long. This time the Russians, under a new general, Count Peter Semyonovich Saltykov, again advanced into Brandenburg. They defeated the Prussian general, Wedell, at Kay on July 23, 1759. When Frederick tried to prevent a Russian union with the Austrians, he suffered a major defeat at the battle of Kunersdorf on August 12, 1759. The Austrians then captured Dresden. Frederick lost control of all Saxony, on which he had relied for supplies. In the following passage he described the rout at Kunersdorf to his reader Catt (see page 129).[5] At the same time he wrote to a friend that he was preparing to die like a king. At this delicate moment the Russians and Austrians disagreed on the next move, and the Russians retired from Brandenburg.

I think you will give more credit to what I shall tell you; this is the truth: having gathered round me all the troops I could, you perceive that I had no time to lose in endeavoring to beat the Russians. Saxony defenseless, the army of the Empire which could easily penetrate as far as Berlin, General Haddick who had occupied the camp

[5] *Frederick the Great, Memoirs of his Reader, Henri de Catt, 1758–1760,* trans. F. S. Flint (London, 1916), II, 163–65. Reprinted by permission of Constable and Company, Ltd.

of Müllrose and who could easily march on the capital, all these considerations, my dear sir, forced me to act with the greatest celerity. It is not true that I tried to push too far the advantages which I had gained over the enemy; as everything was happening exactly as I could wish, I naturally sought to take advantage of the goodwill of my troops. We had completely smashed their left wing, which fell back through a deep ravine until it was behind Kunersdorf. Our first battalions which pursued the enemy through the ravine went forward into this ravine with perhaps too much ardor and some disorder; the other battalions, following too closely and with too much rapidity, were in difficulties, when the Prince of Württemberg, impatient at his idleness, charged the Russian infantry at an inconvenient moment, was repulsed, and threw our troops into disorder; and Loudon, letting loose his cavalry right and left, plunged our troops into confusion, and they fled in the greatest disorder.

You can imagine, my dear sir, the confusion and consternation of my troops. At the mere sound of the Cossacks, the battalions which were formed up in a good position fled some distance, without our being able to reach them and stop them. It would have been all over with us, my friend, if the Russians and the Austrians, taking advantage of their success, had pursued my poor, disheartened troops; but being content with their own self-congratulation on their success and their good fortune, they gave me time to recover; and I, poor devil, who, on the night of the action, had not 6,000 men, had 28,000 at the end of a few days. It is false, you may be assured, that we had, as you were foolishly told, 20,000 men killed, wounded and prisoners. My losses amounted to 10,000 men only all told: my enemies lost 24,000, and this must be so, since they acknowledge it.

All this turned out better than I dared to hope. Thus all the evil as well as all the good which we fear or hope never comes about. I will not tire you with an account of all the means I used to drive off the Russians, to prevent them from besieging Glogau, and to force them to go back into Poland. This would take too long for the moment; but I will read you what I composed. You will see that I did not lose my time, and you will be all the more grateful to me because I was rather ill after the loss of our terrible battle. If it is not so good as it might have been, blame that accursed attack of gout, which gave me a good deal of suffering, and the effects of which I still feel.

War of the Bavarian Succession, 1778

I rely in my future operations entirely upon your well-known zeal for my service. . . .

In 1778, Frederick was sixty-six, but there was still fire in the old warhorse. At this time he turned his entire attention to the question of Bavarian succession. Maximilian Joseph of Bavaria died childless in 1777, and Joseph II of Austria laid claim to about one-third of the Bavarian electorate. Angered at this attempt to upset the territorial balance in southern Germany, Frederick combined with his old enemy Saxony to wage war against Austria. On April 5, 1778, he assembled his generals and gave them the following talk.[6]

Gentlemen!

I have called you together for reasons that concern us all. Most of you have served the greatest part of your lives with one another, and with me; we are grown greyheaded in the service of our country, and we therefore know best ourselves the dangers, difficulties and glory in which we have shared. I have no doubt, but that all of you as well as myself, abhor the spilling of innocent blood, but the danger with which our country is at present threatened, renders it our duty, and makes it even necessary, that we endeavor by the most effectual and most immediate measures to dispel the storm which seems ready to break over our heads. I rely in my future operations entirely upon your well-known zeal for my service, and I shall acknowledge it with gratitude as long as I live. But at the same time I require of you, that you look upon it as your most sacred duty, to show kindness and mercy to our enemies, and to attend in the strictest manner to the keeping up of a rigid discipline among the troops under your command. . . .

The armies never clashed in this "potato war," so-called because each side tried to live off the other's supplies, Austria was soon isolated diplomatically and by the Treaty of Teschen (1779) relinquished her claims to Bavaria.

[6] *Miscellaneous Papers*, pp. 222–23.

2

Frederick as Ruler and Autocrat

Frederick retained his father's system in governing Prussia. An absolute ruler, he considered the state to be a kind of pyramidal structure with himself at the apex. He made all the major decisions—the keynote to his rule was obedience to royal authority. Frederick worked hard to maintain a smooth-functioning governmental structure. He watched every conceivable development, read all the dispatches from his diplomatic agents, discussed business affairs with secretaries, ministers, and local administrators, and personally read all petitions from both highborn and lowly citizens. Nothing was too small to merit his attention. Only reluctantly did he delegate power to others: he wanted to do everything himself.

ON THE PHILOSOPHY OF GOVERNMENT AND THE DUTIES OF SOVEREIGNS, 1781

The sovereign is properly the head of a family of citizens, the father of his people.

In his Political Testament *(1752), Frederick presented his view of politics as "the science of always using the most convenient means in accord with one's own interests." In 1781, he developed his earlier ideas on politics more fully in an* Essay on the Forms of Government and on the Duties of Sovereigns.[1] *Writing as always in French, the elderly ruler revealed the ideas that had guided him in his career as sovereign and administrator. The* Essay *showed him to be something more than a talented dilettante in government. It was privately printed at first for the benefit of Voltaire and other* philosophes *all of whom Frederick wanted to understand that he was an enlightened as well as a competent ruler.*

[1] *Posthumous Works of Frederick II,* trans. T. Holcroft (London, 1789), V, 10–33.

. . . As to monarchical government, of this there are various forms. The ancient feudal government, which some ages since was almost general in Europe, was established by the conquest of the Barbarians. The general of a horde rendered himself sovereign of the conquered country, and divided its provinces among his principal officers; who, it is true, were subject to the lord paramount, and who supplied him with troops when required; but, as some of these vassals became equally powerful with their chief, this formed a state within a state; and hence a series of civil wars, which were the misfortune of the whole. In Germany, these vassals are become independent; in France, England, and Spain, they are suppressed. The only example that remains, of that abominable form of government, is the republic of Poland.

In Turkey, the sovereign is despotic: he may with impunity commit the most atrocious cruelties; but it also often happens, by a vicissitude common to barbarous nations, or from a just retribution, that he in his turn is strangled.

With respect to the true monarchical government, it is the best or the worst of all others, accordingly as it is administered.

We have remarked that men granted preeminence to one of their equals, in expectation that he should do them certain services. These services consisted in the maintenance of the laws; a strict execution of justice; an employment of his whole powers to prevent any corruption of manners; and defending the state against its enemies. It is the duty of this magistrate to pay attention to agriculture; it should be his care that provisions for the nation should be in abundance, and that commerce and industry should be encouraged. He is a perpetual sentinel, who must watch the acts and the conduct of the enemies of the state. His foresight and prudence should form timely alliances, which should be made with those who might most conduce to the interest of the association.

By this short abstract, the various branches of knowledge, which each article in particular requires, will be perceived. To this must be added a profound study of the local situation of the country, which it is the magistrate's duty to govern, and a perfect knowledge of the genius of the nation; for the sovereign who sins through ignorance is as culpable as he who sins through malice: the first is the guilt of idleness, the latter of a vicious heart; but the evil that results to society is the same.

Princes and monarchs, therefore, are not invested with supreme authority that they may, with impunity, riot in debauchery and voluptuousness. They are not raised by their fellow citizens in order that their pride may pompously display itself, and contemptuously insult simplicity of manners, poverty and wretchedness. Government is not intrusted to them that they may be surrounded by a crowd of useless people, whose idleness engenders every vice.

The ill administration of monarchical government originates in various causes, the source of which is the character of the sovereign. Thus a prince addicted to women suffers himself to be governed by his mistresses, and his favorites, who abuse the ascendancy they have over his mind, commit injustice, protect the most vicious, sell places, and are guilty of other similar acts of infamy. . . .

The sovereign is attached by indissoluble ties to the body of the state; hence it follows that he, by repercussion, is sensible of all the ills which afflict his subjects; and the people, in like manner, suffer from the misfortunes which affect their sovereign. There is but one general good, which is that of the state. If the monarch loses his provinces, he is no longer able as formerly to assist his subjects. If misfortune has obliged him to contract debts, they must be liquidated by the poor citizens; and, in return, if the people are not numerous, and if they are oppressed by poverty, the sovereign is destitute of all resource. These are truths so incontestable that there is no need to insist on them further.

I once more repeat, the sovereign represents the state; he and his people form but one body, which can only be happy as far as united by concord. The prince is to the nation he governs what the head is to the man; it is his duty to see, think, and act for the whole community, that he may procure it every advantage of which it is capable. If it be intended that a monarchical should excel a republican government, sentence is pronounced on the sovereign. He must be active, possess integrity, and collect his whole powers, that he may be able to run the career he has commenced. Here follow my ideas concerning his duties.

He ought to procure exact and circumstantial information of the strength and weakness of his country, as well relative to pecuniary resources as to population, finance, trade, laws, and the genius of the nation whom he is appointed to govern. If the laws are good they will be clear in their definitions; otherwise, chicanery will seek to elude their spirit to its advantage, and arbitrarily and irregularly determine on the fortunes of individuals. Lawsuits ought to be as short as possible, to prevent the ruin of the appellants, who consume in useless expenses, what is justly and duly their right. This branch of government cannot be too carefully watched, that every possible barrier may be opposed to the avidity of judges and counselors. Every person is kept within the limits of his duty, by occasional visits into the provinces. Whoever imagines himself to be injured will venture to make his complaints to the commission; and those who are found to be prevaricators ought to be severely punished. It is perhaps superfluous to add that the penalty ought never to exceed the crime; that violence never ought to supersede law; and that it were better the sovereign should be too merciful than too severe.

As every person who does not proceed on principle is inconsistent in his conduct, it is still more necessary that the magistrate who watches over the public good should act from a determinate system of politics, war, finance, commerce, and law. Thus, for example, a people of mild manners ought not to have severe laws, but such as are adapted to their character. The basis of such systems ought always to be correspondent to the greatest good society can receive. Their principles ought to be conformable to the situation of the country, to its ancient customs, if they are good, and to the genius of the nation.

As an instance, it is a known truth, in politics, that the most natural allies, and consequently the best, are those whose interests concur, and who are not such near neighbors as to be engaged in any contest respecting frontiers. It sometimes happens that strange accidents give place to extraordinary alliances. We have seen, in the present times, nations that had always been rivals, and even enemies, united under the same banners. But these are events that rarely take birth, and which never can serve as examples. Such connections can be no more than momentary; whereas the other kind, which are contracted from a unity of interests, are alone capable of exertion. In the present situation of Europe, when all her princes are armed, and among whom preponderating powers rise up capable of crushing the feeble, prudence requires alliances should be formed with other powers, as well to secure aid, in case of attack, as to repress the dangerous projects of enemies, and to sustain all just pretensions, by the succor of such allies, in opposition to those by whom they are controverted. . . .

If [a prince] be the first general, the first minister of the realm, it is not that he should remain the shadow of authority, but that he should fulfill the duties of such titles. He is only the first servant of the state, who is obliged to act with probity and prudence; and to remain as totally disinterested as if he were each moment liable to render an account of his administration to his fellow citizens.

Thus he is culpable, if he be prodigal of the money of the people, dispersing the produce of the taxes in luxury, pomp, or licentiousness. It is for him to watch over morals, which are the guardians of the laws, and to improve the national education, and not pervert it by ill examples. One of the most important objects is the preservation of good morals, in all their purity; to which the sovereign may greatly contribute, by distinguishing and rewarding those citizens who have performed virtuous actions, and testifying his contempt for such as are so depraved as not to blush at their own disorders. The prince ought highly to disapprove of every dishonest act, and refuse distinctions to men who are incorrigible.

There is another interesting object which ought not to be lost sight of, and which, if neglected, would be of irreparable prejudice to good morality; which is that princes are liable too highly to notice persons who are possessed of no other merit than that of great wealth.

Honors, so undeservedly bestowed, confirm the people in the vulgar prejudice that wealth only, is necessary to gain respect. Interest and cupidity will then break forth from the curb by which they are restrained. Each will wish to accumulate riches; and, to acquire these, the most iniquitous means will be employed. Corruption increases, takes root, and becomes general. Men of abilities and virtue are despised, and the public honor none but the bastards of Midas, who dazzle by their excessive dissipation and their pomp. To prevent national manners from being perverted to an excess so horrible, the prince ought to be incessantly attentive to distinguish nothing but personal merit, and to show his contempt for that opulence which is destitute of morals and virtue.

As the sovereign is properly the head of a family of citizens, the father of his people, he ought on all occasions to be the last refuge of the unfortunate; to be the parent of the orphan, and the husband of the widow; to have as much pity for the lowest wretch as for the greatest courtiers; and to shed his benefactions over those who, deprived of all other aid, can only find succor in his benevolence.

Such, according to the principles which we established at the beginning of this Essay, is the most accurate conception we can form of the duties of a sovereign, and the only manner which can render monarchical government good and advantageous. Should the conduct of many princes be found different, it must be attributed to their having reflected but little on their institution, and its derivatory duties. They have borne a burden with the weight and importance of which they were unacquainted, and have been misled from the want of knowledge; for in our times ignorance commits more faults than vice. Such a sketch of sovereignty will perhaps appear to the censorious the archetype of the Stoics; an ideal sage, who never existed except in imagination, and to whom the nearest approach was Marcus Aurelius. We wish this feeble Essay were capable of forming men like Aurelius; it would be the highest reward we could possibly expect, at the same time that it would conduce to the good of mankind.

We ought however to add that the prince who should pursue the laborious route which we have indicated would never attain absolute perfection; because, with all possible good will, he might be deceived in the choice of the persons whom he should employ in administration. Incidents might be depicted under false colors; his orders might not be punctually executed; iniquitous acts might be so concealed as never to arrive at his knowledge; and his ministers, rigorous and consequential, might be too severe, too haughty in their exactions. In fine, it is impossible a monarch should be everywhere, in an extensive kingdom. Such therefore is and must be the destiny of earthly affairs, that the degree of perfection which the happiness of the people requires, as far as it depends on government, never can be attained. Therefore, in this as in everything else, we must of necessity remain satisfied, with that which is the least defective.

The following selections give chronologically, in his own words, evidences of Frederick's attention to administrative details.

REGULATION ON USING SIMPLE PROSE, 1740

Otherwise his Majesty may be induced to extract with his own hand, one of these verbose memorials.

Executives at all stages of history have had to contend with the inflated but obscure official verbiage referred to by former U.S. Representative Maury Maverick as "gobbledygook," after the gobbling of turkeys. Frederick was well aware of this practice. In the following regulation directed to his Supreme Board and the secretaries employed in drawing up official papers, he made it clear that he wanted all such matters expressed in simple, understandable prose. This order gives a clue to Frederick's success as a ruler.[2]

His Majesty, the King of Prussia, our most gracious sovereign, etc., etc. has already frequently desired, that all official papers, questions, and memorials of his Supreme Board of Finances, War, and Domains, may not be drawn up in so prolix and verbose a manner as hitherto, but be made as concise and perspicuous as possible. But as this order has not yet been complied with, and as the questions which are daily sent in, are loaded with many obscure and unnecessary details and narratives, by the perusal of which his Majesty's time is wasted; his Majesty hereby commands his Supreme Board, etc. that the secretaries employed in expediting the said official papers, be directed to draw them up in a manner conformable to the orders and intention of his Majesty, and that the members of the Board themselves see to it. Otherwise his Majesty may be induced to extract with his own hand, one of these verbose memorials, which may be sent in, and draw it up as it ought to be, in order to show the Board the possibility of being clear, and at the same time concise.

FRÉDÉRIC

Potsdam
Sept. 26, 1740
To the Supreme Board, etc., etc.

[2] *Miscellaneous Papers,* pp. 19–20.

ORDER TO SPEED UP LAWSUITS, 1745

Very little strict justice is still to be met with in my dominions.

Frederick made many improvements in the administration of justice. He gave a free hand to Samuel von Cocceji, the author of the judicial reforms for which Frederick himself is often given credit. Cocceji had served as chief justice in the last years of Frederick William's reign, but had been prevented by the envy of his colleagues from introducing needed legal reforms.

On January 14, 1745, Frederick addressed the following order to his ministers, asking that there be reform in the matter of court delays.[3] *In consequence, the Supreme Court of Appeals made decisions on 560 suits in one year, and not one case from the preceding year remained on the list. From this point Cocceji went on to raise the standard of the judicature. In 1752, Frederick wrote of Cocceji's work: "One thing is certain. Injustice in the courts has become comparatively rare, the judges are less corrupt, trials shorter, and there are fewer cases pending."*

My dear Ministers of State, Messrs. von Cocceji, von Broich, and von Arnim,

It cannot but be still recent in your memories, that I have already made and published many orders and regulations, in order to prevent the ruinous delay of lawsuits. But as I still perceive that these orders and regulations, so far from having produced any good consequences, have been neglected, and that very little strict justice is still to be met with in my dominions, but that my subjects have the greatest reason to complain of the delay thereof; I herewith most graciously command you, to make this business, in which my subjects are so deeply interested, your first aim, to consider this the most important duty of your office, and to provide, that in all my courts of judicature such fixed and unalterable rules be established, that every suit, according to the circumstances attending it, may be forwarded and dispatched without delay, and, according to rigid justice, finished and decided within a year from its commencement. I herein depend entirely upon you. After mature deliberation, you will contrive such methods as are most likely to answer this end.

FRÉDÉRIC

Berlin
Jan. 14, 1745

[3] *Miscellaneous Papers,* pp. 21–22.

REFUSAL TO PROMOTE A FIELD MARSHAL'S SON, 1748

He must depend for fame and praise upon his own personal merit.

Frederick had set views on the matter of military promotion. When a Hanoverian field marshal requested that his son be made an officer because of high birth, Frederick judged it to be a ridiculous pretension and dictated the following answer.[4]

Noble and well-beloved,

I have considered the request of your letter, dated May 22, a.c.* and I must acquaint you, that I have a considerable time ago given orders, that no count shall ever be admitted to any considerable rank in my army: for commonly when they have served me a year or two, they leave the army and return home. If your son wishes to enter into my service, he must entirely forget that he is a count; and if he does not improve in his profession, he can never be advanced.

I am, etc., etc.

FRÉDÉRIC

The following was added in the king's own handwriting:

Young counts, if they learn nothing, are ignorant fellows** in every country. The son of the King of England is now a midshipman on board a man-of-war, in order to acquire a knowledge of the maneuvers of that service. If a count means to be of the least use to the world or to his country, he must renounce all pride arising from birth or titles (for these things are baubles) and he must depend for fame and praise upon his own personal merit.

FRÉDÉRIC

[4] *Miscellaneous Papers,* pp. 40–41.
* "This current year."
** German: *Ignoranten.*

REWARD FOR A PEASANT WOMAN, 1748

I will always keep the best I have for you.

Frederick made it a point to be accessible to his people at all hours and places because he believed their welfare was the state's welfare. Any peasant who came to Potsdam was asked whether he came to see the king or to make a complaint or request. Of course, most peasants were still serfs who could not approach their sovereign. The royal reputation was enhanced among the poor folk by tales of his Majesty's kindness to peasants. In the winter of 1748 to 1749, during one of Frederick's journeys through Silesia, the wife of a peasant living near Breslau presented the king with a basket of fruit. She was so touched by the graciousness with which he had received it that she decided to send him another the next year. The offer was accompanied by the following letter.[5] *Frederick replied by sending 200 crowns, "which I have also packed as well as I was able."*

Letter to Frederick

Most dear, and most clement, our lord the King,

As our fruit has not succeeded better this year than the last, you must condescend to receive it, such as it is. I and my husband have picked out the best we could find, and we have packed it up as well as we were able with straw and hay. We hope you will eat it in good health. May God give you a long life, in order that you may be able to come and see us for many years to come. I will always keep the best I have for you. I and my husband entreat you, therefore, to regard us with favor; especially, because our little bit of land produces less than it did, and that we have a debt upon it of 120 crowns, ten *groschen,* and six *fenin.* Moreover, we commend you to the protection of Almighty God; and we shall be, till death, and forever, of your Majesty,

the faithful and devoted subjects,

I and my husband

Frederick's Reply

Good mother,

I am much obliged to you for your fine fruit. If God grants health and life to me, I will return and see you a year hence. Keep something

[5] *Vie de Frédéric II,* trans. Lord Dover, *Life of Frederick the Second, King of Prussia* (London, 1832), I, 436–39.

for me, in order that I may find it when I come to you. With regard to what you tell me of your little bit of land being charged with a debt of 120 crowns, ten *groschen,* and six *fenin,* that is really a bad business. You should be very economical, otherwise your affairs will go back instead of advancing. I send you herewith 200 crowns, which I have also packed up as well as I was able. Pay your debts with them, and free your bit of land. Take care to economize as much as you are able: this is a counsel which I give you seriously, as your attached king,

FRÉDÉRIC

CONVERSATION WITH A SOLDIER, 1760

Oh, you blockhead! I'll sell you this ring for 500, and be a gainer by the bargain.

In early August 1760, toward the end of the Seven Years' War, Frederick's army, consisting of 30,000 men, was encamped near Schweidnitz, twenty-eight miles southwest of Breslau in Silesia. The Prussians were surrounded by Austrians and Russians to the number of 114,000. Frederick's position was desperate—his men had been marching for days, and there was little food.

Fatigued, Frederick, wrapped in his greatcoat, sat down upon the bare ground by one of the camp fires. A soldier of the regiment of Willersdorf observed him, and pulling off his own pouch, offered it to him as a pillow. Frederick lay down, and placed his head upon the pouch. But unable to sleep, he opened his eyes and entered into conversation with the soldier. He asked what country he came from, how long he had been in the service. At last, emboldened by the king's friendliness, the soldier ventured to ask several questions himself. The following conversation ensued.[6]

Soldier. Now, supposing your Majesty were taken prisoner, how could you be ransomed, considering that you are a king?

King. As a general, not otherwise.

Soldier. Hum! I can't think that; you are more than a general.

King. No, indeed, I am not. In my army, my rank is that of a general.

The soldier shook his head, and said, But they would get some valuable booty, were they to take your Majesty prisoner.

King. Upon my word they would not. I have not a penny about me.

[6] *Miscellaneous Papers,* pp. 205–6.

Soldier. Your Majesty must not think to persuade me of that. Shall I believe that you are entirely without money?

King. But I tell you, I am: I am not worth a farthing (*turning his pockets out*). There, you see it is as I said.

Soldier. That is indeed extraordinary. But—you have there a beautiful ring, and I dare say of very considerable value.

The king pulled off his ring, and showed it to the soldier. Well! what do you think it is worth? Guess!

Soldier. I fancy the ring may be worth some 10,000 dollars, or so!

King. Oh, you blockhead! I'll sell you this ring for 500, and be a gainer by the bargain.

Soldier. That I shall never believe. That's certainly not true.

King. Most undoubtedly it is. I will show you now its whole value. These small stones may perhaps be worth 300 dollars. The large stone in the middle is a topaz, worth at most thirty dollars; and besides the setting, which cost a trifle, there is nothing of value in the whole ring.

Soldier. Upon my honor, I should not have thought it.

The morning now began to break, and an adjutant came to make his report. The king rose, ordered him to give the soldier a *Frédéric's d'or,** and said, "There, you see that I have no money."

A GENERAL'S REFUSAL OF THE KING'S COMMAND, 1761

The money they bring I mean to bestow on our field hospitals.

In the fall and winter of 1760 to 1761, Frederick again and again denounced "the plunderings, riotous, and even disgusting savageries" perpetrated by his Saxon enemy. When his complaints to the Polish king went unanswered, Frederick determined on retaliation by sending his men to sequester the furniture of the Polish royal hunting lodge at Hubertusburg. That, he believed, would hit the Polish monarch "in the pit of his stomach." Frederick would use the money for his field hospitals. For the task he called in one of his distinguished officers, a General Saldern, one of the most exact and punctiliously honorable of his commanders. In a remarkable dialogue, Frederick got a flat refusal.[7] *It was a classic case of a conflict between a royal order and an individual conscience. Nothing remained for Sal-*

* About 18 shillings.

[7] Küster, *Charakterzüge des General-Lieutenant von Saldern* (Berlin, 1793), pp. 39–44, trans. in Thomas Carlyle, *History of Friedrich the Second, called Frederick the Great* (New York, 1866), VI, 121–22.

dern but to become ill and retire from the service. The order was carried out by another officer in a scandalous fashion.

King. Saldern, tomorrow morning you go with a detachment of infantry and cavalry, in all silence, to Hubertusburg; beset the Schloss, get all the furniture carefully packed up and invoiced. I want nothing with them; the money they bring I mean to bestow on our field hospitals, and will not forget *you* in disposing of it.

(Saldern, usually so prompt with his "*Ja*" on any order from the king, looks embarrassed, stands silent—to the king's great surprise—and after a moment or two says:)

Saldern. Forgive me, your Majesty: but this is contrary to my honor and my oath.

King (*still in a calm tone*). You would be right to think so, if I did not intend this desperate method for a good object. Listen to me: great Lords don't feel it in their scalp when their subjects are torn by the hair; one has to grip their own locks, as the only way to give them pain.

(These last words the king said in a sharper tone; he again made his apology for the resolution he had formed; and renewed his order. With the modesty usual to him, but also with manliness, Saldern replied:)

Saldern. Order me, your Majesty, to attack the enemy and his batteries, I will on the instant cheerfully obey; but against honor, oath, and duty, I cannot, I dare not!

(The king, with voice gradually rising, I suppose, repeated his demonstration that the thing was proper, necessary in the circumstances; but Saldern, true to the inward voice, answered steadily:)

Saldern. For this commission your Majesty will easily find another person in my stead.

King (*whirling hastily round, with an angry countenance*): *Saldern, Er will nicht reich werden* (Saldern, he refuses to become rich).

QUICKER JUSTICE FOR THE CITIZENS OF FRANKFURT, 1767

Make example of those judges by whose negligence justice is delayed.

Frederick believed it to be his most important task to fulfill honorably his duties as king. "The sovereign," he said, "must act honestly, with wisdom, and complete disinterestedness, as though at any moment he might be called upon to give an account of his administration to his fellow citizens." Above all it was necessary to maintain justice for all the people, rich and poor alike. He felt that the farmers-general of his domains were more protected by the provincial courts than they should have been, and that the complaints of his subjects against their cruel treatment were often disregarded, no matter what the justice of their cause. When he learned that a lawsuit by the citizens of Frankfurt, whose houses had been destroyed by fire, was delayed for three years, he sent this peremptory letter to his High Chancellor.[8]

My dear High Chancellor, M. von Jarriges:

In answer to your report, dated 23d instant, and to the postscript annexed, I acquaint you that, notwithstanding the many reasons you allege, why the suit of the citizens of Frankfurt, whose houses were destroyed by fire, has been delayed these three years, and is not yet decided; I am still of opinion that nothing can excuse or palliate a delay, by which those poor people, who have lost all means of subsistence, and who are still less able to re-establish themselves in their former dwellings, are completely reduced to want and beggary. This is not the only case in which I know that justice has been delayed; I have heard of several more: you will therefore do well to be particularly attentive to the dispatch of depending suits, to examine into the conduct of the different courts, and to *make examples of those judges by whose negligence justice is delayed.*

I am, etc., etc.

FRÉDÉRIC

Potsdam
Sept. 24, 1767

REMINDER TO A LADY TO PAY HER DEBTS, 1772

In every other respect, I am your gracious king.

Mounds of petitions and memorials came to Frederick each day. Any request, no matter how small, received his personal attention. He dispensed justice with an even hand. In October 1772, a lady deeply in debt presented a complaint to the king in which she brought the injustice of her creditors, who de-

[8] *Miscellaneous Papers*, p. 23.

manded interest upon the sums due them, to his attention. By custom, the German courts granted delays to debtors in order to give them time to settle their affairs, during which time none of the creditors could arrest the debtor. In some parts of Germany interest was allowed, but in most other areas the debtor was exempted from paying interest during this term. Frederick replied as follows to the aggrieved lady.[9]

Dear Madam,

The situation of your circumstances, represented to me in your complaint, dated 23d instant, excites my pity, but I can by no means protect you against your creditors in the manner you wish. The delay granted you, cannot excuse you from paying the full interest upon your debts, especially as it is granted with the express condition, that full interest shall be regularly and accurately paid; *and it is impossible for me, or any of my courts, to release you from this obligation. In a suit of this kind, no rank, no high birth, no respect of persons, has the least weight with me;* but in every other respect, I am your gracious king.

FRÉDÉRIC

Potsdam
Oct. 27, 1772

COMMUTATION OF TWO DEATH SENTENCES, 1776

I have great objections . . . to sign the sentence of death.

Frederick never forgot the nightmare of November 6, 1730, when his friend, Lieutenant von Katte, was led to the gallows and hanged (see pages 78–81). The experience gave him a lifelong distaste for executions. On April 23, 1776, when papers for a sentence of death on two young men were presented to him, he quickly ordered commutation.[10]

My dear Minister of State, Baron von Zedliz:

I have great objections in my own mind, to sign the sentence of death, pronounced by the court, against the incendiary Döpel. Both he and his accomplice Weiss are said to be still very young; and on

[9] *Miscellaneous Papers,* pp. 43–44.
[10] *Miscellaneous Papers,* p. 40.

that account it is my pleasure, that neither of them be executed, but that they be confined in the house of correction, and care be taken, that during their confinement, they be better instructed in their duty to society, and made sensible of the dreadful nature of their crime. You are therefore directed to have the warrant altered accordingly.

I am, etc., etc.,

FRÉDÉRIC

Potsdam
April 23, 1776

AN ORDER FOR ECONOMY, 1777

Try not to make the purchase dearer than is indispensable.

At Fordan, a small trading town in the Bromberg Department of West Prussia, there was a grain magazine run by a provisions-master named Bein. In the following royal cabinet order, Frederick advised Bein to take special pains on the purchase of wheat, for the king's eyes were upon him.[11]

Potsdam, April 1777

To the Chief Proviant-Master Bein, at Fordan:

His Royal Majesty of Prussia, Our most all-gracious Lord, lets herewith, to the Head Proviant-master Bein, the grain-prices table of the Bromberg Department be despatched; Wherefrom Bein perceives how low in some places these are, and that at Inovraclaw and Strezeltnow the bushel of rye costs about 14 pence: now, as it is so cheap there, the price in Poland must be still smaller; and therefore it is not to be conceived why the Poles demand such high prices.

Bein therefore is charged to take especial pains, and try not to make the purchase dearer than is indispensable.

RECOMMENDATION FOR MORE HUMANE TREATMENT FOR A MUSKETEER, 1781

Perhaps the fellow is melancholy.

No detail in the life of his musketeers and grenadiers escaped the notice of the Prussian ruler. How he handled the case of one

[11] Trans. in Carlyle, VI, 437–38.

of his soldiers who had attempted suicide is revealed in this letter to one of his high officers.[12]

My dear Major-General Baron von Keller,

I understand that a musketeer in your regiment, one Sutorius, is condemned to six years labor upon the fortifications, for having attempted to destroy himself, which sentence I think much too rigid. Few men in their sound senses will ever attempt to take away their own lives. Perhaps the fellow is melancholy, and endeavored to get rid of existence in a fit of this disorder. Upon this ground I do not confirm the sentence pronounced upon him by the court-martial, but direct, *that instead of being sent to labor upon my fortifications, he be blooded,* and every proper step be taken towards his cure; and that when this is accomplished, he be again taken into my service, admonished and encouraged to behave in future in a more proper and rational manner.

I am, etc., etc.,

FRÉDÉRIC

Potsdam
June 14, 1781

RESPONSE TO A PETITION BY A CATHOLIC PRIEST, 1785

How should heretics be capable of judging in the disputes of a monastery of Franciscans . . . ?

When, on August 3, 1785, Frederick read a petition from a Catholic priest, he replied that the decision belonged to the petitioner's superior, the vice-bishop of Breslau.[13] *In this case the vice-bishop had taken the office of Count von Schaffgotsch, the bishop, who had been obliged to leave the country because of various crimes and misdemeanors. Labeling himself a "heretic," Frederick apparently took some pleasure in witnessing difficulties of this kind.*

To Father Francis Pizner,

His Majesty the King of Prussia, our most gracious Sovereign, etc., etc., hereby acquaints Father Francis Pizner, in answer to his memorial

[12] *Miscellaneous Papers,* p. 30.
[13] *Miscellaneous Papers,* pp. 44–45.

lately received, that the decision of his business positively belongs to the vice-bishop of Breslau, M. von Rothkirch, and he can by no means decide in any question of this nature; *for how should heretics be capable of judging in the disputes of a monastery of Franciscans, concerning the violation of their vows?* There is therefore no other way, but to refer the business to the vice-bishop of Breslau, to whom it has already been reported.

FRÉDÉRIC

Potsdam
Aug. 3, 1785

PROTECTION FOR A COLONEL'S WIDOW, 1786

I will be a father to his children.

Frederick's feats on the battlefield would not have been possible without the fanatical loyalty of his officers and men. Links of sympathy between monarch and fighting troops were strong and endurable. Frederick made it a point to favor those who had served him. On January 21, 1786, he received news at Potsdam of the death of a Colonel von Troschke, for whom he had a special regard. He immediately ordered a letter to be written to the colonel's widow in which he expressed his grief upon losing so brave an officer. He promised to protect her and her family, and asked if her domestic circumstances required his assistance. He added the following lines.[14]

I honored your late husband, as a *specimen* of an excellent officer; but as he alas! is dead, I will be a father to his children; and show those favors which I intended for him, to them and their mother. Send me an exact statement of your circumstances, and I promise to contrive matters so, that the family shall be satisfied.

Frederick also provided for the daughters of the deceased colonel in Protestant convents in Westphalia.

I was glad to receive by your letter of yesterday, an exact account of your domestic concerns; after the loss of my brave colonel von Troschke. I shall now endeavor to give you convincing proofs of my

[14] *Miscellaneous Papers,* pp. 160–61.

favor and protection. I have ordered his salary as governor of Karzig, in Newmark, amounting to 500 dollars per annum, to be continued to you, as a provision for yourself and for the education of your children; and I shall take measures that the value of your estate shall between this and midsummer, be increased to the sum of at least 20,000 dollars. This will be to you and your family an indelible proof of the favor of your gracious king.

FRÉDÉRIC

Potsdam
Jan. 21, 1786

3

Frederick as Letter Writer

Frederick was an inveterate letter writer. Throughout his life he habitually turned to the pen to express himself in communications to the great, the near-great, and the lowly. Of the thirty volumes of his works, twelve are devoted exclusively to his correspondence. This section contains a selection of Frederick's letters illustrating the wide range of his interests and the variation of his moods.

THE SIXTEEN-YEAR-OLD FREDERICK TO HIS FATHER, 1728

I beg my dear papa to be kindly disposed toward me.

Relations between father and teen-age son were strained. Frederick William banished his son from his sight except at meals, where the prince royal was required to sit at the foot of the table. More often than not the young man would rise hungry because the dishes that reached him were empty. On occasion the angered father would hurl a soup plate at the head of his heir.

The sixteen-year-old Frederick decided on a desperate move. He composed and sent a pitiful message to his father.[1] *It was a naïve but sincere attempt to win his "dear papa's" heart, but it drove the monarch into a frenzy of anger. The coarse and brutal reply left a mark on the young man. Psychoanalysts today would probably attribute Frederick's hard and scornful character in his mature years to this kind of bullying from his father. This was a generation gap in its most brutal form.*

Letter from Frederick to His Father

Wüsterhausen, 11 September, 1728

For a long time I have not ventured to present myself before my dear papa, partly because I was advised not to do so, but mainly

[1] Quoted in Friedrich Förster, *Friedrich Wilhelm I, König von Preussen* (Potsdam, 1834–1835), I, 362.

because I anticipated an even worse reception than usual and was afraid to disturb my dear papa further by the favor I shall now ask. So I prefer to put it in writing.

I beg my dear papa to be kindly disposed toward me. I assure him that, after a long examination of my conscience, I find not the smallest thing with which I should reproach myself. But if, contrary to my wishes, I have disturbed my dear papa, I herewith beg him humbly for forgiveness, and I hope that my dear papa will forget the fearful hate which appears so clearly in his whole behavior and to which I find it hard to accustom myself. Until now I have always thought that I had a kind father, but I now see quite the opposite. Nevertheless, I shall take courage and hope that my dear papa will think this over and restore me once again to his favor. In the meantime, I assure him that I will never in my life willingly fail him, and, in spite of his disfavor, I shall remain with most dutiful and filial respect, my dear papa's

Most obedient and faithful servant and son,

FRIEDRICH

Frederick William's Reply

A naughty, obstinate boy, who does not love his father. When one has done his best, and especially when one loves one's father, one does what he wants one to do, not only when he is standing by but also when he is not there to see. Besides, you know very well that I cannot abide an effeminate fellow who has no manly tastes, who cannot ride or shoot (let it be said—to his shame!), is untidy in his personal habits, and wears his hair curled like a fool instead of cutting it. I have condemned these things a thousand times, yet there is no sign of improvement. For the rest, you are haughty, as indifferent as a country lout; you converse with no one outside of a few favorites, instead of being friendly and sociable; you grimace like a fool; you never follow my wishes out of love for me but only when you are forced to do so. You care for nothing but having your own way, and you think nothing else is of any importance. That is my answer.

FRIEDRICH WILHELM

FREDERICK'S FIRST FAN LETTER TO VOLTAIRE, 1736

Voltaire cannot be imitated except by Voltaire himself.

The extraordinary friendship between Frederick and Voltaire began when Voltaire was forty-two and Frederick was twenty-four. In a letter dated August 8, 1736, Frederick wrote more than

a thousand words of bad French to the French philosophe. *A sincere fan letter, it was full of praise and philosophical reflections. Enclosed with it was a French translation of some essays by Christian Wolff, a follower of Leibnitz. With these words began a friendship of four decades, broken by quarrels and recriminations (see pages 109–24).*[2]

Berlin, 8th August, 1736

Sir,

Although I have not the satisfaction of knowing you personally, you are nonetheless known to me by your works. They are treasures of the mind, if the expression may be allowed, and compositions elaborated with so much taste, delicacy, and art, that their beauties appear new each time they are reread. I feel I have discovered in them the character of their ingenious author, who does honor to our age and to the human mind. The great men of modern times will one day be obliged to you, and to you alone, if the dispute concerning the ancients and the moderns should again arise; because you will incline the balance to their side.

To the quality of an excellent poet you add an infinity of other knowledge which indeed has some affinity with poetry but has only been fitted to it by your pen. Never before has a poet made metaphysical thought rhythmic; you were the first for whom that honor was reserved. That taste for philosophy which you display in your writings encourages me to send you a translation I have had made of the accusation and justification of M. Wolff, the most celebrated philosopher of our day, who has been cruelly accused of irreligion and atheism because he carried light into the most shadowy recesses of metaphysics and because he treated this difficult subject in a manner as elevated as it was clear and precise. Such is the destiny of great men: Their superior genius ever leaves them naked to the poisoned darts of calumny and envy.

I am now having translated a *Treatise on God, the Soul and the World,* which emanates from the pen of the same author. It shall be sent you, Sir, as soon as it is finished, and I am sure you will be struck by the force of evidence in all its propositions, which follow each other geometrically and are connected together like the links of a chain.

The complacency and support you exhibit toward all who devote themselves to the arts and sciences make me hope that you will not

[2] *Letters of Voltaire and Frederick the Great,* trans. Richard Aldington (London, 1927), pp. 19–23. Copyright © Madame Catherine Guillaume. Reprinted by permission of Rosica Colin, Ltd.

exclude me from the number of those whom you find worthy of your instruction. I mean your correspondence; which cannot but be profitable to every thinking being. Without aspersing the deserts of others, I dare to assert that the whole world cannot show a person to whom you could not act as a master. Without overwhelming you with an incense unworthy to be offered you, I may yet say that I find numberless beauties in your works. Your *Henriade* charms me and triumphs happily over the injudicious criticisms which have been made of it. The tragedy of *César* shows us sustained characters; its sentiments are all magnificent and grand; and we realize that Brutus is either a Roman or an Englishman. *Alzire* adds to the graces of novelty the happy contrast between the manners of savages and of Europeans. Through the character Gusman you show us that Christianity when misconceived and guided by false zeal renders men more barbarous and cruel than Paganism itself. If Corneille, the great Corneille, who attracted the admiration of his age, should come to life again in our days, he would see with astonishment and perhaps with envy that the goddess of Tragedy lavishes prodigally upon you those favors of which she was so sparing to him. What may we not expect from the author of so many masterpieces! What fresh wonders may not issue from the pen which lately designed so wittily and elegantly the Temple of Taste!

This it is which makes me desire so ardently to possess all your works. I beg you to send them to me, Sir, and to communicate them unreservedly. If among your manuscripts there should be any which, with necessary prudence, you think fit to hide from the public eye, I promise you to keep it secret and to content myself with applauding it in private. I know unfortunately that the faith of princes is little to be trusted in our days; yet I hope you will not allow yourself to be moved by general prejudices and that you will make an exception to the rule in my favor.

In possessing your works I should think myself richer than in possessing all the transitory and contemptible gifts of fortune which are acquired and lost by a like chance. The first can be made our own—I mean your works—by the aid of memory, and remain ours as long as it does. Knowing the slight extent of my own memory I reflect long before choosing those things I consider worthy of being placed in it.

If poetry were in the same condition as it was formerly, that is if poets could do nothing but hum over tedious idylls, eclogues cast in one mould and insipid stanzas, or if they could do nothing but raise their lyres to the tone of elegy, I should renounce it forever; but you ennoble this art, you show us new paths and roads unknown to the Lefrancs and the Rousseaus.*

* J. B. Rousseau, the lyric poet; not Jean-Jacques.

Your poems possess qualities which render them respectable and worthy of the admiration and study of good men. They are a course of morality whereby we learn to think and to act. Virtue is painted there in its fairest colors. The idea of true glory is there defined; and you insinuate the taste for knowledge in a manner so fine and so delicate that he who has read your works breathes the ambition of following in your steps. How often have I said to myself: "Wretched man! abandon this burden whose weight exceeds your strength; Voltaire cannot be imitated except by Voltaire himself."

At such moments I have realized that the advantages of birth and that vapor of grandeur with which vanity soothes us is of little service or, to speak truly, of none. These distinctions are foreign to ourselves and but embellish outwardly. How much more preferable are the talents of the mind! How much is due to men whom nature has distinguished by the mere fact that she has created them! She takes pleasure in creating some whom she endows with every capacity needed for the progress of the arts and sciences; 'tis for princes to reward their vigils. Ah! may glory only make use of me to crown your successes! I should fear nothing except that this country is so infertile in laurels that it does not furnish as many as your works deserve.

If I am not so favored by my destiny as to take you into my service, at least I may hope one day to see you, whom I have admired so long and from so far, and to assure you by word of mouth that I am, with all the esteem and consideration due to those who, following the torch of truth, devote their labors to the public, Sir, your affectionate friend,

FRÉDÉRIC P.R. OF PRUSSIA

AN ACRIMONIOUS EXCHANGE WITH LOUIS XV, 1745

How can an alliance subsist, unless the contracting powers concur with an equal ardor for their common preservation?

Frederick was a master of the art of double talk. Among the thousands of letters which he wrote are many in which he disguised his real feelings under masks of politeness and seemingly harmless sentences. He subjected both kings and commoners to this kind of special treatment.

A good example of this form of letter writing came toward the end of the Second Silesian War. The Austrians tried again on September 30, 1745 to smash Frederick's army, only to be defeated at Soor in northeastern Bohemia. Frederick's horse was shot out from under him in the stubborn fighting. In December,

Frederick sent Old Dessauer into Saxony, where the grizzled war horse succeeded in knocking the Saxons out of the war. Deprived of her Saxon ally, insulted by the British, fearful of losing her territories in Italy and the Netherlands to France and Spain, Maria Theresa decided to make peace. The treaty of Dresden was concluded between Prussia and Austria-Saxony on Christmas Day, 1745. Prussia won possession of Silesia.

Meanwhile, the French deserted Frederick. As the Second Silesian War drew to a close, Louis XV, in answer to a forcible appeal for assistance, sent Frederick a letter which appeared to be amiable and civil but which really made it clear that France did not intend to carry out her treaty obligations. Angered, Frederick replied in an equally ironical tone.[3]

Louis XV to Frederick

Sir, and my Brother,

Your Majesty, in your letter of the 15th of November, confirms to me what I already knew respecting the convention of Hanover of the 26th of August. I cannot help being astonished that a treaty should have been negotiated, concluded, signed, and ratified with a sovereign who is my enemy, without my receiving the slightest notice of it. I am not surprised at your refusal to lend yourself to violent measures, and to a direct and formal engagement against me: my enemies ought to know your Majesty better. I consider it a fresh injury to myself, that they should have dared to make to you such unworthy propositions. I counted upon your creating a diversion. I have made two powerful ones myself in Flanders and Italy; while I occupied on the Rhine the attention of the Queen of Hungary's largest army. The expenses I have gone into, and the efforts I have made, have been rewarded by the greatest successes. The effects of these have, however, been much endangered by the treaty, which your Majesty has concluded without my privity. If the Queen of Hungary had agreed to that treaty, all her army in Bohemia would have been suddenly turned against me. These are not the ways in which peace can really be made.

I do not, however, on this account, feel the less dread at the perils and dangers, which you are now in the midst of. Nothing can equal my impatience to hear of your safety; and the assurance of your security and tranquillity will cause mine. Your Majesty has great forces under your command; you are the terror of your enemies, over whom you have gained considerable and glorious advantages; joined to which, the winter, which suspends all military operations, will aid you

[3] *Histoire de mon Temps,* trans. in Dover, I, 386–88, 391–92.

to defend yourself. Who is more capable than your Majesty to afford good counsels to yourself? You have only to follow what shall be suggested to you by your talent, your experience, and, above all, your sense of honor.

With regard to assistance from me, which can only consist in subsidies and diversions, I have given all that was possible; and I will continue to do so in the ways the most likely to ensure success. I am reinforcing my troops. I neglect nothing; but I am hastening whatever preparations may enable me to act, in the ensuing campaign, with the greatest vigor. If your Majesty has any projects in view capable of favoring my enterprises, I entreat you to communicate them to me, as I shall always have great pleasure in acting in concert with you.

Frederick to Louis XV

Sir, and my Brother,

After the letter which I wrote to your Majesty on the 15th of November, I had, I think, a right to expect from you some real assistance. I will not now enter into a consideration of the reasons you may have, for abandoning your allies to the caprices of fortune. Upon the present occasion, the valor of my troops has delivered me from the dangerous position, in which I was placed. If the number of my enemies had overwhelmed me, your Majesty would, apparently, have been contented with pitying me; and I should have been without resources. How can an alliance subsist, unless the contracting powers concur with an equal ardor for their common preservation? Your Majesty tells me to take counsel of myself; and I shall do so, as you think it fitting. Reason tells me to end as speedily as I can a war, which has no longer any object, since the Austrian troops are no longer in Alsatia, and the emperor is no more.

Under these circumstances, any future battles that might be fought, would be only a useless effusion of blood. Reason also advises me to think of my own security; and to reflect upon the great Russian armament, which threatens my kingdom on the side of Courland; and on the army, which M. de Traun commands on the Rhine, and which might easily march toward Saxony: and also to consider the inconstancy of fortune, and that, in the circumstances in which I find myself, I must not expect any assistance from my allies.

The Austrians and the Saxons have just sent ministers here, to negotiate a peace. I have therefore no other part left than to sign it. After having thus acquitted myself of the duty I owe to the state I govern, and to my own family, no object will be more anxiously sought by me, than to make myself useful to the interests of your Majesty. I should be indeed truly happy, if I could be the instrument of the general pacification of Europe. Your Majesty could not entrust your wishes to any one, who is more attached to you than myself, or who would labor with more earnestness to re-establish concord and good intelligence between the different states, whom these long disputes have rendered enemies. I entreat you to continue your friendship to me, which will always be precious to me; and to be persuaded that I am, etc., etc.,

The War of the Austrian Succession continued on for another three years, but Frederick took no further part in it. He was only thirty-three, but he had won world-wide fame, and already he was being called Frederick the Great. A Hohenzollern, he had outmaneuvered his competitors, the Wittelsbachs of Bavaria, the Welfs of Hanover, and the Wettins of Saxony. From now on there would be only two great powers inside the empire—Austria and Prussia. The era of dualism in German history had begun.

A "VICTORY LETTER" TO THE QUEEN DOWAGER, 1757

The Austrians have been dispersed like chaff before the wind.

The continental Seven Years' War began in 1756, when Frederick invaded Saxony on August 29. There was consternation in the capitals of the Great Powers, which on January 10, 1757, declared war on Frederick. But the allies worked slowly. It was not until May 1, 1757 that the Second Treaty of Versailles, this time an admittedly offensive pact, was concluded between Austria and France.

Frederick would have to fight on three fronts. His plan was characteristic: he would take on his enemies one at a time. He struck with four armies invading Bohemia, where the Austrians were concentrated. On May 5, 1757, he issued an order to move along a line facing the Bohemian capital. The Battle of Prague turned out to be a bitter conflict, in which the Prussian infantry attacked again and again, only to be met with a storm of bullets and a line of bayonets. Frederick's heavy guns were trapped in a series of morasses and crevices. The tide was turned by onrushing Prussian cavalry, appearing at precisely the most favorable moment. At last Frederick could take pride in his cavalry.

The bewildered Austrians, leaving 10,000 dead and more than 4,000 prisoners in Prussian hands, fell back into Prague. Frederick lost 11,740 killed and wounded. That night he sent his mother, the queen dowager, news of the battle.[4] It was a "victory letter," but Frederick's invasion of Bohemia was to be an expensive fiasco.

[4] *Vie de Frédéric,* II, xxvi, 75, trans. in Dover, II, 47.

Madam,

My brother and myself are safe and well. The Austrians are in a fair way to make a bad campaign of it; while I find myself free, and at the head of 150,000 men. Add to this, that we are masters of a kingdom, which is obliged to furnish us with troops and money. The Austrians have been dispersed like chaff before the wind. I shall send part of my army to make my compliments to the French; and with the rest I am about to pursue the Austrians.

Five weeks later Frederick again attacked the Austrians at Kolin. This time, however, he was beaten. He was forced to raise the siege of Prague and evacuate Bohemia.

There was no rest for the weary Prussians. From the east, the Russians invaded East Prussia on July 30, 1757 and defeated the Prussians at the Battle of Grossjägerndorf. For some reason the Russians did not exploit their success and, instead, withdrew from East Prussia. Meanwhile, 16,000 Swedes landed in Pomerania to take the territory promised them for participation in the war.

The outlook for Frederick was bleak. Both Austrians and Russians were battering his armies. In addition, a British-Hanoverian force under the Duke of Cumberland was defeated in western Germany on September 8, 1757. But the Prussian monarch was by no means ready to capitulate. His reply was to hit back and strike hard.

A DESPAIRING COMMUNICATION TO WILHELMINA, 1757

I shall even bless Heaven for its mercy, if it grant me the favor to die sword in hand.

Time and time again during the Seven Years' War Frederick was on the verge of disaster. Like D'Artagnan the swordsman, he faced first one enemy on one side and then turned rapidly to meet onslaught from the other. To the southwest were the French, to the south were the Austrians, and to the east were the feared Russians. It took the highest kind of military ability to cope with this pressure from all sides. Frederick won his share of victories, but there were also serious defeats, which brought him close to the end. His situation seemed hopeless. Depressed, despairing, he sent the following letter to his sister Wilhelmina.[5]

[5] *Oeuvres de Frédéric,* xxvii, i, 303–7, trans. in Carlyle, V, 137–39.

Kirschleben, near Erfurt
17th September, 1757

My dearest sister, I find no other consolation but in your precious letters. May Heaven reward so much virtue and such heroic sentiments!

Since I wrote last to you, my misfortunes have but gone on accumulating. It seems as though destiny would discharge all its wrath and fury upon the poor country which I had to rule over. The Swedes have entered Pomerania. The French, after having concluded a neutrality humiliating to the king of England and themselves are in full march upon Halberstadt and Magdeburg. From Prussia I am in daily expectation of hearing of a battle having been fought: the proportion of combatants being 25,000 against 80,000. The Austrians have marched into Silesia, whither the Prince of Bevern follows them. I have advanced this way to fall upon the corps of the allied army; which has run off, and entrenched itself, behind Eisenach, amongst hills, whither to follow, still more to attack them, all rules of war forbid. The moment I retire toward Saxony, this whole swarm will be upon my heels. Happen what may, I am determined, at all risks, to fall upon whatever corps of the enemy approaches me nearest. I shall even bless Heaven for its mercy, if it grant me the favor to die sword in hand.

Should this hope fail me, you will allow that it would be too hard to crawl at the feet of a company of traitors, to whom successful crimes have given the advantage to prescribe the law to me. How, my dear, my incomparable sister, how could I repress feelings of vengeance and of resentment against all my neighbors, of whom there is not one who did not accelerate my downfall, and will not share in our spoils? How can a Prince survive his state, the glory of his country, his own reputation? A Bavarian Elector, in his nonage or rather in a sort of subjection to his ministers, and dull to the biddings of honor, may give himself up as a slave to the imperious domination of the House of Austria, and kiss the hand which oppressed his father: I pardon it to his youth and his ineptitude. But is that the example for me to follow? No, dear sister, you think too nobly to give me such mean (*lâche*) advice. Is liberty, that precious prerogative, to be less dear to a sovereign in the eighteenth century than it was to Roman patricians of old? And where is it said that Brutus and Cato should carry magnanimity farther than princes and kings? Firmness consists in resisting misfortune: but only cowards submit to the yoke, bear patiently their chains and support oppression tranquilly. Never, my dear sister, could I resolve upon such ignominy.

If I had followed only my own inclinations, I should have ended it (*je me serais dépêché*) at once, after that unfortunate battle which I lost. But I felt that this would be weakness, and that it behooved me to repair the evil which had happened. My attachment to the state awoke; I said to myself, it is not in seasons of prosperity that it is rare to find defenders, but in adversity. . . .

But it is time to end this long, dreary letter; which treats almost of nothing but my own affairs. I have had some leisure, and have used it to open on you a heart filled with admiration and gratitude toward you. Yes, my adorable sister, if Providence troubled itself about human affairs, you ought to be the happiest person in the universe. Your not being such confirms me in the sentiments expressed at the end of my *Épitre*. In conclusion, believe that I adore you, and that I would give my life a thousand times to serve you. These are the sentiments which will animate me in the last breath of my life; being, my beloved sister, ever,—Your—F.

FREDERICK AND VOLTAIRE CORRESPOND ON THE VIRTUES OF PEACE, 1759

Socrates or Plato would have thought as I do on this subject.

Frederick was at war with France, but he nevertheless maintained his correspondence with Voltaire.[6] *King and litterateur, they were, said Carlyle, like "a pair of lovers hopelessly estranged and divorced; and yet, in a sense, unique and priceless to each other." Among the frequently recurring topics, one that turned up most often on Voltaire's side was that of peace: "Oh, if your Majesty would only make peace!" Frederick always responded with the theme: "Really, does it always depend on me?" (See pages 109–24 for further discussion of the Frederick-Voltaire relationship.)*

Frederick to Voltaire

Reich-Hennersdorf, 2nd July 1779

Asking *me* for peace: there is a bitter joke. It is to him [*King Louis*] that you must address yourself, or to his Amboise in petticoats [*Madame de Pompadour*]. But these people have their heads filled with ambitious projects: these people are the difficulty; they wish to be the sovereign arbiters of sovereigns; and that is what persons of my way of thinking will by no means put up with. I love peace quite as much as you could wish; but I want it good, solid and honorable. Socrates or Plato would have thought as I do on this subject,

[6] *Oeuvres de Frédéric*, xxiii, 53, 59–60, trans. in Carlyle, V, 490–92.

had they found themselves placed in the accursed position which is now mine in the world.

Think you there is any pleasure in leading this dog-of-a-life [*chienne, she-dog*]? In seeing and causing the butchery of people you know nothing of; in losing daily those you do know and love; in seeing perpetually your reputation exposed to the caprices of chance; in passing year after year in disquietudes and apprehensions; in risking, without end, your life and your fortune?

I know right well the value of tranquility, the sweets of society, the charms of life; and I love to be happy, as much as anybody whatever. But much as I desire these blessings, I will not purchase them by baseness and infamies. Philosophy enjoins us to do our duty; faithfully to serve our country, at the price of our blood, of our repose, and of every sacrifice that can be required of us. The illustrious *Zadig* went through a good many adventures which were not to his taste, *Candide* the like; and nevertheless took their misfortune in patience. What finer example to follow than that of those heroes?

Take my word, our "curt jackets," as you call them are as good as your red heels, as the Hungarian pelisses, and the green frocks of the Roxelans [*Russians*]. We are actually on the heels of the latter who by their stupidities give us fine chance. You will see that I shall get out of the scrape this year too, and deliver myself both from the Greens and the Dirty-Whites [*Austrian color of coat*]. My neighbor of the sacred hat—I think in spite of Holy Father's benedictions, the Holy Ghost must have inspired him the reverse way; he seems to have a great deal of lead in his bottom.

Voltaire's Reply

The Delicés [*some time in August 1759*]

In whatever state you are, it is very certain that you are a great man. It is not to weary your Majesty that I now write; it is to confess myself—on condition you will give me absolution! I have betrayed you; that is the fact. In fact, I have received that fine *Marcus-Aurelius* letter, exquisite piece, though with biting *Juvenal* qualities in it, too; and have shown it, keeping back the biting parts, to a beautiful gillflirt of the court, *minaudière,* who is here attending Tissot for her health; *minaudière* charmed with it; insists on my sending it to Choiseul. "He admires the King of Prussia, as he does all nobleness and genius; send it!" And I did so—and look here, what an answer from Choiseul, and may it not have a fine effect, and perhaps bring peace—Oh, forgive me, Sire. But read that note of the great man. "Try if you can decipher his writing. One may have very honest sentiments, and a great deal of *esprit,* and yet write like a cat."—

"Sire, there was once a lion and a mouse (*rat*); the mouse fell in love with the lion, and went to pay him court. The lion, tired of it, gave him a little scrape with his paw. The mouse withdrew into his mousehole (*souricière*); but he still loved the lion; and seeing one day a net they were spreading out to catch the lion and kill him, he gnawed asunder one mesh of it. Sire, the mouse kisses very humbly your beautiful claws, in all submissiveness:—he will never die between two Capuchins, as at Bâle, the mastiff (*dogue*) of St. Malo has done. He would have wished to die beside his lion. Believe that the mouse was more attached than the mastiff."

—V.

A THANK-YOU LETTER TO THE EX-KING OF POLAND, 1760

Everybody has not such pacific dispositions as yourself.

Frederick kept himself busy writing letters throughout his military campaigns. The winter of 1759 to 1760 passed in negotiations for peace, with no results. Stanislaus Leczinski, the former ruler of Poland, offered the town of Nancy, capital of his duchy of Lorraine, as the site for a peace conference. Frederick, from his headquarters at Freiberg, dispatched the following reply to the ex-king.[7] *Frederick's enemies objected to Nancy, then suggested Breda, then Leipzig, and finally dropped the subject. The Prussian and English monarchs offered peace to the Empress of Russia, but to no avail. The Seven Years' War went on along with Frederick's busy correspondence.*

Sir, and my Brother,

I receive your offer with the most lively gratitude, and ask for nothing better than to accept of it. Any negotiation carried on under the auspices of your Majesty, could not fail of having a happy result; but everybody has not such pacific dispositions as yourself. The courts of Vienna and Petersburg have rejected, in a most unprecedented manner, the propositions, which the king of Great Britain and myself have made to them. They will probably persuade the king of France to take the same course, and to continue the war; in which case these powers will be alone responsible for the blood, which their refusal will cause to be shed. If all princes, like your Majesty, listened to the voice of humanity, of kindness, and of justice, the earth would soon

[7] Quoted in Archenholz, *Histoire de la Guerre de Sept Ans,* trans. in Dover, II, 195–96.

cease to be the scene of devastation, war, and carnage, which it at present is. I am, with sentiments of the greatest esteem and of the most sincere friendship, sir and my brother,

Your Majesty's faithful brother,

FÉDÉRIC*

Freiberg, 8th February 1760

A LETTER OF COMPLAINT, 1760

I have the labors of Hercules to perform.

In his wartime correspondence, Frederick often complained about the fortunes of his life. On June 23, 1760, the Prussians were defeated by the Austrians in the Battle of Landshut. Frederick struck back at the Battle of Liegnitz (Pfaffendorf) and thereby prevented the union of the Austrians and Russians. Soon after the battle, Frederick sent the following letter to his friend, the Marquis d'Argens, in which he wrote dejectedly of his many problems.[8]

Hermansdorf, near Breslau
27th August 1760

Formerly, my dear marquis, the affair of the 15th would have decided the campaign; but at present that action is only a scratch. A great battle must determine our fate. We shall have one, as it appears, soon; and then, if the event be favorable to us, we may rejoice in good earnest. I return you thanks, however, for the sincere interest you take in the advantage we have obtained. It required many stratagems and much address to bring things to that point. Do not talk to me of danger: the last action only cost me a coat and a horse; which is buying a victory very cheap.

I have not received the letter you mention. We are in a manner blocked up, as far as regards correspondence, by the Russians on one side of the Oder, and the Austrians on the other. A small skirmish was even necessary to clear the way for Cocceji,** who, I hope, will be able to convey to you this letter.

I never in my life was in a more dangerous and embarrassing situ-

* Frederick often wrote his signature as Fédéric.

[8] *Oeuvres posthumes de Frédéric II,* trans. in Dover, II, 212–15.

** The aide-de-camp, to whom this letter was entrusted.

ation than during this campaign. Believe me, nothing less than a miracle is still necessary to enable me to overcome all the difficulties, which I foresee. I do my duty as well as I can, when occasion offers; but remember always, my dear marquis, that I cannot command good fortune; and that I am obliged in my plans to leave too much to chance, because I have not means enough to render them more certain. I have the labors of Hercules to perform, at an age, too, when my strength is leaving me, when my infirmities increase, and, to speak the truth, when hope, the only consolation of the unhappy, begins to desert me. You are not sufficiently acquainted with the circumstances of affairs, to have a clear idea of the dangers, which menace the state. I know them, but conceal them. I keep all my fears for myself, and only communicate to the public my hopes, or the little good news, that I can acquaint them with. If the blow I now meditate succeeds, then, my dear marquis, will be the time to express our joy. But till then, do not let us flatter ourselves, lest unexpected bad news should too much deject us.

I lead here the life of a military monk. I have much to think of about my affairs; and the rest of my time I give to literature, which is my consolation, as it was that of the consul, the father of his country and of eloquence. I know not whether I shall survive this war; but if that should be the case, I am resolved to pass the rest of my days in retirement, in the bosom of philosophy and friendship. . . .

FRÉDÉRIC

A SOOTHING LETTER TO VOLTAIRE, 1777

Your age should render your person sacred and inviolable.

The break between Frederick and Voltaire came in 1753 when the latter departed in anger from Potsdam (see pages 120–23). The two began to denounce each other in bitter terms. Frederick called Voltaire a "miser, dirty rogue, coward, and liar." "Voltaire," he wrote, "is the most malevolent madman I have ever met. He is only good to read. You cannot imagine all his duplicities, knaveries, and infamies. I am disgusted that so much wit and learning do not make people better."

Voltaire replied in kind. He excoriated his former patron as "a nasty monkey, perfidious friend, wretched poet, and an ungrateful ally." He even published an anonymous book in which he described in coarse detail Frederick's interpersonal relations.

Yet, a year later, in March 1754, the correspondence was resumed, eventually amounting to 654 letters which sought to re-

capture the old spirit of camaraderie. It was a wild combination of love–hate:

Voltaire: *"For your sake I was banished from my country. I loved you. My only wish was to end my days in your service. And just what was my reward? Deprived of Key, Order, and pension, I was forced to flee. I was hounded as if I were a deserter from your Grenadiers, arrested, insulted, robbed. You have good qualities and great talents. But you have one odious fault. You love to humiliate your fellow man. You have brought shame upon the name of philosophy."*

Frederick: *"You behaved shamefully. You richly deserved to see the inside of a dungeon. Your talents are no more widely known than your disloyalty and malice."*

Voltaire: *"You have done me harm enough."*

Frederick: *"You behaved like a disturber. You have wronged me in every way. I forgave you everything, and I am willing to forget everything. Had you not been dealing with someone madly in love with your noble genius, you would not have gotten out of it as well as you did."*

Voltaire: *"You are necessary to my happiness. I could not live without you or with you. You are the most attractive person I know."*

Frederick: *"I console myself that I live in the age of Voltaire. That is enough for me."*

Voltaire: *"From afar I kiss the victorious hands which have written such inspired and profitable prose."*

By 1777, the feud had cooled so much that Frederick thought it best to send the following letter to his old friend.[9]

Potsdam, 10th February, 1777

Your age should render your person sacred and inviolable. I am indignant, I am angry with the wretches who are poisoning the end of your life. I have often said to myself: "How can it be that Voltaire, the glory of France in his age, was born in a country so ungrateful as to allow him to be persecuted? What a discouragement for the future race! Henceforth where will be the Frenchman who will devote his talents to the glory of a nation which slights the great men it produces and punishes instead of rewarding them?"

Persecuted merit arouses my sympathy and I fly to its assistance though it be at the ends of the earth. If I must give up hopes of seeing the immortal Voltaire again, at least I shall be able to con-

[9] *Letters of Voltaire and Frederick the Great,* pp. 379–81. Copyright © Madame Catherine Guillaume. Reprinted by permission of Rosica Colin, Ltd.

verse this summer with the wise Anaxagoras.* We shall philosophize together; your name will be mingled in our conversations and we shall lament the sad destiny of men who, from weakness or stupidity, are falling back into fanaticism.

Two Dominicans, who have the King of Spain at their feet, dispose of the whole kingdom; their sanguinary false zeal has re-established in all its splendor that Inquisition which M. d'Aranda had so wisely abolished. As the world now goes, the superstitious triumph over the philosophers because the great masses of men have minds which are neither cultivated nor geometric. The mob knows that we appease those we have offended with presents; it thinks the same thing applies to the Divinity and that an infallible way of pleasing God is to give him the smoke which rises from a fire which burns a heretic. Add to this the ceremonies, the declamations of monks, the applause of friends, and the stupid piety of the multitude, and you will see it is not surprising that the purblind Spaniards should still be attached to a cult worthy of cannibals.

Philosophers could prosper among the Greeks and Romans, because the religion of the Gentiles had no dogma; but the dogma of our infamous ruins everything. Authors are obliged to write with a circumspection irksome to truth. The priestly rabble avenge the least scratch endured by orthodoxy; no one dares to show the truth openly; and the tyrants of souls wish the ideas of citizens to be all cast in the same mould.

Nevertheless you will always possess the advantage of having surpassed all your predecessors in the noble heroism with which you have combated error. And just as the famous Boerhaave is not reproached because he did not destroy fever, consumption, or epilepsy, but limited himself to curing in his own time some of his contemporaries; so we cannot reproach the learned doctor of souls at Ferney because he could not destroy superstition and fanaticism, and because he only applied his remedies to those who were curable.

A FINAL MESSAGE TO THE DUCHESS OF BRUNSWICK, 1786

The old must give place to the young.

Frederick's lifelong devotion to letter writing continued even during the days of his last illness. On July 10, 1786, Dr. Zimmermann took leave of Frederick, and set off on his journey to Hanover. He left his patient, as he wrote, "not only in a dangerous but in a desperate condition, with a confirmed dropsy, to all appearance, an abscess in the lungs, and such a prostration

* D'Alembert.

of strength, that he could neither stand nor move without support" (see pages 139–44). In Hanover, Dr. Zimmermann saw Frederick's sister, the Duchess of Brunswick, and not wishing to alarm her, gave her a favorable account of his health. The duchess wrote in terms of hope and confidence to Frederick, who sent her this reply, only six days before his death.[10]

10th August 1786

My adorable sister,

The physician of Hanover must have wished to give you a favorable opinion of his skill; but the truth is, that he was of no use to me. The old must give place to the young, in order that each generation may find a place for itself. Indeed life itself is little else, than the witnessing the births and deaths of one's countrymen. In the meanwhile, I find myself a little easier for the last few days. My heart is always inviolably attached to you, my dear sister. With the highest esteem, believe me ever, my adorable sister,

Your faithful brother and servant,

FRÉDÉRIC

[10] *Vie de Frédéric II*, trans. in Dover, II, 454–55.

4

Ideas and Ideology: Frederick as Advocate

Throughout his life Frederick gave continuing evidence of an argumentative nature. Little escaped the range of his interests. His waking hours were usually given to commentaries on anything and everything that passed before his eyes. Following are several miscellaneous examples—from manifestoes to panegyrics—of how Frederick reacted to what was going on around him. These first-hand passages show Frederick's compulsion to prove the correctness of his point of view and the logic of his actions.

A MANIFESTO DEFENDING AGGRESSION, 1740

We shall give strict orders that our troops shall observe the most exact discipline.

Soon after he ascended the throne, Frederick tangled with a neighboring monarch. The issue at stake was Silesia—one of Europe's largest provinces, consisting of four duchies. Southwest of Brandenburg, between Bohemia and Poland, Silesia was a prize, with rich soil, good pasture land, deep forests, and deposits of coal and iron. From the beginning of his reign Frederick had his eye on this valuable province. He had legal claim, he insisted, for the ducal house was extinguished in 1675, and Austria had wrongfully seized the inheritance.

But squarely in the way stood the determined figure of Queen Maria Theresa, Archduchess of Austria, and Queen of Bohemia and Hungary. Strong-willed, capable, efficient, she was a jealous defender of Habsburg power in Europe. She would maintain the integrity and traditions of her country. "I may be only a poor queen," she said, "but I have the heart of a king."

There was startling news on October 20, 1740—Charles VI, the Holy Roman Emperor, died. Eight days later there was even more electrifying news: Czarina Anna Ivanova of Russia was also dead. Frederick saw an opportunity in the general confusion. He had his experts in the foreign office work night and day on "legal proof" of Prussian rights to Silesia. By early December his troops were concentrated on the Silesian frontier. On December 1, 1740, he issued the following proclamation telling the whole world that he was entering Silesia "without any design of committing the least hostility." [1]

We Frederick, etc. As it has pleased the Almighty to take from this world, the Emperor, Charles VI, and that, by this means, the empire, and the most august house of Austria, remain without a head; so that the latter, considering the extinction of the male line, finds itself likewise, on account of the succession to its dominions, much exposed to dangerous troubles of which a part have manifested themselves already, and others are still ready to break out.

As we have, moreover, always taken part in what tended to the good and preservation of the Duchy of Silesia; the rather, as it serves for a barrier to our dominions, and that this province might, in particular, be exposed to the same troubles, and be invaded to our very great prejudice, as well as that of our frontiers, by those who form pretensions to the hereditary dominions of the house of Austria, from whence the flame of war might extend itself to our own territories, and expose them to evident danger.

Wherefore, in order to prevent consequences so dangerous, upon the appearance of a general war, with which Europe is threatened; and to provide for the defense of the dominion which God has given us, as well as for that of our subjects, conformable to the principles of natural right, which permits all, and every one, to be watchful of their own preservation: As also to prevent diverse views, which are partly kept concealed, but, of which, some have already manifested themselves, and may prove prejudicial to us: And, in fine, for very important reasons on our part, which we shall not fail to make public in due time: We have thought proper to cause our troops to enter the Duchy of Silesia, in order to cover it from being invaded or attacked.

And as, by so doing, we have no intention to prejudice, in the least, her Majesty the Queen of Hungary; with whom we are resolved to keep a strict friendship, as well as with the whole Austrian house; and to do her and them all manner of good offices, in imitation of our ancestors: And as it will sufficiently appear in proper time, that such only is our view. And that we are, besides, actually busied in explaining ourselves, upon this occasion, with her Majesty, the

[1] *Memoirs of Frederick II, King of Prussia* (London, 1757), pp. 30–33.

Queen of Hungary. For this reason, the inhabitants of the Duchy of Silesia, and of the incorporated provinces, of whatever religion or condition they are, may be assured that they have no hostility to apprehend on our part, nor on that of our troops; but that, on the contrary, they shall be maintained in their rights, liberties, and privileges, as well public and private, as ecclesiastical and civil; that they shall have the benefit of our royal protection, in its full extent; that we shall give strict orders, that our troops observe the most exact discipline, and that no persons be molested nor troubled in the peaceable possession of what belongs to them.

On the other hand, as we enter Silesia without any design of committing the least hostility, but only to support its inhabitants, preserve their properties, and provide for the tranquillity of that duchy, which is equally necessary to us: We are in great hopes that they will undertake nothing that may be contrary to these gracious offers, and marks of friendship, or that can oblige us, contrary to our inclination, to take other measures, in which case they can impute only to themselves the bad consequences that may result from them.

Signed, FRÉDÉRIC

At Berlin this first day of December, 1749

Within hours, 40,000 superbly trained Prussians with Frederick at their head marched across the borders of Silesia.

"The man must be mad!" said the king of France.

JUSTIFICATION FOR THE SILESIAN WAR, 1740

It was a means of acquiring reputation, of increasing the power of his state.

Frederick made other attempts to explain and condone his original invasion of Silesia. Later, in a more expansive mood, he was more inclined to reveal his true motives. In his History of My Times, *written in the third person, he admitted that he had been moved by the necessity of acquiring a reputation and increasing the power of Prussia.*[2] *He had been obviously more Machiavellian than altruistic, and had been thinking of something more than "to provide for the tranquillity of that duchy."*

[2] *Histoire de mon temps,* in *Oeuvres de Frédéric le Grand,* 30 vols. (Berlin, 1846), II, 54–56.

The emperor Charles VI ended his days on October 20, 1740. That news arrived at Rheinsberg where the king [*Frederick II*] was suffering an attack of quartan fever. The doctors, infatuated with ancient maxims, would not give him quinine, but he took it in spite of them because he proposed to do things more important than nursing a fever. He resolved to lay claim at once to the territories of Silesia, to which his house had undeniable rights, and to prepare himself to support those claims by force of arms, if necessary. That project fulfilled all his political desires: It was a means of acquiring reputation, of increasing the power of his state, and of terminating all that concerned the litigious question of the Berg-Jülich succession. However, before he made up his mind completely, the king weighed the risks there were in undertaking such a war and the advantages that were to be hoped for from it.

On the one side, there was the powerful house of Austria, which, with vast territories, did not lack resources; there was the daughter of the emperor attacked, who would probably find allies in the king of England, in the Dutch Republic, and in most of the princes of the empire, since they had signed the Pragmatic Sanction. The duke of Courland, who was then governing in Russia, was engaged with the court of Vienna; besides, the young queen of Hungary could attract Saxony to her interests by ceding it some districts of Bohemia; and as for details of executing the trick, the scanty harvests of 1740 made it difficult to provision troops.

On the other hand, a host of reflections revived the hopes of the king. The situation of the court of Vienna after the death of the emperor was very unpleasant: the finances were in disorder; the army was shattered and discouraged by the ill success which it had had against the Turks; the ministry was disunited; and when one considered that, in addition to these factors, there was at the head of the government a young, inexperienced princess who had to defend a disputed succession, the result was that that government could not appear formidable. . . .

That which tipped the balance in favor of the war was the death of Anna, Czarina of Russia, following soon after that of the emperor. By her decease, the Russian crown fell to young Ivan, Grand Duke of Russia, son of a princess of Mecklenburg and of Prince Antoine-Ulric of Brunswick, a good friend of the king of Prussia. It appeared that during the minority of the young czar Russia would be well occupied in maintaining order at home, without supporting the Pragmatic Sanction—a fact which could not fail to be reflected in Germany. Add to these reasons an army all ready to go, supplies all gathered together, and perhaps the desire of making a name for oneself—all this was the cause of the war which the king declared upon Maria Theresa of Austria.

A CELEBRATED INTERVIEW WITH HERR PROFESSOR GELLERT, 1760

You must ride daily, and take a dose of rhubarb every week.

To keep his mind active and to seek solace from the responsibilities of war, Frederick, during the winter from 1760 to 1761, held interviews in his quarters with the learned professors of Leipzig University. He showed an appetite for a snatch of talk with anybody of good sense. Of special interest is his celebrated interview with Professor Gellert, a forty-five-year-old bachelor who lectured on morals and moral sentiment. Frederick knew Gellert's popular books, Fables in Verse *and* On Letter Writing. *Carlyle described Gellert as "a modest, despondent kind of man, given to indigestion, dietetics, hypochondria: of neat figure and dress; nose hooked, but not too much; a fine countenance, and fine soul of its sort." In the interview on December 18, 1760, Frederick spoke German at times, sometimes French; Gellert used mostly German.*[3]

King. "Are you (*Er*) the Professor Gellert?"

Gellert. "Yea, *Ihre Majestät.*"

King. "The English Ambassador has spoken highly of you to me. Where do you come from?"

Gellert. "From Hainichen, near Freiberg."

King. "Have not you a brother at Freiberg?"

Gellert. "Yea, *Ihre Majestät.*"

King. "Tell me why we have no good German authors."

Major Quintus Icilius (puts in a word). "Your Majesty, you see here one before you;—one whom the French themseves have translated, calling him the German La Fontaine!"

King. "That is much. Have you read La Fontaine?"

Gellert. "Yes, your Majesty; but have not imitated: I am original (*ich bin ein Original*)."

King. "Well, this is one good author among the Germans; but why have not we more?"

Gellert. "Your Majesty has a prejudice against the Germans."

King. "No; I can't say that (*Nein; das kann ich nicht sagen*)."

Gellert. "At least, against German writers."

King. "Well, perhaps. Why have we no good historians? Why does no one undertake a translation of Tacitus?"

[3] *Gellert's Briefwechsel mit Demoiselle Lucius* (Leipzig, 1823), pp. 629–32, trans. in Carlyle, VI, 116–19.

Gellert. "Tacitus is difficult to translate; and the French themselves have but bad translations of him."

King. "That is true (*Da hat Er recht*)."

Gellert. "And, on the whole, various reasons may be given why the Germans have not yet distinguished themselves in every kind of writing. While arts and sciences were in their flower among the Greeks, the Romans were still busy in war. Perhaps this is the warlike era of the Germans:—perhaps also they have yet wanted Augustuses and Louis-Fourteenths!"

King. "How would you wish one Augustus, then, for all Germany?"

Gellert. "Not altogether that; I could wish only that every sovereign encouraged men of genius in his own country."

King (starting a new subject). "Have you never been out of Saxony?"

Gellert. "I have been in Berlin."

King. "You should travel."

Gellert. "*Ihre Majestät,* for that I need two things, health and means."

King. "What is your complaint? Is it *die gelehrte Krankheit* (disease of the learned, dyspepsia so-called)? I have myself suffered from that. I will prescribe for you. You must ride daily, and take a dose of rhubarb every week."

Gellert. "*Ach, Ihre Majestät,* if the horse were as weak as I am, he would be of no use to me; if he were stronger, I should be too weak to manage him."

King. "Then you must drive out."

Gellert. "For that I am deficient in the means."

King. "Yes, that is true; that is what authors (*Gelehrte*) in Deutschland are always deficient in. I suppose these are bad times, are not they?"

Gellert. "*Ja wohl*; and if your Majesty would grant us peace (*den Frieden geben wollten*)—"

King. "How can I? Have you not heard, then? There are three of them against me (*Es sind ja drei wider mich*)!"

Gellert. "I have more to do with the ancients and their history than with the moderns."

King (changing the topic). "What do you think, is Homer or Virgil the finer as an epic poet?"

Gellert. "Homer, as the more original."

King. "But Virgil is much more polished (*viel polierter*)."

Gellert. "We are too far removed from Homer's times to judge of his language. I trust to Quinctilian in that respect, who prefers Homer."

King. "But one should not be a slave to the opinion of the ancients."

Gellert. "Nor am I that. I follow them only in cases where, owing to the distance, I cannot judge for myself."

Major Icilius. "He, the Herr Professor here, has also treated of German letter writing, and has published specimens."

King. "So? But have you written against the *Chancery Style,* then (the painfully solemn style, of ceremonial and circumlocution; letters written so as to be mainly wig and buckram)?"

Gellert. "*Ach ja,* that have I, *Ihre Majestät.*"

King. "But why doesn't it change? The devil must be in it (*Es ist etwas Verteufeltes*). They bring me whole sheets of that stuff, and I can make nothing of it!"

Gellert. "If your Majesty cannot alter it, still less can I. I can only recommend where you command."

PANEGYRIC OF VOLTAIRE, 1778

The memory of Voltaire will increase from age to age, and transmit his name to immortality.

Denied Christian burial by the Archbishop of Paris, Voltaire was hurriedly interred at Scellières before the bishop of that diocese had a chance to object. Frederick was appalled by the news. He had had a difficult time with the Frenchman, but he still regarded Voltaire as the authentic and inspired voice of his time. He composed a panegyric which was read at an extraordinary meeting of the Academy of Sciences and Belles Lettres in Berlin on November 26, 1778. These were the concluding remarks.[4]

The cause of Voltaire, supported upon solid foundations, prevailed in all those tribunals where reason was preferred to mystical sophistry. Notwithstanding all the persecutions which he suffered from theological hatred, he always distinguished religion from those who dishonored it; he rendered justice to those ecclesiastics, whose virtues were a real ornament to the Church; and blamed only those scandalous hypocrites, whose morals were a public abomination.

M. de Voltaire, then, passed his life amidst the persecution of those who envied, and the applause of those who admired his greatness. While the invectives of the former were unable to humble his mind, the approbation of the latter did not give him too high an opinion of himself. He was satisfied with enlightening the world, and with inspiring, by his writings, the love of learning and humanity. His morality consisted not merely in delivering good precepts, but in setting a good example. His courage assisted the unhappy family of Calas: he pleaded the cause of the Syrvens, and plucked them from the barbarous hands of their judges; he would have raised from the dead the chevalier La Bare, had he possessed the power of working miracles. How delightful

[4] *The Panegyric of Voltaire, by the King of Prussia* (London, 1779), pp. 48–56.

is it that a philosopher, from the center of his retreat, should exalt his voice, and become the organ of humanity, in order to compel the judges of men to suspend their unjust decrees? This single stroke in the character of Voltaire, is sufficient to entitle him to a place among the small number of the real benefactors of men. Philosophy and religion unite their strength in recommending the cause of virtue.

Who then acted most like a Christian, the magistrate who cruelly banished a family from their country, or the philosopher who protected and received them; the judge who employed the sword of the law to assassinate an idle and unthinking youth, or the sage who wished to save the life of a young man, and to correct his extravagance: the murderer of Calas, or the protector of a forlorn family?

This, gentlemen, will ever render the memory of Voltaire dear to all who are endowed with a feeling heart, or have been born with bowels of compassion. How precious soever may be the qualities of wit, fancy, genius, and knowledge, those presents of which nature is so rarely lavish; they can never be preferred to acts of beneficence and humanity. We admire the first, but we bless and venerate the second.

Whatever uneasiness I feel, gentlemen, in separating myself forever from Voltaire, the moment approaches when I must recall the grief occasioned by his death. We left him in his quiet retirement of Ferney. His affairs induced him to undertake a journey to Paris, where he expected to arrive in time to save the wreck of his fortune from a bankruptcy in which he was involved. He wished not to appear in the capital of his native country without carrying with him a present. His time, continually divided between philosophy and the Belles Lettres, furnished him with a variety of performances, of which he always kept a reserve.

He had lately finished a new tragedy, entitled *Irène,* and wished to produce it at the theatre of Paris. It was his constant practice to subject his pieces to the severest criticism before he exposed them in public; and, agreeable to this principle, he consulted men of taste of his acquaintance concerning his new tragedy, sacrificing a vain confidence to the desire of rendering his labors worthy of posterity. Docile to the enlightened advices of his friends, he set himself with ardor to correct his piece, and employed many nights in this laborious occupation. Whether it was to divert sleep, or to restore the vigor of his senses, he prescribed to himself an immoderate quantity of coffee; fifty dishes a day scarcely satisfied his desire of this beverage, which, agitating his blood, produced a violent inflammation. To allay the fever occasioned by this excess, he had recourse to opiates, which he took in such large doses, as, instead of diminishing his distress, tended greatly to increase it. Soon after the improper use of this remedy he was seized with a kind of palsy, followed by a stroke of an apoplexy, which put an end to his days.

Although M. de Voltaire was naturally of a delicate constitution; and although grief, anxiety, and intense application, had greatly weakened his health, he reached his eighty-fourth year. In his existence, mind prevailed in everything over matter. It was a strong soul which communicated its vigor to a body almost transparent. His memory was astonishing; and he preserved the faculties of thought and imagination to his last breath. With what joy shall I recall to you, gentlemen, the testimonies of admiration and gratitude, which the Parisians bestowed on him during his last visit to his native city! . . .

But can it be believed, that Voltaire, to whom profane Greece would have erected altars, whom Rome would have honored with statues, whom a great empress, protectress of the arts and sciences, wished to commemorate with a monument in her capital city, should almost have been deprived in his native country of a small quantity of earth to cover his ashes! Is it possible that in the eighteenth century, when the light of reason is so generally diffused, when the spirit of philosophy has made so great progress, there should be found *Hierophantes,* more barbarous than the *Heruli,* more fit to live with the savages of Trapobana, than in the center of Paris, who, blinded by a false zeal, and intoxicated with fanaticism, should prevent the performance of the last rites of humanity to one of the most celebrated men that France ever produced!

Yet this absurdity all Europe has witnessed, with a mixture of grief and indignation. But whatever may be the hatred of these fanatics, and the meanness of their vengeance in insulting the dead, neither their envious clamors, nor their savage howlings can injure the memory of M. de Voltaire. The greatest felicity they can expect is, for them and their vile artifices to be forever consigned to darkness and oblivion, while the memory of Voltaire will increase from age to age, and transmit his name to immortality.

CONTEMPT FOR GERMAN LANGUAGE AND LITERATURE, 1780

Literature has not flourished on our soil.

The young Frederick was trained in French by his Huguenot governess, and French came to be and remained his preferred language. He admitted that he spoke German like a coachman. He often complained about his native tongue, which he regarded as fit only for savages—without the grace of other languages. He favored French as a literary medium and wrote his own many works in that language. In the following passage from his De la littérature allemande *(1780) he revealed his contempt for the*

German language and literature.[5] *This attitude, which he maintained throughout his life, was to prove embarrassing to Prusso-German patriots.*

In our own country I hear a jargon devoid of any grace, and which each person manipulates as he pleases, with no discrimination in the choice of terms. Indeed, there is a neglect of the most appropriate and expressive words, and the real meaning is swamped in a flood of verbiage.

I have been seeking to unearth our Homers, our Virgils, our Anacreons, our Horaces, our Demosthenes', our Ciceros, our Thucydides', our Livys. But I find nothing. I should have been spared my pains. Let us admit sincerely and frankly that up to this time literature has not flourished on our soil. . . .

To convince yourself of the bad taste that reigns in Germany, you have only to frequent the theater. You will see the awful plays of Shakespeare translated into our language, and the whole audience transported with delight by these absurd farces, fit only for the savages of Canada. . . . Now we have a *Götz von Berlichingen,* a detestable imitation of these wretched English plays, and the pit applauds enthusiastically and calls for the repetition of its disgusting platitudes. . . .

We shall yet have our classic authors. Everyone will want to read them for both pleasure and profit. Our neighbors will learn German, and our language, polished and perfected by our writers, will be spoken not only in court circles but throughout Europe. This happy time is not yet here, but it will come.

[5] Adapted from Schilling, pp. 297ff.

5
Frederick's Will, 1769

My wishes at the moment when I shall draw my last breath will be for the happiness of my kingdom.

On January 8, 1769, seventeen years before his death, Frederick drew up what was to be his last will.[1] *In this remarkable but little-known document, he gave additional proof of his attachment to his country and family. After his death, the will was opened in the presence of his nephew and successor, Frederick William II, the Princes Henry and Ferdinand, and several ministers. It revealed Frederick's deep sense of duty toward the state and its property. He outlived several of those to whom he bequeathed tokens of remembrance. His two sisters, the Margravine of Anspach and the Queen of Sweden, died, respectively, in 1784 and 1782.*

Life is a rapid passage from the moment of birth to that of death. The destination of man during this brief space is to labor for the welfare of the community of which he is a member. Since I attained to the management of the public affairs, I have striven with all the powers which nature has conferred upon me, and to the best of my humble judgment, to render the State which I have had the honor to govern happy and flourishing. I have established the rule of law and justice; I have introduced order and punctuality into the finances, and into the army that discipline by which it has gained the pre-eminence above all the other troops of Europe. Having thus performed my duties to the State, I should forever be obliged to reproach myself if I were to neglect my family concerns. To prevent all disputes that might arise among my nearest relatives about what I may have to leave, I declare this solemn document to be my last will:

1. I give back cheerfully and without regret this breath of life to

[1] Thomas Campbell, ed., *Frederick the Great: His Court and Times* (London, 1842), pp. 451–57.

bounteous nature, who bestowed it upon me; my body to the elements of which it is composed. I have lived as a philosopher, and wish to be buried as such, without pomp or parade. I desire that I may neither be opened nor embalmed. Let me be deposited in the vault which I had constructed for myself, on the upper terrace at Sans Souci. If I should die during war or on a journey, let me be buried in the nearest convenient spot, and afterwards removed in the winter season to the place at Sans Souci above-mentioned.

2. I bequeath to my dear nephew, Frederick William, as nearest in succession to the throne, the kingdom of Prussia, the provinces, towns, castles, forts, fortresses, all munitions of war and arsenals, of the countries conquered or inherited by me, all the jewels of the crown, the gold and silver service which are in Berlin, my country houses, library, cabinet of medals, gallery of pictures, gardens, etc. I bequeath to him, moreover, the treasure, such as it is, on the day of my death, as a property belonging to the State, which must not be expended but for the defense or the succor of thc people.

3. Should it be found after my death that I have left some small debts, which death has prevented me from paying, my nephew shall discharge them. This is my will.

4. To the queen my consort I bequeath 10,000 dollars per annum in addition to the revenues which she is now receiving, two butts of wine annually, as much wood as she needs for fuel, and game sufficient for her table. The queen has promised, on this condition, to make my nephew her heir. As no place appears more suitable to be assigned for her residence, let Stettin be considered so in name. But I require my nephew to give her apartments suitable to her rank in the palace of Berlin; and he will also pay her every respect which is due to her as the widow of his uncle and as a princess who has never swerved from the path of virtue.

5. Now for the allodial property. I have never been either avaricious or rich, and, consequently, have not much private property at my disposal. I have always regarded the revenues of the State as the ark of the covenant, which no unholy hand ought to touch. I have never applied the public revenues to my personal advantage. My expenses have never exceeded 220,000 dollars a year. My administration of the State leaves me a quiet conscience, and I have no objection to render a public account of it.

6. My nephew, Frederick William, shall be universal heir of my property, upon condition that he pays the following legacies:

7. To my sister of Anspach a snuffbox of the value of 10,000 dollars, which is in my *chatouille,* and a service of porcelain from the Berlin manufactory.

8. To my sister of Brunswick 50,000 dollars, and my silver service with the vine-leaf ornament, and a handsome carriage.

9. To my brother Henry 200,000 dollars, 50 *anthal** of Tokay, and the beautiful lustre of mountain-crystal in Potsdam, the green diamond ring which I wear, two saddle horses with their housings, and a team of Prussian horses.

10. To the Princess Wilhelmina of Hesse, his consort, a revenue of 3,000 dollars, which I derive from a capital invested in the tobacco farm.

11. To my sister the Queen of Sweden, a gold snuffbox, worth 10,000 dollars, 20 *anthal* of Tokay, and a picture by Pesne, which hangs in the palace of Sans Souci, and which was given to me by Algarotti.

12. To my sister Amelia, an income of 10,000 dollars out of the capital invested in the tobacco, a snuffbox out of my *chatouille,* worth 10,000 dollars. 20 *anthal* of Tokay, and the silver plate off which my aides-de-camp dine.

13. To my brother Ferdinand 50,000 dollars, 50 *anthal* of Tokay, a state carriage, horses, and everything belonging to it.

14. To his consort, my niece, an income of 10,000 dollars out of the money lent to the tobacco-farm company, and a snuffbox set with brilliants.

15. To my niece the Princess of Orange, a service of Berlin porcelain, a snuffbox worth 10,000 dollars, 40 *anthal* of Tokay, and a state carriage with a team of Prussian horses.

17. To my nephew, the Margrave of Anspach, I bequeath a yellow diamond, two of my best saddle horses with saddles and furniture, and 30 *anthal* of Tokay.

18. To my nephew, the hereditary Prince of Brunswick, two English horses, with saddles and furniture, and 10 *anthal* of Tokay.

19. To my nephew, Prince Frederick of Brunswick, 10,000 dollars.

20. To my nephew, Prince William of Brunswick, 10,000 dollars.

21. To my niece of Schwedt, consort of the Prince of Württemberg, 20,000 dollars, and a snuffbox set with brilliants.

22. And to her husband, two of my saddle horses with saddles and furniture, and 20 *anthal* of Tokay.

23. To my niece, the Princess Philippine of Schwedt, 10,000 dollars.

* Preuss says, that *anthal* is an Hungarian wine measure, containing the same quantity as the German *Eimer,* that is, 320 bottles. He adds, that the value of an *anthal* of Tokay, at this time, may be calculated from the following entry: "Paid to Count Münchow, Minister of State, on account of the 40 *anthal* of Tokay, bought for the King's Majesty in Hungary, 6875 dollars."

24. To Prince Ferdinand of Brunswick, my brother-in-law, whom I always highly esteemed, a snuffbox set with brilliants, and 20 *anthal* of Tokay.

25. I recommend to my successor, with all the warmth of affection that I am capable of, those brave officers who have fought under me. I beseech him to provide in particular for those officers who have been in my retinue, not to dismiss one of them, nor to suffer any of them, afflicted with illness, to perish in want. He will find in them experienced military men, and, in general, men who have exhibited proofs of intelligence, valor, devotedness, and fidelity.

26. I recommend to him my private secretaries, as well as all those who have been employed in my cabinet. They are clever at business, and can give him information on many points with which they alone are acquainted, and which the ministers know nothing about.

27. In like manner, I recommend to him all who have served me, as well as my valets. I bequeath to Zeysing, for his extraordinary integrity, 2,000 dollars, and 500 for the servants of my wardrobe; and I flatter myself that they will be allowed to retain their salaries till they have been elsewhere suitably provided for.

28. To each of the staff officers of my regiment and that of Lestwitz, and also to those of the *garde-du-corps,* I bequeath a gold medal, struck on occasion of the successes of our arms and of the advantages gained by our troops under my command. To each soldier of these four battalions, I bequeath two dollars, and the same to each of the *garde-du-corps.*

29. If I should before my death add hereto a codicil written and signed by myself, it shall have the same effect and validity as this will.

30. If any of my legatees dies before me, the legacy is cancelled.

31. If I die in the field, my universal legatee is not bound to pay the legacies till peace is restored. During the war, nobody has a right to demand anything.

32. I further recommend to my successor to honor his blood in the persons of his uncles, aunts, and other relatives. Chance, which presides over the destiny of men, likewise determines the accident of primogeniture; and if a man is a king, he is not on that account of more worth than others. I recommend to all my relations to live in harmony, and not to forget in case of emergency to sacrifice their personal interest to the welfare of the country and the State.

My wishes at the moment when I shall draw my last breath will be for the happiness of my kingdom. May it be ever governed with justice, wisdom, and firmness; may it be the happiest State for the mildness of its laws; may it be the best administered in regard to the finances; may it be the most valiantly defended by an army aspiring solely to honor and noble glory! O that it may continue to enjoy the highest prosperity till the end of time!

33. I appoint the reigning Duke of Brunswick executor of this my last will. From his friendship, sincerity, and integrity, I reckon upon his acceptance of this office.

PART TWO

THE WORLD LOOKS AT FREDERICK THE GREAT

6

The Early Days

Thus far we have observed Frederick the Great through his own words at various stages of his career. Now let us turn to eyewitness observations by those who knew him well, from his adored sister Wilhelmina, to the French sage Voltaire, to diverse visitors at Potsdam.

Eyewitnesses testify to Frederick's unhappy early days. Embittered, detesting the hard regimen to which he was subjected, the royal prince showed a preference for gay clothes, French verse, extravagant entertainment, and friends of questionable morals. He resented his father's tyranny, religious zeal, and stinginess. Yet, from this harsh education Frederick was to emerge cured of his youthful follies.

Frederick's early years were described in detail by his sister, Wilhelmina, who was two and a half years older than he. Devoted to her brother, Wilhelmina was not an altogether objective eyewitness, but allowing for sibling attachment, her accounts give an absorbing picture of a miserable adolescence.

FREDERICK WILLIAM'S INSTRUCTIONS, 1719

Then my son must go at once to bed by half-past ten.

The education of a prince is always a solemn and serious affair. For young Fritz it was loaded with conflict. There was no difficulty in the very early years, when he was under feminine control. For the first seven years of his life he was in the care of two women of the Berlin court, both of whom adored him. The "honorary governess" was Frau von Kamecke, wife of the royal major-domo, who passed on the specific orders of the king. The second governess was Madame de Roucoulles, a kindly French Huguenot whom the lad loved and whose gentle voice was in contrast with that of his gruff father. From her young Frederick imbibed a love for French speech and culture that was to last all his life.

The education of the seven-year-old crown prince was turned over to masculine tutors, Lieutenant-General Finck von Finckenstein, Lieutenant-Colonel von Kalkstein, and Jaques Egi du Duhan de Jandun. The father drew up a set of instructions for his son's tutors, in which every minute of the day was prescribed. The king took into consideration the contemporary medical opinion that too much sleep was bad for a growing boy. Of greater importance was the military precision of the molding process. Everything possible was done to see that the young lad breathed military air. The king provided a costly toy for his son: a miniature arsenal modeled on the Berlin Zeughaus *(armory), which included tiny replicas of every tool of war used by the Prussian Army. However, most important was the Spartan treatment ordered by the king.*[1]

On Sunday morning, Frederick is to rise at seven. As soon as he has put on his slippers, he is to get on his knees by his bedside and pray to God briefly, but loud enough so that everyone in the room can hear. The prayer must be learned by heart: "Lord God, Holy Father! I thank Thee from the bottom of my heart that Thou has so graciously preserved me through the night. Make me useful for Thy holy will. Prevent me from doing anything today or any day for the rest of my life that could separate me from Thee. For the sake of our Lord, Jesus Christ, my Redeemer, Amen!" This must be followed by the Lord's Prayer.

Immediately after this has been done, my son is to dress himself quickly, wash properly, tie up his queue, and powder. Dressing and the short prayer must be finished within a quarter of an hour, so that it will then be a quarter past seven. When this is finished, all his servants and Duhan shall enter to recite the great prayer on their knees. Then Duhan shall read a chapter from the Bible, and sing a good hymn, until it is a quarter to eight. Then all the servants shall make their exit, and Duhan shall read the Gospel of the day with my son, explain it briefly, and thus demonstrate the meaning of true Christianity. In addition, he is to repeat a part of the catechism of Noltenius [the court chaplain]; this is to continue until nine o'clock. Then the chaplain is to come down to me with my son. In the evening he must

[1] Adapted from Förster, I, 357–59.

say good-night to me at half-past nine, then go immediately to his room, undress very quickly, wash his hands, and then Duhan shall recite a prayer on his knees, sing a hymn, at which all his servants shall again be present. Then my son must go at once to bed by half-past ten.

Monday he shall be awakened at six o'clock. At once, without complaint, he must rise immediately and kneel down, saying a short prayer, as on Sunday morning. As soon as this prayer is finished, he shall, as quickly as possible, put on his shoes and gaiters, wash his face and hands (without soap), put on his jacket, comb his hair, and have his queue tied but not powdered. While the latter is being done, he shall have tea and breakfast at the same time, and all this must be finished before half-past six. Then Duhan and all his servants shall come in; a great prayer will be recited, a chapter read from the Bible, and a hymn sung, as on Sunday. This shall last until seven o'clock, when the servants must take their exit. From seven to nine Duhan shall work with him in history. At nine o'clock Noltenius shall come to instruct him in Christianity until a quarter to eleven. At this time he shall wash his face quickly with water and his hands with soap, dress himself in white, powder, and put on his coat. He shall come to the king at eleven o'clock, with whom he shall stay until two o'clock. Then he shall return to his rooms. Duhan will meet him there to describe maps to him from two to three o'clock; he shall also explain to him the power and weakness of all European states, together with the size, wealth, and poverty of the towns. From three to four o'clock Frederick will work at morality; from four until five Duhan shall write German letters with him and help him acquire a good style. At five o'clock he shall go to the king, ride and enjoy himself in the fresh air, and do what he likes, so long as it is not against God. [*A similar procedure is outlined until Saturday.*] . . .

On Saturday morning until half-past ten o'clock everything that he has learned during the entire week in history, writing, and arithmetic, as well as in morality, is to be repeated in order to learn whether or not he has profited therefrom. The General Count von Finckenstein and the Colonel von Kalkstein shall be present. If he has profited, then Fritz may take the afternoon off, but if he has not, then he must repeat from two until six o'clock everything he has forgotten in the preceding days.

ATTEMPT TO RUN AWAY, 1730

I am treated like a slave.

As long as the king was away from the court, Frederick and sister Wilhelmina enjoyed some peace and quiet. But as soon as their father returned, the crown prince and his sister were subjected again to irrational abuse. Wilhelmina reported: "He never saw my brother without threatening him with his stick, and [my brother] often said to me that he would respectfully bear all ill-treatment save blows, and that if it came to these he would run away."

When Frederick's friend, Karl von Keith, left to become an officer in the army, the royal prince found another favorite in a young lieutenant named Hans Hermann von Katte, the son of a field marshal. Young Katte had a dark complexion scarred by smallpox. His thick black eyebrows, drawn low over his eyes, met above his nose, giving him an odd, staring expression. But through industry, travel, and study, as well as his friendship with the French ambassador, Katte acquired a veneer of polish and sophistication. This wild young man was to exert a strong influence on the impressionable crown prince. The two resolved to escape. Wilhelmina described the situation immediately before the flight.[2]

We had scarcely escaped from one crisis when we entered upon another. My brother was so irritated at the ill usage he received from the king that he was considering seriously what decision he should come to. He never let the queen suspect anything, but daily came secretly to see me.

"I am perpetually being told to have patience," he said, "but no one knows what I have to endure. I am treated like a slave, am beaten every day, and have no relaxation of any kind. I am forbidden to read, to study the sciences or music, and am scarcely allowed to speak to anybody. My life is in perpetual danger, I am surrounded by spies, I have not even enough clothes, and am wanting in most other necessaries of life; but the last terrible scene with the king at Potsdam has quite overcome me. He sent for me one morning. As soon as I entered the room he seized me by my hair and threw me on the ground. After having beaten me with his fists, he dragged me to the window and tied the cord, which fastened back the curtain, round my throat. I had, fortunately, time to get up and seize hold of his hands, but as he pulled with all his might at the cord round my throat, I felt I was being strangled, and screamed for help. A page rushed in to my assistance, and had to use force in freeing me from my father's hands.

"Tell me now what remains to me but flight. Katte and Keith are both ready to follow me to the end of the world. I have passports and letters of credit, and have arranged everything in such a manner that

[2] *Memoirs of Wilhelmina, Margravine of Bayreuth,* trans. and ed. by Princess Christian of Schleswig-Holstein (New York, 1888), pp. 118–20.

I cannot possibly run any danger. I shall fly to England, where I shall be received with open arms, and shall have nothing more to fear from my father's anger. I shall confide none of these intentions to the queen. First of all because she gossips with Ramen; and secondly, because should such an occasion arise, she could then swear that she knew nothing about the whole business. As soon as my father undertakes another journey, for that makes everything safer for me, I shall carry out my plan, for everything is in readiness."

I cried incessantly during this speech, and afterwards asked him if he had reflected as to the results of this step, and how terrible they would be. Mademoiselle von Sonnsfeld, who was present, spoke in the same strain to him, but we both saw that our representations were quite useless.

Soon after this the king went to Potsdam. During his absence I took the Holy Sacrament, and on my return from the Dom (Cathedral) on Sunday I found Katte waiting for me. Ramen's rooms were just opposite, and she was standing at her door, and Katte was unfortunately imprudent enough to give me a letter from my brother in her presence.

"I have just come from Potsdam," Katte said, "where I have been staying secretly for three days to see the crown prince, and he entrusted this letter to my care."

I took it from him without saying a word, and went my way, much annoyed, as anyone may suppose, at his want of tact. As soon as I reached my room I opened the letter and read as follows:—

> Dear Sister,
>
> I am beside myself. The king ill-treats me worse than ever. I can stand this existence no longer. The queen puts the final touch to this misery by her infatuation for this maid Ramen. The king knows everything that takes place every day in her apartments, because Ramen keeps him informed of it all through his valets. These villains ought to be hanged on the highest gallows. The king returns to Berlin on Tuesday; but, as it is still a secret, do not tell the queen, or else she will at once inform that wicked creature.
>
> Good bye, dear sister,
> Yours always entirely.

I was now in a terrible difficulty. I could not show this letter to the queen, and yet I feared that Ramen would have told her I had received it. After thinking it well over, I threw the missive into the fire.

THE HANGING OF LIEUTENANT KATTE, 1730

Had I a thousand lives, my beloved prince, I would lay them all down for you.

When Frederick and Katte carried out their plan to escape, they were arrested as "deserters." Katte was quickly condemned to death by an official court-martial. Frederick William was adamant. There would be no reprieve from the death sentence—Lieutenant Katte would be executed. In the gray of a winter morning on November 6, 1730, the young officer was brought to Küstrin garrison, and the imprisoned Frederick was escorted to a lower room to see his friend as he passed on his way to the scaffold. Following is Wilhelmina's description of the sad event.[3] *Frederick's sister made no mention of Katte's last words to Frederick as given by Carlyle:* "La mort est douce pour un si aimable prince" (*Death is sweet for so lovable a prince*").

After the execution the body lay all day upon the scaffold by royal order. It was buried at night in the common churchyard.

Seckendorff now stepped in as mediator, and begged for mercy for both criminals, particularly my brother. It was granted him only with much trouble, for my father's rage had increased. For Katte he could obtain nothing, not even a reprieve. His sentence was therefore pronounced. He heard it without moving a muscle, and with the most heroic firmness. He merely answered, "I submit to the king's will, and to that of Providence. I can die without fear, for I have nothing to reproach myself with, and I suffer for a good cause." He then prepared himself for the awful trial before him. Next day he was told that the king wished his execution to take place away from Berlin. This rather startled him, but he soon regained his composure.

As soon as he was left alone, he called the officer of the guard, and gave him the snuffbox containing the portraits of my brother and me, saying, "Keep this, and think sometimes of me. Do not, however, show the box to anyone, as it might do harm to the high personages who are represented on it." Katte then wrote three letters, one to his grandfather, one to his father, and one to his brother-in-law. When the clergyman came to him, he said, "I have greatly sinned before God. My great ambition was the cause of many faults, of which I repent sincerely. The crown prince's favor made me blind to all else. I now know how vain are all earthly things. I repent truly of all my sins, and pray death to lead me to everlasting peace." The day was spent in conversing in this manner. Towards evening, Major Schenk came with tears in his eyes and told Katte that everything was ready for his departure, adding: "The king has commanded me to be present at your execution, and to accompany you to the place where it is to be carried out. I have twice over begged to be excused from this mission, but the

[3] *Memoirs of Wilhelmina*, pp. 161–64.

king insisted, so I could but obey. Would to God that his heart had been softened, and that I might have been the bearer of your pardon."

"You are very kind," Katte replied, "but I do not wish to escape from my fate. I give life for a master whom I love most dearly, and, by doing so, give him the greatest proof of my devotion. Happiness without end awaits me." With these words he stepped cheerfully and smilingly into the carriage.

Before starting, he took leave of many officers and soldiers of the gendarmerie, who had assembled to witness his departure. It was nine o'clock in the morning when he reached Küstrin. The scaffold had been erected in front of my brother's windows, from which the bars had been removed. It was on a level with the window, and only a few paces from it.

As soon as they had reached the interior of the fortress, Schenk said to Katte, "Keep up your courage, for a fearful trial is before you."

"Say rather that it is the greatest comfort that could have been given me," he replied.

My unfortunate brother had, the day before, witnessed all these preparations without knowing their purpose. He expected his own death warrant. Early in the morning the governor of the fortress, General Lepel, and the president, Münichow, entered my brother's prison and endeavored to prepare him as best they could for the terrible news they had to communicate to him. They brought him a plain brown suit of clothes, the counterpart to that which Katte wore (my brother would not take it off afterwards, till it had to be literally torn off him). As soon as the crown prince heard what was in store for him, he was seized with frantic despair, which grew only greater and greater as he was forced to approach the window. He tried to throw himself out of it. Then he exclaimed, "For God's sake postpone the execution! I will write to the king that I will solemnly renounce the crown if only I can save Katte's life."

As my brother saw him mount the scaffold he called out to him, "I am miserable, dear Katte. I am the cause of your misfortune, oh, that I were in your place!" Katte then kneeling down, replied, "Had I a thousand lives, my beloved prince, I would lay them all down for you." One of the attendants then stepped forward to blindfold him, but he waved them back. He then said in a firm voice "My God, into thy hands I commend my spirit." He had scarcely uttered these words when his head fell. In falling he had still stretched out his hand towards the window at which my brother was standing. The poor prince had fainted away. He was laid on his bed, where he remained insensible for several hours. Fever then attacked him, and his condition was not to be described. Katte's body had been left lying in such a position that my brother could not escape seeing it. As no one knew what to do with the crown prince, and the doctors feared for his life, they sent for a clergyman. But the cruel emotions my brother had been through were not so easily got over, and he became calmer only when quite exhausted. Great bodily weakness, accompanied by floods of tears, at last succeeded the violent fits of despair, and he sank into melancholy, which lasted some time. Even now we never dare mention this terrible scene to him. Katte's body remained lying on the scaffold till sundown. It was then buried in a corner of the fortress near the bastions.

FREDERICK AT THE WEDDING OF WILHELMINA, 1731

He answered me rather coldly, and said but little.

A royal commission headed by the Prussian war minister, Field Marshal von Grumbkow, went to Küstrin and released Frederick from prison. Frederick took the oath of allegiance, after which his sword was returned to him. He immediately wrote a letter of apology to his father:

Most illustrious and most merciful father. Your Majesty my most gracious father has quite rightly conceived a just wrath and repugnance against me for my disobedience as his Majesty's subject and soldier as well as my behavior as his Majesty's son. With the utmost subservience and respect I now submit myself to my most gracious father and beg him to pardon me. It is not so much the loss of my liberty as my own reflections which have brought me to reason in regard to my crimes. I remain with respect and humility, to the end of my days.

The king condemned his son to remain in Küstrin and work as a clerk in the local administrative council. He would work each day from 7–11:30 A.M. and from 3–5 P.M., listening and learning, and doing occasional clerical duty. On Sundays he was to attend three church services. The only books he could have were the German Bible and Arndt's Treatise on True Christianity. *There would be no French books, no flute, no letters. Frederick accepted all this with good grace.*

When his father visited him, Frederick, in the presence of spectators, fell at the king's feet and begged forgiveness. Frederick William ordered him to get up and then he launched into a diatribe on his son's misdeeds.

Meanwhile, the king continued his strategy of subduing his family. Believing it time to marry off Wilhelmina, he offered her a "free choice"—between three names: the Duke of Weissenfels, elderly, penniless; Margrave Frederick William of Schwedt, the nephew of Old Dessauer; and Frederick of Brandenburg-Kulmbach, future Margrave of Bayreuth. The queen wanted her daughter to marry the British Prince of Wales. Trapped, Wil-

helmina decided on the future Margrave of Bayreuth, which led to an unhappy marriage. The queen raged; the king wept tears of joy and told Wilhelmina that he might even allow Fritz to attend her wedding.

What happened at the wedding on November 20, 1731 was described by Wilhelmina in her memoirs.[4] *Apparently the deep attachment between brother and sister had cooled somewhat.*

The king had designated Küstrin as his [*Frederick's*] prison, and to punish him still further, my father would not allow him to put on his own uniform. He made him wear a plain French suit of clothes, which the king looked on as a mark of shame. My brother had this suit made after the same cut as that which Katte wore on the day of his execution. The king ordered, furthermore, that my brother was to work every day in the Finance Department as a simple lawyer's clerk. This position is generally given to young men who wish to improve their minds. When they have served some time in this capacity they are promoted. This post is also given only to the smaller gentry or to young men in the middle classes. My brother and I sometimes wrote to each other, Major Sonnsfeld managing the correspondence for us. I had not forgotten the promise Grumbkow had given me, in the king's name, that my brother should be set entirely free soon after my marriage. I asked Sastot to tell Grumbkow, and to ask him to remind the king that he must keep his word. Grumbkow let me know that I might make myself quite happy on this point, as he would make it his especial business to speak with the king on the subject.

The first two days after my wedding passed by quietly. Of an evening we went to play at cards in the queen's rooms. My mother's temper grew worse and worse: she could no longer bear me. The Margrave of Anspach was a very ill-bred young prince, and wished to ingratiate himself with my mother at our cost. He told her every kind of gossip about Prince Henry of Bayreuth, and only added fuel to the fire. The principalities of Anspach and Bayreuth are close to each other, and have unfortunately always been at enmity, which was the more to be regretted as failing male heirs in the one, the succession then falls on the other. Anspach was much vexed at the alliance Bayreuth had just made, not on political grounds, but merely from jealousy.

On the 23rd, the king gave a ball in the state rooms of the castle. As I was very fond of dancing, I gave myself quite up to the pleasure of the occasion. Grumbkow, with whom I was dancing, said several times to me, "Your Royal Highness is so engrossed by the ball, that you do not observe what is taking place." At last I asked him what there was

[4] *Memoirs of Wilhelmina,* pp. 208–11.

to see. "Goodness me," he answered, "what has come to you today? Go and embrace your brother, who is standing there." I was so overcome with joy, that had Grumbkow not supported me, I should have fallen to the ground. At last I found this beloved brother standing near my mother, who was playing at cards. I clasped him in my arms. I was quite beside myself with happiness. I laughed, I cried and talked the most utter nonsense. As soon as the first moments were over, I threw myself at my father's feet, and in my deep and heartfelt gratitude, said so many touching and tender words, that he began to cry. Upon this the whole company also began to weep, and there was nothing to be seen but pocket handkerchiefs, and the scene resembled the most affecting situation in a tragedy.

My brother was so much altered that I should scarcely have known him again. He had not grown taller, but his grief had made him very stout. His former slimness of figure had quite disappeared. He was very broad in the shoulders, and his head seemed sunk between them: he was no longer so handsome as he had been. I could not cease caressing him in my joy at his return. He answered me, however, rather coldly, and said but little. I presented the hereditary prince to him, but he did not speak to him. This behavior seemed strange to me, and I was at a loss to understand it. I did not dare ask him why he acted thus, as the king was watching us narrowly. The queen seemed rather pleased to see my brother again, but her happiness in no way resembled mine. My mother never loved any of her children. She cared for them only as they served her ambitious purposes. The gratitude my brother owed me for effecting the reconciliation with the king spoiled her pleasure. If she alone had been the cause of it, she would have behaved quite differently.

At last we went to dinner, to which four hundred couples sat down. They were mostly persons of good birth. My father was not present: he dined with my brother. . . .

. . . The next day the king sent the crown prince to see me. He remained a whole hour. We had much to say, giving our respective accounts of all that had occurred since we had parted. He was very reserved with me, and all his assurance of affection and friendship seemed forced. He looked several times at Prince Henry, and said a few formal words to him. I could not make him out; he seemed to me to be no longer that beloved brother who had cost me so many tears, and for whom I had sacrificed so much. I tried to hide what I felt, and to be the same as ever with him. The king gave him an infantry regiment, and returned him his sword and uniform. He also gave him a yearly income, and settled that he was to live at Ruppin, where his regiment was quartered.

7

Personality and Character as Observed by His Contemporaries

Generations of readers have been absorbed by the character of the great Hohenzollern. The following section is composed of selections from among the thousands of reactions to Frederick. Each gives one clue to a many-faceted personality.

COURAGE: THE PRINCE ROYAL BEFORE HIS BAPTISM OF FIRE, 1734

This was the last time I saw him in the same intimate way as of old.

The twenty-two-year-old Fredcrick was so disgusted with his own marriage that he welcomed the opportunity of going off to war. The chance came in 1734, when he saw active service for the first time. Once again the French were attacking the empire in the War of the Polish Succession (1733–1735). Frederick served in the indecisive campaign of the old Prince Eugene, the legendary hero of battles against French and Turks. In the siege of Philippsburg, Frederick, while riding on reconnaissance, continued his conversation without halt while cannon shots splintered trees beside him. In the following passage from her Memoirs, *Wilhelmina related the meeting with her brother just before he went to Philippsburg.*[1]

The king had meanwhile left to join the army. My brother and all the princes followed him a few days later. The king had gone by way of Cleves, but my brother wrote me word he should pass through Bayreuth. As the king had, however, strictly forbidden him to stop there, he begged me to meet him on the 2d of July at Berneck, two miles from Bayreuth, where he should make a halt of an hour. I took good care not to lose this opportunity of seeing my beloved brother,

[1] *Memoirs of Wilhelmina,* pp. 353–55.

and started quite early in the morning for Berneck, accompanied by my governess, M. von Voit, and M. von Seckendorf. My husband, attended by my chamberlain and Baron Stein, followed us, to welcome the crown prince in the margrave's name. We arrived at ten o'clock at Berneck. The heat was intense, and I was very tired with the journey. I waited in the house prepared for my brother's reception till three o'clock in the afternoon. A fearful thunderstorm came on. I never witnessed one more terrible. The thunder resounded among the rocks which surround Berneck till the world seemed approaching its end. A perfect deluge of rain followed on the thunder. It struck four o'clock, and yet my brother never came. I could not understand what had happened to him, while the different people I had sent on horseback to look for him did not return either. At last, in spite of all my entreaties, my husband started off in quest of my brother. . . .

At length I reached Himmelscron at midnight. Half dead from fear and fatigue, I threw myself on my bed. I was haunted by the dread that some accident must have happened to my brother and my husband. The hereditary prince arrived at four o'clock, without, however, bringing me any tidings of my brother. Somewhat pacified by my husband's return I fell asleep, but was awakened almost directly by a message that M. von Knobelsdorf wished to speak to me, having been sent by my brother. I jumped up at once from my bed and rushed to meet him. He informed me that my brother had only expected me next day, and had therefore stopped to rest at Hof. If I liked, he would meet me at some spot near Bayreuth, which he would reach at eight o'clock, and remain there a few hours to see me. No time was therefore left for sleep. I ordered my carriage and started to join the crown prince.

My brother overwhelmed me with affection. He found me in a deplorable condition, and so altered he could hardly help crying. I could scarcely stand I was so weak, and fainted constantly. He told me that the king was greatly irritated against the margrave because he would not allow his son to take part in the campaign. I expained all my father-in-law's reasons to my brother, and defended his actions in the matter. "Very well, then," the prince replied, "your husband must leave the army, and give up the command of his regiment to the king. At the same time, you need have been in no anxiety, for I know from reliable sources that no blood will be shed." "Yet for all that," I added, "preparations are being made to lay siege to Philippsburg." "That is true," he answered, "but no battle will be fought there." While we were talking my husband joined us, and entreated my brother to help him to get away from Bayreuth. They both stood talking together for some time. My brother told me afterwards that he would write the margrave a very civil letter, and place the matter in such a light before him that it could not fail to have good results. "We will remain together," he added, turning to my husband; "nothing will make me happier than to have my dear brother always about me." The crown prince wrote his letter, and gave it to Baron Stein to deliver to the margrave, after which we took a tender farewell of each other. My brother promised me to obtain the king's leave to pay me a visit at Bayreuth on his return. This was the last time I saw him in the same intimate way as of old. He changed greatly afterwards.

IMPATIENCE: FREDERICK READY TO MOUNT THE THRONE, 1734

Our old master has nearly reached his end; he will not last out this month!

In October 1734, Frederick, fresh from his baptism of fire, visited Wilhelmina in Bayreuth. His sister's account of this visit may have been exaggerated, as were many of her tales. But it was an unflattering portrait of Frederick, who was already making plans for his actions after the death of his father.[2] *The king was dangerously ill from dropsy, but thanks to the skill of his surgeons he made a marvelous recovery and lived for six more years.*

My brother arrived at our house on the 6th of October. He seemed to me to be unable to control himself, and in order to avoid all conversation with me, said he was obliged to write to the king and queen. I sent for pens and paper, and he sat down and wrote in my room. It took him one good long hour to write two short notes of a few lines only. Afterwards he had the whole court presented to him, but took no particular notice of its members beyond looking mockingly at each of them. We then went to dinner. The whole of his conversation consisted of perpetual satirical remarks about everything he saw, while he repeated to me over and over again the words "little Sovereign and little Court" at least a hundred times. I was irritated beyond measure, and could not understand how he could have altered so much toward me. The etiquette at all the courts of Germany allows only those that have the rank of captain to dine at the table with the royal personages, lieutenants and ensigns dining at a third table. My brother had a lieutenant in his suite, and insisted on his dining at his table, saying that the king's lieutenants were worth the margrave's ministers. I appeared not to notice this uncivil remark.

As we were sitting alone together in the afternoon, my brother said,

[2] *Memoirs of Wilhelmina,* pp. 364–66.

"Our old master has nearly reached his end; he will not last out this month! I know he made you many fine promises, but I shall not be able to fulfill them. Half the sum the king has lent you I will leave you. I think you can both be satisfied with that." I answered him that my love for him had no selfish ends in view, and that I should never ask him for anything but the continuance of his friendship. I would rather not accept a penny from him than be a burden to him.

"No, no," my brother replied, "you are to have the hundred thousand *thalers*.* I have settled them on you. People will be much surprised when they find how differently I act to what they expect. They imagine I shall waste my treasures, and that money will become as common at Berlin as stones. I shall take good care it is not so. I shall increase the army, but all the rest will remain on its old footing. The queen, my mother, shall be treated with every possible respect and honor, but she shall not interfere in the affairs of the State. If she does so she will meet her match in me."

I was struck dumb as I heard the crown prince say all this, and did not know whether I were sleeping or waking. My brother afterwards asked me about the affairs of the principality, about which I gave him nearer details. "When your foolish father-in-law is dead, I would advise your getting rid of the whole court, and living like private people, in order to pay off your debts. You do not, in fact, require so many people and you must discover how to reduce the salary of those whom it is necessary for you to keep. You were accustomed at Berlin to have only four dishes at dinner, and you must be satisfied with the same here. I will ask you both to come to Berlin from time to time, and that will save you the expense of housekeeping."

My heart had all along felt fit to break, but now as I listened to this unworthy talk of my brother's I burst into tears. "Why do you cry?" he asked me. "Go along with you, you are depressed and in a melancholy humor, and require some distraction. The music is waiting for us. I will drive your sad thoughts away by playing to you on the flute." With these words he gave me his hand, and led me into the other room. I sat down to the harpsichord, which I covered with my tears. Mademoiselle von Marwitz sat down opposite to me, so that no one should observe my distress.

On the fourth day of his stay with us the crown prince received an urgent message from the queen entreating him to hasten his return as the king was at the point of death. This news overwhelmed me with grief. I loved the king, and felt that owing to the turn circumstances had taken I could no longer rely on my brother. During the last two days before he left he was more amiable toward me. My love for him made me find excuses for his shortcomings, and I fondly believed we

* Fifteen thousand pounds.

were again reconciled to each other. The hereditary prince meanwhile did not let himself be deceived. He told me many things which afterward came true. My brother took his departure on the 9th of October, leaving me in great uncertainty regarding himself.

DISSIMULATION: PATRON FOR BALLET DANCER LA BARBERINA, 1744

. . . where they did—nothing but drink tea.

Frederick was proud of the opera house which he had built at Berlin shortly after his accession in 1740, and he took great joy in attending the performances there. His love for this form of music led him on a campaign to obtain the services of a beautiful Italian ballet dancer named La Barberina. In 1744, he had her virtually kidnapped and brought to Berlin. Professionally, she was an enormous success. Tongues began to wag with the gossip that La Barberina included the king himself among her numerous lovers. Frederick, whose distaste for women had led to unflattering rumors, was not at all averse to stories about his friendship with the ballet dancer. For four years he was her patron and he saw to it that she was paid huge sums for her appearances. She finally fell into disfavor when she married the son of Chancellor Cocceji. The story of La Barberina was told in this passage by Dr. J. G. Zimmermann.[3] *(See pages 132–36 for Dr. Zimmermann's "small mutilation.")*

But pictures were not the only means by which the king wished to insinuate that he yet was very fond of women. He would also make people believe that he lived in a very intimate connection with the famous dancer Barberina. Once on a masquerade at Berlin, he walked with her, unmasked, arm in arm; and then retired with this beautiful Italian, into a closet, where they did—nothing but drink tea.

This sweet woman was the only one with whom Frederick the Great, when king, seemed to be in love, and for this reason, her history, without impropriety, may be introduced into the history of such a man. Mr. Denina has done this, without being sufficiently informed. Madam Barberina never returned, as he says, from Berlin to Venice. She never eloped from Berlin with an Englishman; and, consequently, the king could never be influenced by this motive, to have her taken up at Venice.*

[3] Dr. J. G. Zimmermann, *Select Views of the Life, Reign, and Character of Frederick the Great, King of Prussia* (London, 1792), I, 58–61.

* *Essai sur la vie et le régne de Frédéric II,* p. 114.

The Prussian resident at Venice had engaged her for the opera at Berlin, at seven thousand dollars a year. A contract in due form was drawn up between her and the resident. At the time that this was done, she had quarreled with her lover, a Scotchman of the name of Mackenzie. The two lovers were reconciled, and Madam Barberina did not choose to fulfill her engagement. The king bid his resident sue her before the Senate of Venice. The Senate laughed, and refused justice. About that time, the baggage of a Venetian ambassador to the British court, Signor Campello, was passing the Prussian dominions, on its way from Hamburg to London. The king gave orders to arrest it, and to declare at Venice, that nothing of this baggage should be given up, before Madam Barberina was surrendered to him. Campello had many near relations in the Senate; and this candid and enlightened court of justice, found now that the king was perfectly in the right.

The fair dancer, duly escorted, was sent by the Senate of Venice to the confines of Austria; and thence by the courts of Vienna and Dresden, to the borders of Brandenburg. Mr. Mackenzie followed her everywhere, but, on the desire of his family, was obliged to leave Berlin, and to return to England. Madam Barberina soon forgot him; for she pleased the king, and her pay was increased to twelve thousand dollars. She married afterwards a son of the High Chancellor Cocceji, now President of the Regency at Glogau, and is still living. Mackenzie, as easily may be conceived, bore an inveterate spite to Frederick, and being a near relation and intimate friend of Lord Bute, inspired him likewise with his implacable hate. It is well known from Frederick's *History of the War of Seven Years,* how, toward the end of this war, Bute treated the reviving hero. The refusal of a fair dancer to a favorite of this lord, had, of course, the same influence upon the conclusion of that war, as a pair of gloves, refused by the Duchess of Marlborough, on the end of that for the Spanish Succession.

MILITARY GENIUS: BATTLE OF HOHENFRIEDBERG, JUNE 4, 1745

A fault committed in war never escapes with impunity.

Many eyewitnesses testified to Frederick's military genius. On January 20, 1745, Emperor Charles VII died in Munich. No longer could Frederick claim to be acting as the champion of the Holy Roman Empire. There was even more disquieting news: Maximilian Joseph, Charles VII's son, followed the advice of his dying father and made peace with Maria Theresa, signing the separate treaty of Füssen with Austria. Austria restored all con-

quests to Bavaria, and the Elector of Bavaria promised Francis Stephen, the husband of Maria Theresa, his vote at the coming imperial election.

And that was not all the bad news for Frederick. Maria Theresa was doing her best to strike back at him. On January 8, 1745, she concluded the Union of Warsaw, a new alliance with Saxony, England, and Holland against Prussia. The Austrian queen was refusing to be the weak woman Frederick wanted her to be.

At 4 A.M. on June 4, 1745, the Prussians swooped on the half-asleep Saxons, first raining cannon balls on them. Then the infantry pushed ahead. Prince Charles, assuming that the distant thunder meant that the Saxons were smashing the Prussians, decided to remain in bed. But soon there came news of disaster. By the time Charles could get into his trousers it was too late to do much about it. The Prussians had cut his troops to pieces.

By 9 A.M. it was all over. The entire Austro-Saxon army was in retreat, losing 6,000 men, including four generals and 200 officers. Frederick's performance was masterful. He even personally led three battalions on an Austrian gun emplacement in one of his greatest victories.

The story of Hohenfriedberg was told by a Prussian officer in the following account testifying to Frederick's "masterful stroke." [4]

The King of Prussia's conduct, both before and on the day of this memorable action, deserves the highest commendation. The situation of affairs, with regard to his own forces, as well as to the enemy's, required some decisive event. By keeping merely on the defensive, and only endeavoring to keep our adversaries from penetrating into Silesia, over the mountains, the king must have sacrificed a great many men, weakened his provinces and finances, by procuring subsistence for his army at his own expense, and all this at the hazard of not succeeding at last. For the enemy, on the other hand, was stronger than we, or believed to be so. He had behind him all the strength of Bohemia; and even supposing that a whole campaign could have been spent in skirmishing, his experience in this kind of warfare, and the superiority of his light troops, gave us no ground to hope for equal success everywhere. Moreover, we must add to these considerations, that the king, having occasion for all his troops to make head against Prince Charles

[4] *The King of Prussia's Campaigns,* trans. from the French (London, 1768), pp. 137–43.

of Lorraine and the Duke of Weissenfels, must have abandoned Upper Silesia, whence the body of insurgents might have spread itself over the country, and make it very difficult for us to find subsistence, especially as they had lately made themselves masters of the fortress of Cofel by surprise. It was therefore absolutely necessary to bring the enemy as soon as possible to a battle, to present him with opportunities for that purpose, and allure him to the point the king had in view; that is, to beat him, clear Silesia from his parties, and carry the theatre of the war into Bohemia.

It was therefore a masterly stroke in the king, to pretend to be afraid of the superiority of the combined army, and spread the report that he would not wait for it in the neighborhood of Schweidnitz; but take a sure post between Breslau and Glogau on the river Oder, for the convenience of his convoys. In consequence of these affected appearances, he caused the mountains of Upper Silesia and the country of Glatz to be evacuated, assembled all his different corps, and kept himself closely covered in his camp between Schweidnitz and Striegau, using all imaginable precautions to conceal from the enemy his real designs, and the number of his troops; being fully persuaded, that, if Prince Charles would but come down into the plain, it would be in his power to force him to a battle.

The event justified the wisdom of the king's measures; and if one must be a great general to contrive fine projects, and draw the plans of them, he must not be less so, to take advantage of the proper season for executing them with vigor and dexterity. And in this case also his Majesty discovered the reach of his understanding. When the king saw that his stratagem was successful, and that Prince Charles and the Duke of Weissenfels were falling into his snare, he laid hold of the favorable moment, with surprising readiness; and justly supposing that the combined army, having come down from the mountains about sunset, would not have time to make the proper dispositions during the night, attacked and surprised it at the break of day, and gained over it a most complete victory. It may be said, that this was doing business with a good grace, and at the critical nick of time; and if we have seen Silesia saved, and our army subsisted at the expense of Bohemia, we owe this happy revolution wholly to the prudent foresight of our august monarch.

The same cannot be said of the combined army and its conduct. The general plan of invading Silesia was proper, without doubt. The court of Vienna proposed to terminate the war against our master by this single campaign, and to secure that end, something more was necessary than mere excursions; but in my opinion, their execution of this plan stood in need of some amendments.

GRIEF: REACTION ON DEATH OF HIS BROTHER, 1758

As heaven is my witness, I cherished him sincerely.

Eyewitnesses carefully observed Frederick's interpersonal relations. Outside of his special love for Wilhelmina, Frederick seldom showed any inclination to draw close to his three younger brothers, Augustus William, Henry, and Ferdinand. He always treated them as if he were a harsh and critical father. Frederick was ten years older than the next brother, Augustus William, a serious-minded young man who was made Prince of Prussia in 1744. In 1757, in the midst of the Seven Years' War, at a time when the Prussians were in a difficult military position, Frederick gave a command to Augustus William, who was completely outmaneuvered by the Austrians. Angered, Frederick refused to speak to his brother, dismissed him, and informed him that he could not expect another appointment. The unfortunate Augustus William died a year later, in June 1758, of a tumor on the brain.

In his Memoirs, *Henri de Catt revealed how Frederick wept when, on June 18, 1758, he was informed of the death of the brother whose heart he had broken.*[5] *His reaction was composed of equal elements of guilt, self-pity, and self-justification.*

18th June 1758

In going to his Majesty, who had ordered me to be in attendance at two o'clock, I learned from an aide-de-camp that he had received the sad news of the death of the Prince of Prussia, his brother, and that he had been severely struck by this blow. I entered, and I saw the king seated, with his elbow on the table, and a handkerchief in his hand, with which he was covering his forehead. He looked at me for a few minutes, then, rising, he said to me, with his eyes full of tears:

"Ah, my friend, what disastrous news I have received! My poor brother is no more," and he sobbed.

I was keenly touched, and mingled my tears with his. He saw my sorrow, and, placing his hand round my neck, which surprised me, I confess, he said to me: "My friend, he is no more for me, this brother whom I have so much cherished. You are very good to grieve with me; the life which you lead with me is very sad, and how many misfor-

[5] *Frederick the Great, Memoirs of his Reader, Henri de Catt, 1758–1760,* trans. F. S. Flint (London, 1916), I, 187–90. Reprinted by permission of Constable and Company, Ltd.

tunes still await us! But, my friend, I can support them all: losses of the heart, of friendships are the sole heart-rending and irreparable losses: my dear brother is no more."

. . . How much I counted in that moment of bitterness on the force of reason and of his philosophy, which, while approving such legitimate and natural tears, could yet moderate and mollify them.

"I am satisfied of what your kind heart dictates to you in this moment, but, my dear sir, I have called and

J'appelle à mon secours raison, philosophie,
Je n'en reçois, hélas, aucun soulagement:
A leurs belles leçons insensé qui s'y fie:
Elles ne peuvent rien contre le sentiment.
J'entends que la raison me dit que vainement
Je m'afflige d'un mal qui n'a point de remède;
Mais je verse des pleurs dans ce même moment
*Et sens qu'à ma douleur il vaut mieux que je cède.**

Indeed, he did shed tears; after an hour of a sitting so painful for the heart, the king said to me:

"I cannot, my dear sir, stay in my room any longer; I feel as though I am stifling. I am going for a ride on my horse, and to breathe the air and give myself up alone to my sad thoughts. If you will have the kindness—this was his expression—to return again at about five o'clock, you will oblige me. It is pleasant to pour out your grief in company with the very rare person who knows how to share it with you."

The king in fact did set out on his horse, and rode at a walking pace for about an hour, followed by a groom. I saw him start and return, with a pain I cannot describe.

I appeared at five, as he had ordered me.

"My ride did me some good: I can at least breathe; but my heart is still oppressed. I cannot reconcile myself to the idea of seeing a brother whom I cherished carried off, and, as heaven is my witness, I cherished him sincerely: and believe me that there are very few men like me who love their family as I cherish mine. Nothing equals my satisfaction when I can give them real proofs of this, and I have never missed an opportunity, my family must do me that justice. Private individuals cannot love each other more than I love my relations, and this attachment is not common, I confess, among those who are often so improperly—at least as regards morals—called the great of the earth. I

* Chaulieu, 22: On the death of the Marquis de la Fare, in 1748. ("I call to my aid reason, philosophy: I receive from them, alas! no comfort: he is mad who trusts in their fine lessons: they can do nothing against our feelings. I hear my reason telling me that I grieve in vain for an evil which has no remedy; but I shed tears at that same moment, and feel that it is better to give way to my sorrow.")

must tell you with the same frankness that this brother whom I have just lost, and whom I shall long regret, for so many reasons, deserved all my affection, for the excellence of his heart, his attachment for me, and his zeal for the country."

The king would have doubtless said more on this subject, if a heap of letters had not been brought in to him.

"Here is work to do. Good evening, my dear sir, and think of me in my bereavement."

DEPRESSION: DEFEATED AT THE BATTLE OF HOCHKIRCH, FREDERICK CONTEMPLATES SUICIDE, 1758

There, my friend, is all that is required to put an end to the tragedy.

During his campaigns, Frederick would often descend from heights of euphoria to depths of depression. In 1758, his triumph at Zorndorf was counterbalanced by a defeat at Hochkirch, where he tried to outmaneuver his Austrian antagonist, Daun, out of Silesia. In telling the story of the battle, Henri de Catt threw much light on Frederick's personality, especially his tendency to fall into depression.[6]

Unfortunately, the king had to be up earlier than he thought. Between four and five o'clock, the enemy appeared with a large body of Croats, supported by regular infantry, and threw back the camp guards of cavalry which we had on our right flank, Zieten's hussars and the free companies stationed in the brushwood on the right of the camp: the battalions on this right wing scarcely had time to get under arms before the enemy attacked. Such was the beginning of this murderous battle which lasted from four o'clock in the morning until nine. The king, exposed all the while to cannon fire and often to musketry fire, his horse being wounded, gave astonishing proofs of an unshakable firmness and of that coolness which has distinguished him so much on other occasions. He retreated, in the presence of a victorious enemy, with such a bearing and in so admirable an order that the enemy did not venture to follow him. He remained between Pommritz and Hochkirchen, and, although reinforced by all his troops who had not fought, he did not leave this place, being satisfied with what he had done, and doubtless looking upon it as an advantage which he had not greatly looked for. . . .

[6] *Memoirs of de Catt*, I, 33–42. Reprinted by permission of Constable and Company, Ltd.

I was called on this unfortunate day at three o'clock in the afternoon. My heart, which was full of sorrow, feared this first moment in which I should see the king. I entered his room in a state of extreme emotion. He came up to me with a rather open air, and, in a quiet voice, he repeated to me some lines from *Mithridate,* looking at me in a very singular manner. . . .

After a pause of a few minutes, he said:

"My friend, I am a poor conquered man: this is a terrible misfortune to happen to me. Ah, how limited are the views of prudence and experience, and how the future is covered with a thick veil. This is a disaster, a surprise which must be mended. We can truthfully say with François I: All is lost, except honor. My troops fought with courage, and, as for myself, I certainly did not spare myself."

At this word, I began to speak, for, until that moment, he had not left me a moment in which to say anything.

"Yes, Sire, you were not careful enough of yourself. The whole suite, the whole army is of opinion that your Majesty exposed yourself too much. What would become of us if we lost the father! Those, Sire, were the words of the soldiers and of the officers, who all trembled for you."

And this was true. I saw the tears moistening his cheeks.

"What you tell me touches me. Why, my dear sir, should I not expose myself for all these worthy people who are sacrificing their lives for me? The peril was too great for me not to share it. The most accursed accident that has ever happened to me was in progress, and I had to risk my head and my person to save the unfortunate remains of the wreck."

"It is because that head is necessary, Sire, to save us from being wrecked that you must be careful of it."

"Well, well, if not I, it will be my brother."

Some generals were announced.

"Here are some officers to whom I must give orders. If you are not too bored with a poor unfortunate, I beg you to come back again here for a few moments."

I went out. At five o'clock I was called again. The king seemed to me gloomier and more downcast than he was when I first saw him.

"My dear Marshal Keith is no more. This is a real loss to society and to the army. What will my lord, his brother, say about the loss of a brother of whom he was exceedingly fond! So soon as I have a little more leisure, I will write and assure him that I share his grief as if it were my own, and I will celebrate in verse our common loss. It is impossible for me to tell you how many particular reasons I have to regret the poor Marshal; I have also many for sincerely regretting Prince Francis of Brunswick. He was killed by a cannonball: he had ability combined with marked bravery; this bravery is hereditary in the family. What a number of brave men I am losing, my friend, and how I detest this trade to which the blind chance of my birth has condemned me. But I have upon me the means of ending the play, when it becomes unbearable to me."

Doubtless I put on an air, at these words, which struck the king. He said to me:

"Lord, you are changing color!"

He undid his collar, pulled out from beneath his shirt a ribbon, at the end of which was an oval golden box which rested on his chest.

"There my friend, is all that is required to put an end to the tragedy."

He opened the little box, in which were eighteen pills, which we counted.

"These pills," he said, "are of opium. The dose is quite sufficient to take me to that dark bourn whence we do not return."

After showing me this, he hung it round his neck again, and let it fall into its place on his chest.

"Now, my dear sir, you will be kind enough to help me fasten my collar, for I am so clumsy as not to be able to do this, and I do not wish anybody except yourself to know of my little resource."

CURIOSITY: A FRENCH SCHOLAR'S ACCOUNT OF FREDERICK'S PERSONALITY, 1765

Oh! for this last [Rousseau], he is a madman.

"He is a mere coxcomb, a coxcomb and a French wit who will spoil all my labor." This judgment by Frederick William was directed at his eldest son's preference for all things French. When he obtained power, Frederick was anxious to bring French literary lights to Berlin and Potsdam. Among them was the French scholar Dieudonné Thiebault, whom he invited to become Professor of Belles Lettres in the Royal Academy of Berlin. The Frenchman later wrote an account of his reception in Potsdam, which reveals Frederick's sense of curiosity, as well as his hostility to the German language. It also describes an exchange between Frederick and the great philosophe *Jean-Jacques Rousseau, who with characteristically nasty comments rejected Frederick's invitation to come to Prussia.*[7]

On my arrival at Berlin, on the 16th of March 1765, my first concern was to write to M. le Catt, reader or secretary of orders to the king, requesting him to inquire and communicate to me the com-

[7] Dieudonné Thiebault, *Original Anecdotes of Frederick the Second, King of Prussia* (London, 1885), I, 1–11.

mands of his Majesty, both in respect to what related to myself personally, and to a packet with which I had been charged for him by M. d'Alembert, who had signified his desire that I should deliver it in person to the king. On the next day I received an order to be at Potsdam the day after, by three o'clock in the afternoon at the latest. I accordingly arrived on the day, and before the hour prescribed, at M. le Catt's, whom I found still at table.

I was the more curious to take a near view of Frederick, and to judge for myself of his character, as I had hitherto held an uncertain opinion respecting him. All Europe was unanimous in considering him as a man of great military talents and genius; but nothing could be more discordant than the existing opinions in regard to his character, his social, political, and moral qualities. By some he was considered a wise man and a great king, and no less a distinguished scholar and an amiable philosopher; by others, he was represented as a tyrant, a man vain in the extreme of his acquirements, a true and skillful Machiavelianist. At one time, virtues almost supernatural were ascribed to Frederick, at another, the most odious vices, or the most atrocious actions. . . .

We arrived just as the secretaries of the cabinet had entered for the purpose of signing of letters, a business that could not be over in less than half an hour. That we might lose no time, my guide conducted me to the apartment of my Lord Marshal, a respectable old man, the intimate friend of the king, and whose establishment in the palace was very near his Majesty. This nobleman received me as great men, if they have understanding and respect themselves, never fail to receive strangers; that is, with dignity, politeness, and simplicity. "You see me," said he, "in the apartment of a great man, that which belonged to M. d'Alembert. Tell him, when you write to him, that it was in his own apartment, by his own fireside, I inquired of you after his health, and requested you to present him with my compliments." Some details respecting my journey, and various literary matters, made up the conversation during the half hour; at the end of which we received notice that the secretaries had departed. We accordingly quitted my Lord Marshal, and proceeded to the king's apartment.

The day began to decline; M. le Catt made me go before him, and kept two or three paces behind me: the king was standing, and appeared to have been walking about the room. On seeing me he approached, saying: "Good evening, Sir, I am very glad to see you, and to make acquaintance with you." From this moment his questions succeeded each other so uninterruptedly that our conversation became extremely rapid; nor did it alter in this particular during the whole time of his detaining me, which was nearly two hours. He obtained from me, however, but one of my bows, the small space he left between us, and my eagerness to answer him, having put the other two entirely out of the question. It was with difficulty that I found an opportunity to deliver M. d'Alembert's packet. I had been frequently warned that he required direct, frank, short, and ready answers: from me he certainly received most frequently half phrases, and occasionally only one or two words.

He began with asking me how I spelled my name; in what part of France I was born; if my parents were alive; what was my father's profession; if I had any brothers or sisters; how old I was; what had been my pursuits in life; where I had lived; if I were married; to what family my wife belonged; what had been my principal studies; if I had printed any of my productions; in what state of health I had left d'Olivet and d'Alembert; and what route I had taken on my way to Berlin? On my replying to this last question, that I had passed through Stuttgart, Nuremberg, and Dresden, he appeared surprised at the considerable circuit I had made. When I had explained to him that my reason for taking this road was to avoid others still more difficult, particularly in winter, and that it was a M. Barré, a merchant at Berlin, who, having been at Paris, had traced my route; he asked me how my wife and I had been able to make ourselves understood in a country where certainly no French was spoken. "I bought a German grammar at Strassburg," said I, "at the end of which there is a tolerably copious vocabulary, adapted for the use of foreigners. When I wanted anything, I had recourse to my vocabulary, and if I found myself unable to pronounce the name of the article I stood in need of, I pointed to it in the book, and thus procured it. At Nuremberg I met with a captain of your army, who was returning from Savoy, his native country; he was acquainted with the two languages, and, as we pursued the rest of the journey together, he served as our interpreter. "What was the name of this captain?"—"*Favrat.*" We then entered into conversation respecting this officer and his brother, and it appeared to me a favorable opportunity of obliging my traveling companion by repeating what he had related to me of his military operations in some of the places through which we had passed, and particularly his entrance as a prisoner into the city of Dresden, covered with six wounds, almost naked, and in the depth of winter. But, notwithstanding all my endeavors to relate these circumstances in a natural manner, and as if actuated by no particular motive, I soon discovered that I was on dangerous ground, and therefore abandoned so imprudent a subject as soon as I could. In fact, the king suddenly became serious and thoughtful, began to look around him, and appeared occupied with other thoughts. . . .

. . . He returned by a happy transition to that of the French language, and inquired who, in my opinion, were the living authors that wrote the French language with the greatest correctness? I named d'Olivet, d'Alembert, Buffon, J. J. Rousseau. . . . Here he interrupted me, exclaiming, "Oh! for this last, he is a madman."—"Sire, that is no reason why he should not write correctly."

The king soon after put an end to the interview, expressing himself much satisfied with having seen me, and after assuring me that he placed great reliance on my zeal. He then wished me a good evening, and a pleasant journey, and detained M. le Catt, saying, "Catt, I wish to speak with you." Le Catt, however, came to me in a few minutes in an adjoining apartment, and informed me that his Majesty was so well satisfied with me, that he had directed him to write to both M. d'Alembert and M. d'Olivet, to thank them for their choice of me, and also to prepare another letter to be sent to the Academy of Berlin, commanding that I should be there received into its class of *belles lettres,* with a pension of two hundred rix-dollars.

Conversing with M. le Catt, respecting the interview I had with the king, I expressed my surprise at the earnestness with which he had said of J. J. Rousseau, *Oh! he is a madman.* "This earnestness," replied my conductor, "is connected with a recent anecdote which I will relate to you. Some months ago my Lord Marshal, the friend of J. J. Rousseau, appearing much distressed at the persecutions the philosopher of Geneva experiences even in Switzerland and Neuchâtel, of which this nobleman is governor, the king said to him, *'Well, Sir, write to your friend that, if he will come to my states, I will insure him a safe asylum, and a pension of two thousand livres. We will give him a comfortable house at Panckow, contiguous to the gardens of Schönhausen: the house shall have a garden and a field attached to it, that he may be able to keep a cow and poultry, and cultivate his own vegetables. There he may live without inquietude and free from necessities: his solitude may be complete, and he may wander at pleasure in the groves of Schönhausen, where the queen inhabits only during a few of the summer months.'*

My Lord Marshal, delighted with this plan, lost not a moment in writing the proposed letter, which, when finished, he brought to the king previous to its departure. The king took up a pen and added these words: . . . *'Come, dear Rousseau, I offer you a house, a pension, and liberty.'* A short time produced an answer conceived in the following terms: . . . *'Your Majesty offers me an asylum, and promises me liberty. But you have a sword, and you are a king: you offer a pension to me who never did you a service, but have you bestowed one on each of the brave men who have lost either a leg or an arm in doing you service? . . .'* You may easily imagine that ever after, when the name of Rousseau came in the king's way, he did not fail to add to it the epithet you have heard, and with which, at the time, this negotiation was concluded."

DISTRESS: DEATH OF PRINCE CHARLES OF LORRAINE, 1779

The poor Prince Charles is no more.

Frederick became more and more unhappy as his contemporaries died one by one. In 1779, he invited an accomplished courtier, the Prince de Ligne, to Potsdam, where the two discussed "the great times of Augustus and Louis XIV, the eccentricities of Voltaire, the vanity of Maupertuis, and the hypochondria of the Marquis d'Argens, whom the king used to induce to keep his bed for four and twenty hours, by merely telling him he looked ill; and what not besides?" In his memoirs the Prince de Ligne recorded Frederick's reaction when he learned of the death of the Prince of Lorraine.[8]

Another day, when I came to him, he said to me, "I am grieved to announce bad news to you. They write me word that Prince Charles of Lorraine is at the last extremity." He looked at me, to see what effect his communication had upon me, and when he saw my eyes full of tears, he changed, by the easiest transitions, the conversation; talked to me of war, and then of Marshal Lacy. . . .

The next day, the king, as soon as he saw me, came up to me, and said to me, with an air of great feeling, "If you must learn the loss of a man who loved you, and who was an honor to humanity, it is better it should be from one, who was as much attached to him as myself. The poor Prince Charles is no more. Others may, perhaps, replace his loss in your heart; but few princes can replace him, for the beauty of his mind, and his many virtues." While saying this to me, he became extremely affected. I said to him, "Your Majesty's regrets are a consolation to me; and you did not wait for his death to praise him: there are some fine lines about him in the poem on the *Art de la Guerre*." I was myself much affected: however, I managed to recite them; and I thought *the author* seemed to be pleased with me, for remembering them. "The prince's passage of the Rhine," said he, "was a grand thing; but the poor prince always depended upon so many people! I have never depended upon anything but my head—sometimes I have depended upon it too much—for my success. He was ill served, and but little obeyed: neither one nor the other has ever happened to me."

[8] *Mémoires et mélanges historiques et littéraires, par le Prince de Ligne,* trans. in Dover, II, 409–12.

8

Eyewitnesses on Life at Potsdam

For his palace Frederick selected a sylvan paradise overlooking Potsdam from the top of a hill, eighteen miles southwest of Berlin. Here, from 1745 to 1747, he built a smaller version of Versailles, a home fit for a philosopher-king. Every inch of the palace reflected Frederick's taste. The inspiration was French, with just enough originality to merit the designation, "Frederician rococo." Frederick lived in Sans Souci from early spring to late autumn each year until his death. To Potsdam came a stream of visitors, including the following who left eyewitness accounts of the daily life there.

A BRITISH VISITOR, 1740

During the whole audience the king was in extreme good humor.

On August 17, 1740, before he built Sans Souci, Frederick received in audience at Potsdam a British diplomat named Dickins. At this time the British king, George II, who was at Hanover on a visit, was much concerned about the Spanish War, which he feared might bring France and the whole world upon him. Whether or not Prussia was for or against the Spanish War was an issue of moment to the British. Dickins' official report from the archives gives clear indication that Frederick was going to be a monarch who knew his own mind.[1]

Audience lasted above an hour: king turned directly upon business; wishes to have "Categorical Answers" as to three points already submitted to his Britannic Majesty's consideration. Clear footing indispensable between us. What you want of me say it, and be plain. What I want of you are these three things:

1. Guarantee for Jülich and Berg. All the world knows *whose* these duchies are. Will his Britannic Majesty guarantee me there? And if so, how, and to what lengths will he proceed about it?

[1] Dickins, in *State Paper Office,* 17 August, 1740, quoted in Carlyle, III, 38–39.

2. Settlement about Ost-Friesland. Expectancy of Ost-Friesland, soon to fall heirless, which was granted *me* long since, though Hanover makes hagglings, counterclaimings: I must have some settlement about that.

3. The like about those perplexities in Mecklenburg. No difficulty there if we try heartily, nor is there such pressing haste about it.

These are my three claims on England; and I will try to serve England as far in return, if it will tell me how. . . . England I consider my most natural friend and ally; but I must know what there is to depend on there. Princes are ruled by their interest; cannot follow their feelings. Let me have an explicit answer, say at Wesel, where I am to be on the 24th. . . .

During the whole audience, the king was in extreme good humor, and not only heard with attention all the considerations I offered, but was not the least offended at any objections I made to what he said. It is undoubtedly the best way to behave with frankness to him.

A DAY AT POTSDAM, 1759

He always retires bowing in the most courtly manner.

At his accession Frederick established a routine which he scarcely varied throughout his reign. Many authors have written about the regularity of his daily tasks. The following passage, found in the British Museum, gives an eyewitness account of Frederick's daily life at Potsdam in 1759, when he was forty-seven years old. The title page of the book, published in London that same year, bears this identification: "Translated from a Curious Manuscript in French Found in the Cabinet of the Late Field Marshal Keith." Interspersed with a discussion of the dress and way of living of its subject was praise for "the mighty deeds of such a hero." [2]

The king of Prussia is about forty-seven years of age, in stature about five feet six inches, extremely well made, but somewhat remarkable in his deportment, contracted by a long-constrained carriage peculiar to himself; notwithstanding which he is infinitely polite. His countenance is agreeable and sprightly; his voice musical and fine, even when he swears, which he rarely does, except when in a passion. He is better versed in the French language, and speaks it more fluently

[2] *A Succinct Account of the Person, the Way of Living, and of the Court of the King of Prussia* (London, 1759), pp. 5–13.

and correctly than the German, and never makes use of the latter, but to those whom he knows to be ignorant of the former. His hair is of a dark fine chestnut color, and always in queue; he takes a secret pleasure in dressing it himself, which he always does without the assistance of anyone. He never wore a nightcap, nightgown, or slippers, but only puts on a linen cloak when he powders his hair. Three times in the year he has a new suit of the uniform of the First Battalion of his Guards, which is a blue cloth, faced with red and silver Brandenburgs, after the Spanish manner, with tassels at the end, and the Brandenburgs close to the edge; his waistcoat is plain yellow, a *point d'Espagne* hat, and white feather. On a particular occasion, when he had a mind to shine (as he termed it) he ordered a grogoram* uniform to be made for him. He wears boots abroad and at home, and was never seen to appear in shoes, even at his public court days; this trifle gives him an air very constrained and particular to his foreign courtiers.

He always rises about five in the morning, and is busy (at least continues alone) till three-quarters after six. At seven he dresses, and then receives such letters, petitions and memorials as are presented to him, and directs such answers to be made, and prescribes such methods to be taken, as the circumstances of each require; and having dispatched these, at nine his ministers (or rather his domestics) attend on him, and continue with him till eleven, at which time precisely he goes upon the parade to relieve his guards, and sees them perform their various exercises and evolutions, and is very exact in correcting any mistake, and never fails to give them the word of command himself, unless he is indisposed; it is not therefore to be wondered, that most of the generals of other princes endeavor to imitate the Prussian exercise and discipline, as they are the best now in Europe.

After this is done, which employs him till about half an hour after eleven, he returns, and continues in the Great Hall of his Palace, and grants public audience to any of his subjects, and permits them to present their own petitions; and so desirous is he to distribute justice, and relieve the complaints of all his subjects from injuries and oppressions, that he strictly commands his executive officers to hear, determine, and adjudge all disputes without delay, or tedious proceedings in courts of law, and has thereby thrown cavil out of the wavering scales of justice, and poised them equally to all. Having received such petitions, and directed his justiciary officers to expedite such remedies as are requisite and legal, he returns to his closet, and, although only his own domestics are present, he has so habituated himself in bending his body into a bowing posture, that he always retires

* Grogoram or grogram, a coarse fabric made of silk and mohair, stiffened with gum.

bowing in the most courtly manner, and this it is thought has occasioned his remarkable deportment. As soon as he enters his closet, he resumes his business alone, or finishes with his ministers, if anything remains undone before his going to the parade, which frequently is the case; for let the business be never so important, he is punctual in relieving his guards at the stroke of eleven.

He sits down at half an hour after twelve in general, accompanied with his own ministers, and those of foreign princes, who are at Potsdam, and the officers of his First Battalion of Guards. His table consists of twenty-four covers, although it frequently exceeds that number; he never has more than sixteen dishes of all sorts and denominations, which are all served up at the same time. If there be anything extraordinary, such as sea fish, or game, he privately defrays that out of his own purse, and it is not included in the ordinary expense. He is very elegant and particular in his desserts of fruit. The dinner time does not exceed an hour; after dinner he walks about a quarter of an hour, conversing with some of the company, and then retires to his closet, bowing in his usual manner as he goes out.

He continues in private till five o'clock, when his reader, who is usually the Marquis d'Argens, comes to him and reads till seven, and his reading is succeeded by a concert, which lasts till nine. He takes great delight in, and understands music extremely well, and few can equal him upon the flute. His daily concert consists chiefly of wind instruments, which are the best in Europe; namely, three eunuchs, a counter tenor voice, and Mademoiselle Astra, an Italian. These singers cannot be equaled, for he will admit of none that are not superlatively excellent. There is seldom any singing except in the company of favorites, although sometimes on a particular occasion, young lords making interest with the king's favorites gain admittance.

At nine, some of the Voltaires, Algarotti, Maupertuis, and the other wits, never exceeding eight, including the king, and one or two of the king's favorites who usually sup with him, meet in an apartment for that purpose; and supper is served up at half an hour after nine, which never consists of more than eight dishes, which are all introduced at the same time. From the time of supper, which continues till about eleven, wit flies about very freely till twelve, during which time the king lays aside his Majesty, and is only distinguished from the rest of the company by his superior wit and *bons mots.* At the stroke of twelve the king withdraws to bed, and is so exact, that the most entertaining subjects never make him exceed the time above five or ten minutes. . . .

The daily expense of his table for the kitchen is fixed at thirty-three German crowns, or five guineas and a half English money. For this sum he has twenty-four dishes, sixteen for dinner, and eight for supper;

the former consists of twenty-four covers, and the latter of eight; if there be more than twenty-four covers, he pays the overplus to the purveyor of the kitchen, at the rate of a crown a head. All the sea fish and game is not included in this expense, but is charged to the king over and above the five guineas and a half. Out of the thirty-three crowns, the purveyor pays for wood and coals, and buys the kitchen furniture, such as tables, kitchen linen, and in general everything that belongs to it, the wages of the cooks excepted, which the king is charged with extraordinarily. There are four cooks employed in the kitchen, a French one, an Italian, an Austrian, and a Prussian, and each of them dresses four dishes for the dinner, and two for the supper, so that in this variety of cookery, it is calculated that every man's palate may be pleased, which is the intent of the king in having four cooks of the four different countries of which his company generally consists. Whether the king be present or not, he gives a dinner all the year through to the officers of his First Battalion; and allows them a bottle of wine, and a bottle of beer alternately each day between two. There are also made ready every day at twelve o'clock, three large dishes of roast or boiled meat, bread and beer for the officers of his two other battalions of Foot Guards, and everyone may take of this as he pleases; it is a sort of whet before dinner, the price of which is also fixed with the purveyor of the kitchen, who provides at his own discretion a certain quantity.

No officer or soldier who is in garrison at Potsdam, dares presume to go without the gates, although it be but for a walk, without leave first signed by the king, which is very rarely granted; so strict is he in regard to discipline; and in general, nobody who is at Potsdam, can leave it without a letter of license.

A BRITISH GENERAL AT POTSDAM, 1774

The movement was conducted with a spirit and order . . . that was astonishing.

By the early 1770s, Frederick's annual military reviews had become famous all over Europe. Intelligence officers of the major countries were eager to be present. In the summer of 1774, Field Marshal Conway, an officer of considerable reputation in England, came to Germany to see the Prussian reviews. A letter which Conway wrote to his brother, the Marquis of Hertford, gives an enlightening picture of Potsdam.[3]

[3] Quoted in Sir Robert Murray Keith, *Memoirs and Correspondence* (London, n.d.) II, 21ff.

Berlin, July 17th, 1774

. . . On the third day (yesterday evening, in fact), I went, by appointment, to the new palace, to wait upon the king of Prussia. There was some delay: his Majesty had gone, in the interim, to a private concert, which he was giving to the princesses [Duchess of Brunswick and other high guests]: but the moment he was told I was there, he came out from his company, and gave me a most flattering gracious audience of more than half an hour; talking on a great variety of things, with an ease and freedom the very reverse of what I had been made to expect. . . . I asked, and received permission, to visit the Silesian camps next month, his Majesty most graciously telling me the particular days [the military reviews] would begin and end (27th August–3d September, Schmelwitz near Breslau, are time and place). This considerably deranges my Austrian movements, and will hurry my return out of those parts: but who could resist such a temptation! —I saw the Foot Guards exercise, especially the splendid First Battalion. I could have conceived nothing so perfect and so exact as all I saw:—so well dressed, such men, and so punctual in all they did.

The new palace at Potsdam is extremely noble. Not so perfect, perhaps, in point of taste, but better than I had been led to expect. The king dislikes living there: never does, except when there is high company about him: for seven or eight months in the year, he prefers little Sans Souci, and freedom among his intimates and some of his generals. . . . His music still takes up a great share of the king's time. On a table in his cabinet there, I saw, I believe, twenty boxes with a German flute in each: in his bedchamber, twice as many boxes of Spanish snuff, and, alike in cabinet and in bedchamber, three armchairs in a row for three favorite dogs, each with a little stool by way of step, that the getting up might be easy. . . .

The town of Potsdam is a most extraordinary and, in its appearance, beautiful town; all the streets perfectly straight, all at right angles to each other: and all the houses built with handsome, generally elegant fronts. . . . He builds for everybody who has a bad or a small house —even the lowest mechanic. He has done the same at Berlin. Altogether, his Majesty's building operations are astonishing. And from whence does this money come, after a long expensive war? It is all fairyland and enchantment—*Magnum vectigal parsimonsia,* in fact! . . . At Berlin here, I saw the porcelain manufacture today, which is greatly improved. I leave presently. Adieu, dear brother; excuse my endless letter (since you cannot squeeze the water out of it, as some will!)—Yours most sincerely,

Henry Seymour Conway

A BRITISH VISITOR ON FREDERICK AT THE AGE OF SIXTY-SEVEN, 1779

He seemed to exert himself with all the spirit of a young officer.

Visitors to Potsdam came away with similar impressions of Frederick during his later years. The aged monarch continued to perform the duties of office despite increasing infirmities. He still rose at four in the morning in summer and at five in winter, and carried on his administrative work in the same careful manner as in earlier days. Two differences—he now omitted supper and went to bed earlier. Here is an account of his activities in 1779 by a visitor, an otherwise unknown Dr. Moore.[4]

The King of Prussia is below the middle size, well made, and remarkably active for his time of life. He has become hardy by exercise and a laborious life; for his constitution originally seems to have been none of the strongest. His look announces spirit and penetration. He has fine blue eyes; and, in my opinion, his countenance, upon the whole, is agreeable. Some who have seen him are of a different opinion; all who judge from his portraits only, must be so; for although I have seen many, which have a little resemblance to him, and some which have a great deal, yet none of them do him justice. His features acquire a wonderful degree of animation while he converses. He stoops considerably, and inclines his head almost constantly to one side. His tone of voice is the clearest and most agreeable in conversation I ever heard. He speaks a great deal; yet those who hear him regret he does not speak a great deal more. His observations are always lively, very often just; and few men possess the talent of repartee in greater perfection.

He hardly ever varies his dress, which consists of a blue coat, lined and faced with red, and a yellow waistcoat and breeches. He always wears boots with hussar tops, which fall in wrinkles about his ankles, and are oftener of a dark brown than a black color. His hat would be thought extravagantly large in England, though it is of the size commonly used by the Prussian officers of cavalry. He generally wears one of the large side corners over his forehead and eyes, and the front cock on one side. He wears his hair queued behind, and dressed with a single buckle on each side. From their being very carelessly put up,

[4] Dr. Moore, *View of Society and Manners in France, Switzerland, and Germany*, quoted in Dover, II, 417–21.

and unequally powdered, we may naturally conclude, that the *friseur* has been greatly hurried in the execution of his office.

He uses a very large gold snuffbox, the lid ornamented with diamonds, and takes an immoderate quantity of Spanish snuff, the marks of which very often appear on his waistcoat and breeches. These are also liable to be soiled by the paws of two or three Italian greyhounds, which he often caresses. . . . A few days ago I happened to take a very early walk, about a mile from the town (Potsdam), and seeing some soldiers under arms in a field, at a small distance from the road, I went toward them. An officer on horseback, whom I took to be the major, for he gave the word of command, was uncommonly active, and often rode among the ranks, to reprimand or instruct the common men. When I came nearer, I was much surprised to find that this was the king himself. He had his sword drawn, and continued to exercise the corps for an hour after. He made them wheel, march, form the square, and fire by divisions and in platoons, observing all their motions with infinite attention; and, on account of some blunder, put two officers of the Prince of Prussia's regiment in arrest. In short, he seemed to exert himself with all the spirit of a young officer, eager to attract the notice of his general by uncommon alertness.

9

Frederick in the Eyes of the Great Voltaire

Frederick's long and famous friendship with Voltaire began with mutual admiration (*see pages 42–45*) *and ended with angry recriminations. In the early days the French* philosophe *had a weakness for both royalty and clever young men. He was flattered by the hero worship of the enlightened prince in barbaric Prussia. "In whatever corner of the world I end my life," wrote Voltaire, "be certain,* Monseigneur, *that I shall constantly wish you well, and in doing so wish the happiness of a nation. My heart will be among your subjects; your fame will ever be dear to me."*

With such gushing phrases began the friendship that was to be broken by quarrels and accusations. Let us observe the relationship through the eyes and pen of the gifted Frenchman.

THE FIRST MEETING, 1740

I was praised by a king, from the crown of my head to the sole of my foot.

Frederick was enchanted by communications from the great man in Paris, and especially by the gift of Voltaire's philosophical works. On November 4, 1736, the Prince Royal sent a gracious letter, followed three days later by a poem:

Your name, illustrious by your learned works,
Deserves a place with heroes and with kings.

The correspondence went on in this vein, with tears of joy on both sides. Voltaire spoke of Frederick as the darling of mankind: "You think like Trajan, . . . you talk French like our best writers. . . . Under your auspices Berlin will be the Athens of Germany, perhaps of Europe. . . . Happy is he who can serve you, happier still he who enters your presence." How much of this Voltaire really meant is subject to suspicion. Later he confessed: "All those epithets cost me nothing!" He did not think that Frederick spoke French "like our best writers." In fact, Frederick's French was so poor that Voltaire made sure to correct the grammar before sending copies along to his friends.

Gifts were exchanged. Frederick sent portraits of himself, trinkets, and a cane with the golden head of Socrates. Voltaire, said Frederick, could be compared with Socrates except for the calumnies which had blackened the name of the Greek philosopher.

Frederick became more and more anxious to see his distinguished admirer. From Potsdam came invitation after invitation. "I confess I am eager to meet in your person the finest product of this century." Voltaire was not at all opposed to meeting the Prussian king. He was not being treated as he deserved in Paris. Why not visit the Prussian court? A royal figure with Frederick's intelligence, if trained by Voltaire, *might be able to add something of value to humanity. He would meet this unusual monarch and teach him to be a poet-philosopher.*

Voltaire's letters became more and more florid. "Socrates is nothing to me; it is Frederick whom I love." "In Berlin you are composing French verse as it was written in Versailles in the golden age of taste and pleasure." "The olives, the laurels and the myrtles put out their leaves again and Frederick appears."

In early June 1740, a week after he ascended the throne, Frederick wrote his first letter as king to Voltaire. It was a short note ending with: "Love me always and always be sincere with your friend Fédéric." Soon there came news to Paris of Frederick's enlightened measures. Voltaire was even more anxious to see his dear friend, whom he now addressed as "Votre Humanité." *He longed "to see Solomon in his glory."*

At long last, the first meeting took place on September 11, 1740. Frederick was on his way to Brussels, where he was supposed to meet Voltaire, and was only 150 miles away when he fell ill. The two saw each other in the derelict castle of Moyland on Prussian soil near Cleves.

The beginning of the friendship was described by Voltaire in this passage.[1]

I was conducted into his Majesty's apartment, in which I found nothing but four bare walls. By the light of a bougie,* I perceived a small truckle bed,** of two feet and a half wide, in a closet, upon

[1] *Memoirs of the Life of Voltaire, Written by Himself* (London, 1784), pp. 42–49.

* A wax candle.

** A low bed on wheels.

which lay a little man, wrapped up in a morning gown of blue cloth. It was his Majesty, who lay sweating and shaking, beneath a beggarly coverlet, in a violent ague fit. I made my bow, and began my acquaintance by feeling his pulse, as if I had been his first physician.

The fit left him, and he rose, dressed himself, and sat down to table with Algarotti, Keyserling, Maupertuis, the ambassador to the States-General, and myself. While we were at supper, we treated most profoundly on the immortality of the soul, natural liberty, and the *Androgines* of Plato.

While we were thus philosophizing upon freedom, the Privy-Counsellor Rambonet was mounted upon a post horse, riding all night toward Liége, at the gates of which he arrived the next day, where he proclaimed, with sound of trumpet, the name of the king his master, while two thousand soldiers from Vesel were laying the city of Liége under contribution. The pretext for this pretty expedition was certain rights, which his Majesty pretended to have over the suburbs. It was to me he committed the task of drawing up the manifesto, which I performed as well as the nature of the case would let me; never suspecting that a king, with whom I supped, and who called me his friend, could possibly be in the wrong. The affair was soon brought to a conclusion, by the payment of a million of *livres,* which he exacted in good hard *ducats,* and which served to defray the expenses of his tour of Strasbourg, concerning which he complained so loudly in his poetic prose epistle.

I soon felt myself attached to him, for he had wit, an agreeable manner, and was moreover, a king; which is a circumstance of seduction hardly to be vanquished by human weakness. Generally speaking, it is the employment of men of letters to flatter kings; but in this instance, I was praised by a king, from the crown of my head to the sole of my foot, at the same time that I was libeled, at least once a week, by the Abbé des Fontaines, and other Grub Street poets of Paris.

Some time before the death of his father, the King of Prussia thought proper to write against the principles of Machiavelli. Had Machiavelli had a prince for a pupil, the very first thing he would have advised him to do, would have been so to write. The Prince Royal, however, was not master of so much finesse; he really meant what he wrote, but it was before he was a king, and while his father gave him no great reason to fall in love with despotic power. He praised moderation with his whole soul; and in the ardor of his enthusiasm, looked upon all usurpation as absolute injustice.

This manuscript he had sent to me at Brussels, to have it corrected and printed; and I had already made a present of it to a Dutch bookseller, one Venduren [*sic*], one of the greatest knaves of his profession. I could not help feeling some remorse, at being concerned in printing this anti-Machiavellian book, at the very moment the King of Prussia, who had a hundred millions in his coffers, was robbing the poor people at Liége of another, by the hands of the Privy-Counsellor Rambonet.

I imagined my Solomon would not stop there. His father had left him sixty-six thousand four hundred men, all complete and excellent troops. He was busily augmenting them, and appeared to have a vast inclination to give them employment the very first opportunity.

I represented to him, that perhaps it was not altogether prudent to print his book just at the time the world might reproach him with having violated the principles he taught; and he permitted me to stop the impression. I accordingly took a journey into Holland, purposely to do him this trifling service; but the bookseller demanded so much money, that his Majesty, who was not, in the bottom of his heart, vexed to see himself in print, was better pleased to be so for nothing, than to pay for not being so.

While I was in Holland, occupied in this business, Charles the Sixth died, in the month of October, 1740, of an indigestion, occasioned by eating champignons, which brought on an apoplexy, and this plate of champignons changed the destiny of Europe. It was presently evident, that Frederick the Third [*sic*] King of Prussia, was not so great an enemy to a Machiavelli as the Prince Royal appeared to have been.

Although he had then conceived the project of his invasion of Silesia, he did not the less neglect to invite me to his court; but I had before given him to understand I could not come to stay with him; that I deemed it a duty to prefer friendship to ambition; that I was attached to Madame du Châtelet.

VOLTAIRE'S SOJOURN IN BERLIN, 1750

I led the life of liberty, and had no conception of anything more happy than my then situation.

Frederick sent another invitation to Voltaire in 1745. "Come and visit me. I promise a fresh crown of our finest laurels." The French philosophe *was torn between two loves—his mistress Madame du Châtelet, then living apart from her soldier-husband, and Frederick, King of Prussia. From Potsdam came word that Frederick wanted "to possess Voltaire."*

The course of the relationship took a fateful turn in September 1749 when Madame du Châtelet died in childbirth. Voltaire was crushed with grief, although he was not the father of the child. He soon recovered. By June 1750, he was ready for Berlin. Typically, he requested 40,000 thalers *for traveling expenses, which*

Frederick most reluctantly granted him. Together with his niece, Voltaire set out for another meeting with his Prussian friend.

The two greeted each other joyously. Said Voltaire: "You are the greatest monarch that ever sat on a throne." Frederick replied in equally sugary terms, calling his visitor "a pillar of taste, of arts, of eloquence, son of Apollo, the Homer of France."

Voltaire at first settled in an apartment assigned to him in Berlin. He was made a chamberlain, given the decoration Pour le Mérite, *and a pension. The opening days were glorious, as described by Voltaire in his* Memoirs.[2]

Madame du Châtelet died in the palace of Stanislaus, after two days illness; and we were so affected, that not one of us ever remembered to send for priest, Jesuit, or any of the Seven Sacraments. It was we, and not Madame du Châtelet, who felt the horrors of death. The good King Stanislaus came to my chamber, and mixed his tears with mine: few of his brethren would have done so much on a like occasion. He wished me to stay at Lunéville, but I could no longer support the place, and returned to Paris.

It was my destiny to run from king to king, although I loved liberty even to idolatry. The King of Prussia, whom I had frequently given to understand I would never quit Madame du Châtelet for him, would absolutely entrap me, now he was rid of his rival. He enjoyed at that time a peace, which he had purchased with victory; and his leisure hours were always devoted to making verses, or writing the history of his country and campaigns. He was well convinced, that in reality his verse and prose too, were superior to my verse and prose, as to their essence; though as to the form, he thought there was a certain something, a turn, that I, in quality of academician, might give to his writings; and there was no kind of flattery, no seduction, he did not employ to engage me to come.

Who might resist a monarch, a hero, a poet, a musician, a philosopher, who pretended too to love me, and whom I thought I also loved? I set out once more for Potsdam, in the month of June, 1750. Astolphus did not meet a kinder reception in the palace of Alcina. To be lodged in the same apartment that Marshal Saxe had occupied; to have the royal cooks at my command, when I chose to dine alone; and the royal coachmen, when I had an inclination to ride, were trifling favors.

Our suppers were very agreeable. I know not if I am deceived, but I think we had a deal of wit. The king was witty, and gave occasion to wit in others; and what is still more extraordinary, I never found

[2] *Memoirs of the Life of Voltaire,* pp. 123–29.

myself so much at my ease. I worked two hours a day with his Majesty, corrected his works, and never failed highly to praise whatever was worthy of praise, although I rejected the dross. I gave him details of all that was necessary in rhetoric and criticism, for his use; he profited by my advice, and his genius assisted him more effectually than my lessons.

I had no court to make, no visits to pay, no duty to fulfill; I led the life of liberty, and had no conception of anything more happy than my then situation. My Frederick-Alcina, who saw my brain was already a little disordered, redoubled the potions that I might be totally inebriated. The last seduction was a letter he wrote, and sent from his apartments to mine. A mistress could not have written more tenderly; he labored in his epistle to dissipate the fear which his rank and character had inspired: It contained these remarkable words:

"How is it possible I should bring unhappiness on the man I esteem, who has sacrificed his country, and all that humanity holds dear to me. I respect you as my master, and love you as my friend. What slavery, what misfortune, what change can be feared, in a place where you are esteemed as much as in your own country, and with a friend who has a grateful heart. I respected the friendship that endeared you to Madame du Châtelet, but after her I am one of your oldest friends. I give you my promise you shall be happy here as long as I live."

Here is a letter, such as few of *their Majesties* write: It was the finishing glass to complete my drunkenness. His wordy protestations were still stronger than his written ones. He was accustomed to very singular demonstrations of tenderness to younger favorites than I, and forgetting for a moment I was not of their age, and had not a fine hand, he seized it and imprinted a kiss; I took his, returned his salute, and signed myself his slave.

BEGINNING OF THE MAUPERTUIS AFFAIR, 1752

I cannot consent to his being held up to ridicule without being compromised myself.

Among the intellectuals invited to Berlin by Frederick was Pierre Louis Moreau de Maupertuis, a distinguished French natural philosopher. Maupertuis became not only a member of the Berlin Academy but also its president. There were differences about the ability of the French scholar, but some, including Frederick, were deeply impressed. Others spoke of Maupertuis's "tiresome discourses," and still others regarded him as a pseudo-scholar.

There were disagreements between Voltaire and Maupertuis

before the open rupture. What appeared to be the cause of their first misunderstanding was a trifling observation from Maupertuis to which Voltaire made a flippant reply. Both were returning from Sans Souci about half-past one in the morning, in one of the royal carriages, when Maupertuis exclaimed ironically: "It must be confessed, that we spent a charming evening." "I never spent a more stupid one," replied Voltaire. Apparently, the difficulty was that at the supper from which they had just come, Voltaire had been in an unusual melancholy state of mind, while Maupertuis shone. The latter was boasting and Voltaire took it for sarcasm or an affront.

From that day on, the two never spoke to each other, nor would they come near one another. Frederick, hoping that the rivalry would not come to an open break, tried to reconcile them several times, but without success.

Maupertuis then became involved in a scholarly quarrel with a Dutch mathematician named Koenig. The issue involved who had been the first to discover a new law of mathematics associated with Newton's law of gravitation. Frederick took the side of his appointee, Maupertuis; Voltaire, angered, defended Koenig.

In his Memoirs *Voltaire described the opening of the quarrel.*[3]

Algarotti, Darget, and a Frenchman, whose name was Chasol, one of the king's best officers, left him all at once. I was preparing to do the same, but I wished, before I went, to enjoy the pleasure of laughing at a book Maupertuis had just printed. It was the best of opportunities, for never had anything appeared so ridiculous or absurd. The good man seriously proposed to travel directly to the two Poles; to dissect the heads of giants, and discover the nature of the soul by the texture of the brain; to build a city, and make the inhabitants all speak Latin; to sink a pit to the center of the earth; to cure the sick, by plastering them over with gum resin; and, finally, to prophesy, by enthusiastically inflating the fancy.

The king lauged, I laughed, everybody laughed at his book; but there was a scene acting at that time of a far more serious nature, concerning I know not what mathematical nonsense that Maupertuis wanted to establish as discoveries. A more learned mathematician, Koenig, librarian to the Princess of Orange at The Hague, showed him his mistake, and that Leibnitz, who had before time examined that old idea, had demonstrated its falsity in several of his letters, copies of which he sent Maupertuis.

Maupertuis, President of the Academy at Berlin, enraged that an

[3] *Memoirs of the Life of Voltaire,* pp. 136–42.

associate and a stranger should prove his blunders, took care first to persuade the king, that Koenig being settled in Holland, was of course his enemy; and next, that he had said many disrespectful things of his Majesty's verse and prose to the Princess of Orange.

This precaution taken, he suborned some few poor pensioners of the Academy, his dependents, had Koenig condemned as a forger, and his name erased from the number of Academicians. Here, however, he was anticipated, for Koenig sent back his patent-academician-dignity to Berlin.

All the men of letters in Europe were as full of indignation at the maneuvers of Maupertuis as they were weary of his book, and he obtained the contempt and hatred even of those who did not understand the dispute. They were obliged to content themselves at Berlin with a mere shrug of the shoulders; for the king having taken a part in this unfortunate affair, no person durst speak. I was the only one who spoke out. Koenig was my friend; and I had at once the satisfaction to defend the liberty of the learned, the cause of a friend, and of mortifying an enemy, who was as much the enemy of modesty as of me.

I had no intention to stay at Berlin; I had always preferred liberty to everything; few men of letters have a proper sense of it; most of them are poor; poverty enervates and even philosophers, at court, become as truly slaves as the first officer of the crown. I felt how displeasing my free spirit must be to a king more absolute than the Grand Turk. It was a pleasant monarch, in the recesses of his palace, we must confess: he protected Maupertuis, and laughed at him more than anyone. He wrote against him, and sent his manuscript to my chamber by one Marvitz, a minister of his secret pleasures; he turned to ridicule the pit to the center of the earth, the method of cure with plaster of gum resin, the voyage to the South Pole, the Latin city, and the cowardice of the Academy, in having suffered the tyranny exercised upon poor Koenig. But his motto was, *No clamor when I don't cry*; and he had everything burnt that had been written upon the controversy, execpt his own work.

Loud proponent of tolerance, Voltaire was decidedly intolerant when it came to literary battles. Angered to the point of apoplexy by his feud with Maupertuis, he decided to write a shattering satire about his opponent. He took the name Akakia *from that of a doctor of François I who originally called himself* Sans Malice, *but later translated the name into Greek as* Akakia. *Resurrecting the name, Voltaire gave it to an imaginary doctor, "physician to the Pope." Voltaire had this doctor write a letter complaining of the wrong that had been done to the medical profession by a young student, "who must have assumed the name of a distinguished president of the Academy." The student wanted to sell a recent book concerned with the dissection of Patagonian giants, blowing up the Pyramids, and the lack of payment to doctors. In this way Voltaire expected to ward off any complaints by Maupertuis.*

The problem now was to get the book published. Voltaire had already written an essay about Bolingbroke, which he had read to Frederick and for which he had obtained permission to have it published by the royal press. Frederick noted his permission on the last page of the manuscript. Voltaire sent both his Bolingbroke essay and Doctor Akakia *to the printers—as if the single permission covered both. In this deceitful manner, Voltaire had a diatribe published for which Frederick ordinarily would never have granted permission.*

THE PUBLICATION OF *DOCTOR AKAKIA* AND A BROKEN FRIENDSHIP, 1752

Oh Vulcan, cruel and devouring God, receive thy prey!

Frederick quickly learned about Voltaire's satire, Doctor Akakia *—nothing that took place in his court could evade his attention. The royal patron invited Voltaire to the palace in a very polite note. When Voltaire arrived, the following conversation took place.*[4]

Frederick: They say you have written a satire against Maupertuis, which is as witty as it is malicious: I am going to speak to you on that subject with freedom, and as, I think, I ought to speak to a friend. It is not my intention to argue, that Maupertuis has not done you any injury, or that you have not caused him any. I agree, on the contrary, that you both have a right to complain; and, in short, I feel and acquiesce in the opinion, that you are in the right to complain, and I should deliver him up to you without difficulty, if I were to take his case only into consideration; but I beg you will observe, that I have called that man into my service; that I have placed him at the head of my Academy; that I have granted to him the same treatment as to my ministers of state; that I have admitted him into my most familiar society; and that I have permitted him to marry one of the ladies of honor of the queen, the daughter of

[4] Quoted in Francis Espinasse, *Life of Voltaire* (London, 1892), pp. 237–40.

one of my ministers, a Lady de Bredow, belonging to one of the most ancient and most considerable families of my kingdom. I have done so much for him, to the knowledge of all Europe, that I cannot consent to his being held up to ridicule without being compromised myself. If you cover him with disgrace, I shall certainly be ridiculed; and if I suffer that, I cause a real scandal: I shall be blamed for it, and all the nobility of this country will experience a mortification, which will be imputed to my forbearance.

I beg you will consider these circumstances, and see what I can expect from your friendship, and what you owe to mine, and to reason. I know what it costs an author to sacrifice one of his works; above all, when it is filled with happy ideas, and when the details are as agreeable as they are ingenious; but who ought to care less than yourself for a sacrifice of this sort? A thing which would be irreparable for any other person, is nothing to Voltaire; a man who, above all others, in the world, has the most fruitful and the finest genius. You are so rich, both in ideas and talents. Your glory is established by so many more important productions! And what do you want besides, but the wish to make as many more worthy of yourself? You must not doubt, nevertheless, that, in sacrificing the work in question, you will give me a proof of friendship, which, according to the circumstances, I shall so much the more appreciate. I do not hesitate in telling you, that you will render me one of the greatest services. Depend upon it, I shall never forget it. You may, on your side, expect everything from my friendship.

Voltaire: Well, I will bring the manuscript of my *Doctor Akakia,* and place it in the hands, and at the disposal of your Majesty. I have always been too much devoted to your Majesty, not to sacrifice, to the assurance of your kindness, that little revenge, which had appeared to me just, moderate, and consequently innocent. I should certainly make greater sacrifices, if they were required from me by your wishes.

Frederick: Lose no time. I shall wait for you; such noble designs must not be postponed.

Voltaire (after returning with the manuscript): Sire, here is the innocent going to perish for the people! I put it into your hands, order its condemnation.

Frederick: Ah, my friend, what fate is mine! to order a punishment for that which deserves to be crowned with glory. Well! let us submit to fate with dignity; let us be as just as possible; let us revenge the victim by its sacrifice. Read; I shall save what I can, and it will be a precious reminder which my memory will keep with care; read, and may the pages devoured by the flames claim my just admiration. O Vulcan! never was a more memorable thing done, or a greater tribute paid to your honor.

At this point Voltaire read the whole satire. Both men began shaking with laughter. At the same time, Frederick made it clear that this could not be published. Voltaire, who had already sent copies abroad for safekeeping, nobly followed Frederick's suggestion and flung the manuscript into the fire. "Come, my friend," said the king, "cheer up, since it is necessary. O Vulcan, cruel and devouring God, receive thy prey!" Frederick, apparently wanting to keep the manuscript among his treasures, plucked it out of the flames. Voltaire threw it back. The king, as the cost of a singed sleeve, retrieved it.

Meanwhile, the two philosophers joined hands and executed a fantastic dance around the flames. Seldom has such a ludicrous scene taken place between two such distinguished men. Doctor Akakia *was read to the end and then burnt.*

The affair was by no means ended by the Indian war dance around the flames. Voltaire still had a copy of the manuscript and he lost no time in getting it printed. Meanwhile, Frederick had second thoughts about the whole nasty business. This was his Berlin Academy, his President Maupertuis, his intellectual hierarchy, and no one, not even the sharp-tongued Voltaire, was going to make them look ridiculous. He wrote an indignant letter to Voltaire.

Your effrontery astonishes me after what you have just done, which is as clear as day. You persist, instead of avowing yourself culpable. Don't imagine that you will make me believe black is white: when one doesn't see, it's because one doesn't wish to see; but if you push this affair to the end, I shall have everything printed; and people will see that if your works deserve statues, your conduct deserves chains.

The publisher has been questioned, and has told everything.

Frederick knew exactly what was going on. He waited until the edition was finished by the royal press, and then ordered it to be seized. Voltaire, also presupposing what was taking place, took care to acquire secretly four copies of each sheet as they left the press, and sent them to Holland.

After placing a sentry at Voltaire's door, Frederick sent to him a document for his signature: it was a promise that he would not do it again. Written in the king's own hand, it ended: "I promise his Majesty that, as long as he does me the favor of putting me up in the château, I will not write against any person of any government, etc."

Voltaire did not sign. He replied by letter stating that he had never written against any government, not even his own, and he had left France to end his life at Frederick's feet. He begged Frederick to examine the real inwardness of his quarrel with

Maupertuis. He beseeched his patron to spare an elderly man overwhelmed with sickness and pain. That old man would die as closely attached to his Majesty as on the day of his arrival at the Prussian court.

Frederick did not retreat. He informed Maupertuis that Voltaire was so frightened that he would never repeat the offense. Within a few hours word came to Prussia that an edition of Doctor Akakia *printed in Leipzig had arrived in Berlin.*

Angered, Frederick ordered that the book be burned by the public executioner on a Sunday afternoon in the middle of a Berlin market place. Voltaire saw the ceremony from the window of a friend's house. "Oh!" he cried, "see the wit of Maupertuis, which is smoking in the air! What a dark and thick smoke! What a deal of lost wood!"

Word of the quarrel flew through the salons of Europe. Printing presses worked night and day turning out new editions of Doctor Akakia. *Some 30,000 copies were sold in Paris as soon as they were printed.*

The masks were off: the two friends were now about to become enemies. The offense was too great, the scandal too public.

VOLTAIRE'S REQUEST FOR SICK LEAVE, 1753

> *Dat be it, Montseer, ouf dey vurks ouf poesy ouf de king mine master.*

Voltaire still carried on his duties, but the old spark was gone. He began to avoid meals and insisted that the food was too heavy. Because Sans Souci had no adequate fireplaces, he was continually cold. He became more and more lonely as he wandered around the gardens by himself. The story was told (perhaps Voltaire himself invented it) that one of the gardeners got the impression that the king had put a man's clothes on a monkey and set him loose in the gardens.

Early in 1753, Voltaire asked for a "sick leave." Frederick replied that he could leave whenever he wished, but he must return his badge of office (the chamberlain's key), the order Pour le Mérite, *and whatever of the king's verses, including some obscene ones, he had in his possession. Voltaire smuggled his savings out of the country and waited until he had received his quarterly allowance before making his move.*

On March 26, 1753, Voltaire left Potsdam, taking his key, order, and the king's verses with him, and headed for Paris via Leipzig and Frankfurt-am-Main. En route, while in Leipzig, he made arrangements to publish his original lampoon against Maupertuis in even more abusive form.

Frederick exploded with anger when he heard news of his guest's "escape." He feared that Voltaire intended to publish his (Frederick's) verses that he had taken with him. He sent an order to the Prussian envoy in Frankfurt, a certain Herr Freytag, to confiscate the book when Voltaire reached the city.

When Voltaire arrived in Frankfurt, he was stopped by Freytag, who demanded that he hand over key, order, and *poems. Voltaire protested that he had left the verses in Hamburg. Convinced that the Frenchman was lying, Freytag spent the next several hours examining Voltaire's baggage. During the course of the search, Voltaire fainted. On becoming conscious, he was required to promise on his word of honor not to leave Frankfurt. On June 17, the box arrived from Hamburg and Freytag got the precious poems. At this point Voltaire lost his head and tried to escape. He was recognized at the gate of the city, arrested, and with the collaboration of city officials, thrown into a jail cell.*

Voltaire's own account of what happened when he arrived at Frankfurt was told in his Memoirs.[5] *Note how the irrepressible Frenchman, despite his humiliation, anger, and fear, mocked the illiterate Freytag.*

Leaving my palace of Alcina, I went to pass a month with the Duchess of Saxe-Gotha, the best of princesses, full of gentleness, discretion, and equanimity, and who, God be thanked, did not make verses. After that I spent a few days at the country house of the Landgrave of Hesse, who was still a remove farther from poetry than the Princess of Gotha. Thus I took breath, and thence continued, by short journies, my route to Frankfurt, where a very odd kind of destiny was in reserve for me.

I fell ill at Frankfurt, and one of my nieces, the widow of a captain who had belonged to the regiment of Champagne, a most amiable woman, with excellent talents, and who, moreover, was esteemed at Paris as belonging to the Order of Good Company, had the courage to quit that city, and come to me on the Main, where she found me a prisoner of war.

This fine adventure happened thus: One Freytag, who had been banished from Dresden, after having been put in chains, and condemned to the wheelbarrow, became afterwards an agent to the King of Prussia, who was glad to be served by such-like ministers, because they asked no wages but what they could steal from travelers.

[5] *Memoirs of the Life of Voltaire,* pp. 146–54.

This ambassador, and one Schmitt, a tradesman, formerly condemned and punished for coining, signified to me, on the part of his Majesty the King of Prussia, that I must not depart from Frankfurt till I had given back the precious effects I had carried off from his Majesty. "My very good messieurs, (said I,) I have brought nothing out of that country, I can assure you, not even the least regret; what, then, are these famous jewels of the crown of Brandenburg, that you thus re-demand?—"*Dat it be, Montseer,* (answered Freytag) *ouf dey vurks ouf poesy ouf de king mine master.*"—"Oh! (answered I,) with all my heart; he shall have his works in verse and prose, though I have more title to them than one, for he made me a present of a fine copy, printed at his own expense; but, unfortunately for me, this printed copy is at Leipzig, with my other effects."

Freytag then proposed that I should stay at Frankfurt till this treasure arrived from Leipzig, and signed the following curious quittance:

Montseer, so soon as shall dey great pack come ouf Leipzig, mit de vurks ouf poesy be given mit me, you shall go ouf vere you do please. Given at Frankfurt de vurst of June, 1753.—Freytag, resident ouf de king mine master.

At the bottom of which I signed—*Good, vor dey vurks ouf poesy ouf de king your master.*—With which the resident was well satisfied.

On the twelfth of June the great pack of poesy came, and I faithfully remitted the sacred deposit, imagining I might then depart, without offense to any crowned head; but at the very instant when we were setting off, I, my secretary, my servants, and even my niece, were arrested. Four soldiers dragged us through the midst of the dirt, before M. Schmitt, who had I know not what right of Privy Counsellor to the King of Prussia. This Frankfurt trader thought himself at that moment a Prussian general; he commanded twelve of the town guards, with all the importance and grandeur an affair of such consequence required. My niece had a passport from the King of France, and, moreover, never had corrected the King of Prussia's verses. Women are usually respected amidst the horrors of war, but the Counsellor Schmitt, and the President Freytag, endeavored to pay their court to Frederick by hauling one of the fair sex through the mud. They shut us up in a kind of inn, at the door of which the twelve soldiers were posted. Four others were placed in my chamber, four in the garret, where they had conducted my niece, and four in a still more wretched garret, where my secretary was laid upon straw. My niece, it is true, was allowed a small bed, but four soldiers, with fixed bayonets, served her instead of curtains and chambermaids.

In vain we urged we had been invited to the court the emperor had elected at Frankfurt, that my secretary was a Florentine, and a subject of his Imperial Majesty; that I and my niece were subjects of the most Christian king; and that there was no difference between us and the Margrave of Brandenburg. They informed us, that the margrave had more power at Frankfurt than the Emperor.

Twelve days were we held prisoners of war, for which we paid a hundred and forty crowns, or seventeen pounds ten shillings a day. Madame Schmitt had seized on all my effects, which were given back one half lighter: One need not wish to pay dearer for the poesy of the King of Prussia. I lost about as much as it had cost him to send for me and take lessons, and we were quits at parting.

VOLTAIRE'S DECLARATION FROM A PRISON CELL, 1753

I declare myself a criminal . . . if. . . .

Meanwhile, from his prison cell at Frankfurt, Voltaire issued a "declaration," which he hoped would bring about his quick release.[6] *It was compounded in equal parts of his resentment at the ignominy of being jailed, plus blazing anger at his treatment. To be on the safe side, he couched his statement in a subservient and somewhat wheedling tone.*

DECLARATION
of Mr. ****
Detained in Prison in Frankfurt by the King of Prussia

I flee dying. I declare before God and before humanity that I no longer remain in the service of his Majesty, the King of Prussia. I am not fleeing any less attached nor any less obedient to his wishes, for the small amount of time I have to live.

I was arrested in Frankfurt because of a book of poetry, which I had been given as a present. I must remain in prison until the book is returned from Hamburg. I have surrendered to his Prussian Majesty's minister all those letters which I had preserved as token of kindness through which he had honored me. I shall take back to Paris all the other letters which he allows me to take back.

His Majesty wished to see again a contract, which he had made with me. I was ready to return it, as all the rest, as soon as it could be found. I shall surrender it, or put into writing that this was not a contract, but rather a small token of the king's kindness, not being of any consequence, having been written at that time on half of a very small sheet which D'Argent carried from my chamber to the

[6] M. M. C. F. Ecuïer, *Mémoires secrets pour servir l'histoire de notre temps,* (London, n.d.), 22–25.

king's apartment at Potsdam. It did not contain anything else from me other than a "thank you" for the pension, which his Majesty the king conferred on me as a favor with the permission of the king my master, which he could give to my niece after my death, and the cross and chamberlain's key. The King of Prussia had deigned to place on back of the sheet of paper as much as would involve me.

With warm heart I signed the offer, as I had been wanting to do for fifteen years. This paper, which is absolutely useless to his Majesty, to me, and to the public, certainly will be surrendered as soon as it is found among other papers. I cannot nor do I want to make the least use of it. To remove all suspicion, I declare myself a criminal against the sovereign power (*lèse-Majesté*), against the King of France, my master, and the King of Prussia, if I do not return the paper the instant it should fall into my hands.

My niece, who is dear to me in my ill-fortune, engages herself in the same errand. If she finds it, and knowing that my papers can be sent to Paris, I annul the said writing entirely. I declare never to demand anything of his Majesty the King of Prussia, and not to expect anything in the cruel condition in which I find myself, any more than the compassion that your Majesty can give to a man, who has sacrificed all and lost all for having been attached to you; who has served you zealously, who has been useful to you, who has never failed your person, and who has shared in your kindness of heart.

I am forced to dictate this declaration, not being able to write. I sign with the most profound respect, the most pure innocence, and the deepest pain.

Not until July 6, 1753, some five weeks after he had arrived in Frankfurt, was Voltaire able to leave and continue his journey to Paris. The glorious friendship was ended.

10

Dr. Zimmermann on the Case of the Miller Arnold, 1779–1780

Away! away! Herewith you are cashiered.

Proud of his legal code, Frederick took special interest in the proper administration of justice. He once described himself as "l'avocat du pauvre," *as the "champion of the poor." On one occasion a miller, whose windmill stood on ground which was needed for the royal garden, refused to sell his property. "Not at any price?" said the king's agent. "Remember that the king can take it from you for nothing, if he wished." The miller replied: "Have we not the* Kammergericht *(Supreme Court) at Berlin?" That became a popular anecdote in Prussia.*

There was another miller, whose case became a cause célèbre *throughout Europe. When Frederick chose to show his concern for the underdog, he himself became the victim of a set of bizarre circumstances.*

Many reports were circulated about this case, which turned out to be one of the most prominent events of Frederick's reign. Following is an account by one of his physicians, Dr. J. G. Zimmermann, who repeated the story as it was told to him by "a well-informed man." Though it may not be accurate in spots, this report is in all probability close to the truth of what happened.[1]

Miller Arnold lived in Newmark, tenant of a mill, which he rented from a nobleman of the name of Gersdorf, one of the king's counsel for that province. The water that drove the mill rose within the estate of this nobleman, and passed through several ponds before it reached the mill. He found it convenient to lead this water round one of those ponds, without altering, however, its course to the mill. Arnold was deeply in debt, and at last unable to pay his rent. This occasioned a commission of bankruptcy against him, and the mill was put to sale.

The miller's wife was intimately connected with a lawyer, clerk to

[1] Zimmermann, *Select Views,* II, 84–97.

Colonel Heuking's regiment, quartered in the neighborhood. To this dear friend she complained of her distress. He drew up a memorial to the king, wherein he said: "By the commission of bankruptcy issued against Arnold, he was greatly injured. The mill water was taken from him, and he, nevertheless, had been obliged to pay the whole rent. This had involved him in debt, and the now intended sale of the mill could not fail to complete his ruin."

Frederick, struck with the contents of this petition, sent it to the High Court of Justice at Berlin, giving them to understand, "that though it was not usual with him to interfere in judicial matters, yet Arnold's complaint seemed to set forth so atrocious an injury, that he could not forbear enjoining them, with the utmost attention to inquire into it, and to do justice to the petitioner."

This inquiry was made, and the rule of the Inferior Court at Küstrin confirmed; however, without informing the king of the legal causes of this judgment, which, no doubt, ought to have been done. For, though it is very comforting to be in the right, yet we should never neglect what duty, or even prudence directs us to observe toward our sovereign.

Arnold, in the most lamentable manner, petitioned the king again. Frederick, wondering at his having received no report from the High Court of Justice, ordered it to be sent. The judges, having returned all the papers and records, concerning this lawsuit, to the Inferior Court, begged, for this reason, to be excused: And, upon his asking "why these papers might not be had again?" answered, that "the third instance of revision being open to the petitioner, it was still in his power to recover whatever was due to him."

But the sentence of the Senate of Revision was not more favorable to Arnold than the former judgments; and the judges neglected again to state to the king the true circumstances of the case, and to explain the legal grounds upon which they proceeded against the insolvent miller. As, therefore, this barefaced petitioner appeared again before Frederick, lamenting that, notwithstanding his royal protection, he must fall a sacrifice to the partiality and iniquity of his judges, he was induced to suspect, that his Courts of Justice had strong reasons to conceal from him the particulars of Arnold's cause, and the grounds of their proceedings, which now appeared to him in the most odious light.

Thus prepossessed against his Court of Justice, he betook himself to an expedient of getting at the truth, which he often tried, though not always with success. He ordered the next commander of a regiment, with the assistance of a lawyer, to inquire into Arnold's cause. This commander was Colonel Heuking, who knew nothing about the matter, and the assisting lawyer was the intimate friend of Mrs. Arnold, and the author of all the petitions by Arnold delivered to the king. We may easily conceive the contents of the colonel's report. "It must be obvious," said he, "to anyone who had an opportunity of examining the local circumstances of Arnold's case, that this unfortunate man was used by his judges in the most iniquitous and oppressive manner."

The king now thought himself possessed of the most convincing proofs, that his Courts of Justice, in three instances had pursued the most grinding plan of iniquity and oppression. Resolving to inflict an exemplary punishment on these vile corruptors of public justice, by a cabinet's order, directed to the High Chancellor, Baron Furst, he bade the three judges Friedel, Ransleben, and Graun, who at Berlin had tried Arnold's cause, the very same day to appear before him. The High Chancellor, foreseeing what might happen, nobly determined not to forsake the three judges, who had conducted the trial with the greatest impartiality and candor, and, though uncalled for, went with them to the king.

Frederick had a toothache. His cheeks wrapped up, he lay on a sofa, darting dreadful looks at the unexpected appearance of the High Chancellor, which he attributed to quite other causes. He flew into the wildest passion. The High Chancellor attempted to defend the judges; but the king exclaimed, "What do you want, Sir? Who sent for you? I know you full well: Away! away! Herewith you are cashiered." He added some harsh expressions, and, after the unfortunate High Chancellor had left the room, burst like a thunderstorm upon the three judges, and inveighed terribly against their unpardonable injustice. Like men did these three gentlemen defend themselves. With the most exalted heroism one of them said to Frederick:

"Sire, I have tried Arnold's cause with the strictest adherence to impartiality and justice; and, should your Majesty order me ten times to alter the judgment, I would not; because I could not do it without violating my oath and hurting my conscience."

At this speech, Frederick, like a whirlwind, sprung from his seat, flew out of the room, called the guard, and said, "That's devilish insolence, however!" Now, the three judges stood trembling like aspen leaves, for fear that he was out of his senses. The king, perceiving this agitation, turned to them with great kindness, and said, "Never fear, your persons shall not be hurt; I must only have you arrested!". . .

The guard came, and the three judges were sent to the common town jail. Frederick insisted upon having all the papers and records belonging to Arnold's lawsuit: they lay several days on his table: he perused them; and is said to have once exclaimed: "Should I have done wrong!" However, the impudent report of Colonel Heuking, or rather of Mrs. Arnold's gallant, got the better of his doubts; and, on the 11th of December, 1779, he sent to Baron Zedliz, his minister of state for the judicial department, a short instruction how the prosecution against the three judges ought to be conducted, and their sentence worded.

Baron Zedliz referred it to the criminal court, who pronounced judgment according to justice and duty. The king reversed this sentence, and prescribed again how the three judges should be punished. Baron Zedliz ordered a copy to be made of the very words of the monarch, which, of course, had the form, not of a sentence, but of an order, and sent him this copy. The king, sensible of the impropriety of this form, wanted to have it altered, and for that purpose, returned the copy to Baron Zedliz. But this minister, with the noblest intrepidity, told the king: "That of all the members of the criminal court, not one could, or would sign such a judgment; and that his conscience did not even allow him to countersign it."

Greater courage did Frederick never show in the field, than the High Chancellor Furst, Baron Zedliz, and all the judges proved in this dreadful cause: in all likelihood he was sensible of it, for he gave Zedliz no answer. But his sentence, signed by him alone, January 1st, 1780, was put into execution. The mill was restored to Arnold, and his judges were condemned to pay him damages and costs; the High Chancellor was cashiered, and Count Finckenstein, son to the minister of state, and president of the Regency at Küstrin, experienced the same fate. All the members of this court lost their places, and were imprisoned for twelve months. Out of the three Berlin judges, Friedel and Graun were discarded, and, for twelve months, sent to Spandau; but the third, Mr. Ransleben, who, in the instance of revision, had drawn up the judgment against Arnold, was acquitted, because Frederick found it recorded, that he several times had insisted upon informing the king of the nature and circumstances of Arnold's cause, that he might be convinced of the legality of their proceedings and sentence. But he had been overruled by all the other members of the court, and this excused him with the king.

The sensational case stimulated a wave of petitions and appeals from millers and others throughout Prussia, all of whom felt that the good Frederick was well able to handle venal judges. Frederick had proved his point, but soon he began to have misgivings. He remitted four months of the sentences given his judges.

The truth emerged after Frederick's death. Miller Arnold had not actually suffered any loss of water power. He was exposed as a notorious perjurer, who made a specialty of rushing into lawsuits. The innocent judges were rehabilitated by a royal decree.

11

Contemporary Views on the Medical History of Frederick the Great

Throughout his life Frederick suffered from a variety of illnesses including asthma, hemorrhoids, colic, indigestion, and a host of other ills. He had a long experience with doctors and his opinion of them was low. The pattern remained much the same: he would call them, ask their opinion, take their medicines, submit to such palliatives as vomiting, and then angrily dismiss the healers from his presence. Following are contemporary accounts of Frederick's medical difficulties.

READER CATT ON THE ILLNESSES OF FREDERICK DURING HIS CAMPAIGNS, 1758

How happy you are not to know this infernal malady.

Henri de Catt was a young Swiss teacher who, while on a holiday, met Frederick on a canal boat in Holland. Frederick engaged him as a "reader," or rather "listener," which really meant duties as a literary crony, listening with reverence as the king declaimed his odes, tragedies, and funeral orations. Catt joined Frederick at Breslau in March 1758 and remained with him for twenty-four years until their relations chilled in the last years of the king's reign. In his Memoirs, *which covered only two years from 1758 to 1760, when Frederick was in the midst of the Seven Years' War, Catt gave an absorbing portrait of the monarch. The following passages, dated June 1758, concern Frederick's bouts with annoying illnesses.*[1]

[1] *Memoirs of de Catt,* II, 156–57, 161–63, 182–83. Reprinted by permission of Constable and Company, Ltd.

3rd June, 1758

The king left Schmirsitz at three o'clock, and arrived at six in the evening at Klein-Latein, where he set up his headquarters, which were covered by Lattorff's first battalion; the second occupied Gross-Latein, and Mochring's hussars were advanced as far as the heights of Czakow. This is what his Majesty told me, and he seemed to me, during the moment I was with him, to be in a bad humor, as I judged by what formed the subject of his conversation; but I could not perceive its application. . . .

"I think that I shall not remain very long in this confounded village, and that, in a few days, we shall return to our Schmirsitz. God knows what awaits me there. I do not know what has disappointed me today. I have been hypochondriacal since this morning. Perhaps the uneasiness which I feel is caused by the hemorrhoids, which are beginning again. In order not to bore you and to make you as gloomy as I am myself, I wish you good evening." . . .

4th June

I was called on this day earlier than usual. It was two o'clock. I was afraid the king was ill, but, on entering, I was undeceived, and this caused me much pleasure.

"I was quite right in what I told you yesterday, my dear sir, that the hemorrhoids were causing my uneasiness. They appeared in the night, and so great that I lost nearly three cups of blood. I am now quite well, just like any other man, and ready to cut capers for you, if you like."

I said nothing, and there were no capers. If I had said the word, he would have cut me half a dozen immediately, which would have pained me on his account. . . .

5th June

The king, who had felt so well, so cheerful, so nimble, as he said, after his bleeding piles, was made very ill by the macaroni of which he had eaten too much for his dinner. He had a rather violent and painful colic, for which it was necessary to have recourse to the usual remedies, enemas, digestive and antispasmodic powders. I was not called on this or the following day. The first enemas not having operated, it became necessary to give rather a large number. This colic alarmed me, and I inquired frequently of the surgeon how it was progressing, and whether it might not have unpleasant consequences.

"None sir, be reassured; this colic will not be the last. In spite of the hundred and one experiences which the king has had with this confounded macaroni, he always comes back to it. Even then, if he only ate a little, it would not matter so much; but he eats copiously of it. When you see him again, he will tell you that he has suffered very much from a violent colic, caused by something or other, for he eats so little! Be on your guard not to let him suspect that you know what has happened. He would think immediately that I have informed you, and he would not pardon me. Be easy in your mind; this evening perhaps, perhaps tomorrow, he will play on the flute, at the same time telling me that he is still suffering very much."

7th June

The surgeon was a good prophet. When I was called at three o'clock, I expressed my concern to the king at his recent sufferings.

"Ah, my dear sir, I have had the worst colic that could be imagined. It was beyond all joking, and I do not know how I brought it on myself. If you saw the little I ate, you would say: 'But how can a man live on so little food and be so active?' I think that my beast of a colic was a consequence of the hemorrhoids, which had suddenly stopped. How happy you are not to know this infernal malady. Before they appear, you have the most unheard-of uneasiness, and when they have come, you feel sick, and a constant desire to vomit. They would lead me a vile life, if I were not as moderate as possible in what I eat. When I suffer from this complaint, my intellectual faculties do not perform their operations with the ease which I should desire. Good or bad health forms our ideas and all our philosophy. . . .

8th June

We arrived at Schmirsitz in the afternoon; I was called at six o'clock.

"I shall now stay in this spot firm as a rock until the taking of the town, if M. Balbi does not lose his head and make me lose the place. Tomorrow I will go and see a little of what is happening. I have ridden about a good deal today, and led my hemorrhoids and my colic a dance." . . .

13th June

The king, being very much occupied by some dispatches which he had received, did not send for me on this day, nor on the following because of a new indigestion. I was uneasy about his health, but his surgeon reassured me.

"We have eaten today," he said to me, "a little too much pie; we have had an indigestion, an enema, and my powders will do wonders; tomorrow, he wishes to go to the siege; he is already in bed now, at seven o'clock." . . .

DR. ZIMMERMANN'S DEFENSE OF FREDERICK AGAINST ACCUSATIONS OF HOMOSEXUALITY

It was his will and express order, after his death, not to be undressed.

As a young man, Frederick was brutally denounced by his father for his "effeminate amusements." His marriage was unhappy, and he seldom saw his wife. At his court in Potsdam, ladies were rarely seen, which gave rise to much scandal. Throughout Europe during his lifetime, it was rumored that Frederick was a homosexual, who was sickened by the sight of women but was always fond of young men.

The debate on Frederick's manliness continued long after his death, as one biographer after another cagily hinted at "the Grecian illness." In the following passage, a contemporary physician, Dr. J. G. Zimmermann, gave his own version of the "delicate matter."[2] *He was no ordinary physician, but titled "First Physician to His Brittanic Majesty at Hanover," who in 1786 was called to Potsdam to treat Frederick in his final illness (see pages 139–44). Dr. Zimmermann's diagnosis was a strange tale of a "small mutilation," which exonerated Frederick of homosexuality. According to this explanation, Frederick tried to conceal his mutilation by allowing himself to be charged with the "vicious failing of so many Grecians and Romans, of which he never was guilty."*

Frederick lost a great deal of "sensual pleasure," says Mr. Bushing, a Prussian ecclesiastic counsellor, "by his aversion to women; but he indemnified himself by his intercourse with men, recollecting from the history of philosophy, that Socrates was reported to have been very fond of Alcibiades."

Not only Mr. Bushing, however, but also Voltaire, la Beaumelle, the Duke de Choiseul, innumerable Frenchmen and Germans, almost all the friends and enemies of Frederick, almost all the princes and great men of Europe, even his servants—even the confidants and friends of his later years, were of opinion, that he had loved, as it is pretended, Socrates loved Alcibiades. And I shall prove that this opinion of all Europe, of all the servants and confidants of Frederick, is a gross mistake, and that they cast an undeserved aspersion upon his character and fame.

Whoever writes on Frederick's life and character, cannot treat a more

[2] Zimmermann, *Select Views,* I, 45–58, 61–67.

important subject than this. Perhaps from every quarter they will tell me, that I had better be silent upon so delicate a matter. But, should it be buried in eternal silence, what can and will be said on this subject, the truth would never be known; and, from century to century, one author would copy it from the other, that Frederick loved, as Socrates did Alcibiades.

If Frederick could love thus, thought I often, he was at least not evirated [*emasculated*] as many Frenchmen presumed to assert; and, for this reason, I have often heartily laughed at the French lieutenants and ensigns, who, in the beginning of the Seven Years' War, (before the battle of Rossbach, however,) would often say: "How can the Marquis of Brandenburg [*Frederick*] venture upon any kind of war with us, as he is even unable to sleep with a woman."

Emasculated was Frederick not, but six months after his marriage, rescued from death by a cruel surgical operation. This was the first and most important of all his cabinet secrets.

Something must have been rumored of this operation long before, and caused the report of his emasculation. But it was a glaring contradiction, at the same time, to upbraid Frederick with a Grecian taste in love. I can explain this contradiction in such a manner as will clear his name from an aspersion, which would have been as indelible and immortal as his fame.

Before his marriage, Frederick did not at all dislike women. In these years his constitution rather gave him a strong inclination for the sex. But the rudeness with which his father once treated a handsome lady, suspected to please the prince, withdrew him from what is called love, —deprived him of this heavenly sensation, and drove him to what is not love,—the enjoying of ladies of pleasure. It was from necessity and principles that afterwards he forsook the fair; but he never ceased to be greatly amiable, when he was speaking or writing to ladies. All his lifetime, this amazing man had it in his power to charm everyone by an inexpressible civility and gratefulness, if he chose to do it.

At the very time that his father was going with him to Brunswick, there to consummate his marriage, Frederick labored under a loathsome disease, never more troublesome than at such a time.*

He disclosed his terrible embarrassment to the margrave, Henry of Schwedt. The margrave advised him to apply to his physician at Malchow, who, he said, in a very short time, had often relieved him in a similar situation.** Frederick sent for this man, called the doctor of Malchow, and his complaint was stopped within four days. Frederick fancied himself radically cured, and the quack took care not to undeceive him. He went to Brunswick, and his marriage was consummated.

* A *gonorrhoea maligna.*

** Frederick, supposing the margrave had given him this advice out of spite, could never abide him afterwards.

At first the Prince Royal was certainly adverse to it, because his father forced him to this marriage. But that aversion was very soon done away by the charms of the truly excellent and amiable princess. He conducted her to Rheinsberg, and the first six months their union seemed to be blessed with all the happiness of the most fortunate connubial state.

A worthy writer is, therefore, much mistaken,* when he assures us, that Frederick lived with his princess in Platonic abstinence. He slept with her every night during the first six months of their marriage. The lady of Baron Veltheim,** then maid of honor to the princess, has certified it to Baron Horst.

These six months were scarcely passed, when the disorder stopped by the quack of Malchow, broke out again with redoubled violence, and many ill symptoms. Frederick was seized with a violent illness. This disease, and especially its cause, was carefully concealed. "It was but a slight distemper," would they say, in the usual court language. However this slight distemper grew so dangerous, and the gangrene was so very near, that nothing could, and did, save Frederick's life, but a cruel incision.

With a mind, so great and powerful, it was rather error than weakness which made him mistake this kind of emasculation, by no means complete, for that shameful mutilation, which he could not abide. He did not know that a man's character dwindles into pusillanimity and cowardice, when, he is evirated by an operation totally different. In this case, certainly the character shrinks into meanness, timidity, peevishness and malice. Some wit or petty smartness may remain; but gone forever is all true greatness and vigor of the soul, all briskness, intrepidity and courage. The cruel operation, which saved Frederick's life, was not of that kind, and, therefore, *he* remained what *he* was, a man of the highest mental powers, the greatest and most intrepid hero of his age.

Altogether against his inclination and his will, he saw himself obliged to separate from his highly amiable and dearly beloved princess, and to pretend some natural aversion, caused by a forced marriage. He now publicly professed nothing but the greatest esteem for his princess. But, that no one might suppose him unable to feel all the sensations of human nature, (which he certainly felt) for some time he laid hold of every opportunity of declaring his delight in beautiful women. The portraits of charming female dancers are still extant, with which, for this reason, he adorned his apartments.

For the very same purpose he would affect to be highly delighted with obscene pictures. He succeeded in this attempt, chiefly through a very obscene painting, described by Voltaire, though its existence be

* Mr. Fisher in his *History of Frederick the Second,* Vol. I, pp. 9 and 48.

** The father of the late Hessian minister at the British court.

very erroneously denied by his corrector, Mr. Nicolai,* who presumes to assert, that Frederick the Second never liked, or pretended to like, such pictures, and that, quite to the contrary, as such an indecent, though highly beautiful picture of a satyr, and a nymph by Cignany, was once offered to the king; he called out, at its first sight, "Fie, fie! away with it!"

The Prussian Minister of State, Baron Horst, wrote me, May 3d, 1789: "I remember very well, in the year 1747, to have seen at Potsdam such a picture by Pesne, as Voltaire describes. It hung in the second room from the great saloon, where the officers of the guards used to dine. But this picture was far from being the most obscene in the king's palaces. . . .

Before and after the time that Frederick was pleased to hang out [his] affection for the beautiful Barberina, influenced by the same principle and motive, he displayed the quite opposite disposition of Socratic love.** But this also was nothing but simulation, nothing but a cloak of what he fancied to be nothing less than an emasculation. This fondness for young men he did not only affect before the Seven Years' War, but also after it. But never did he feel this fondness, and never was he guilty of this excess, though he made every effort in his power to persuade the world that he was. In the fourth canto of his *Palladion,* he openly speaks of this Grecian taste in love with great regard. In the first rank he places Socrates with his Alcibiades; after them, Eurialus and Nisus; and then he says: "All the slanderers of Caesar were wrong, in calling him the husband of all the married Roman ladies; he, on the contrary, was the wife of their husbands"; and, at the end, he calls even the holy apostle John, a Ganymedes! ***

Thus Frederick made use even of blasphemy, to cloak the cure of the doctor of Malchow. He knew very well, that the world did really believe, what he wanted to impose on them. He knew that his pages and servants, all his courtiers in Potsdam and Berlin, his companions, favorites, and all the confidants of his later years, suspected, that he had loved many a handsome youth, not quite so as Socrates did the beauti-

* *Anecdotes of Frederick II.* Numb. 3, pp. 316, 317. Notwithstanding this correction and assertion, Mr. Nicolai tells us, in his description of Berlin and Potsdam, Vol. III, p. 1209: "In the royal Gallery at Sans Souci, hung on the third wall, No. 39, the *Surprised Lovers,* by Giulio Romano." I saw this picture in the year 1786, in that gallery, and it certainly is one of the most obscene pictures in the world.

** I know very well how it has been proved over and over again, that Socrates was not guilty of this taste in love, so very common in Greece. With the Grecian culture, this taste went along to Rome; then again from Constantinople to Italy, France, England, and Germany. Some years since it found as many admirers at Bern, in Switzerland, as formerly in the cloisters of French Jesuits, and at some *eminently enlightened* German courts. All this I only say, however, for the purpose of explaining my meaning; and I misuse the innocent name of Socrates, that it may be easier to find decent expressions, for a thing so indecent and impure.

*** *Oeuvres posthumes de Frédéric le Grand,* Vol. IV, p. 92.

ful Alcibiades, but as the Jesuits, according to his own relation,* so many a handsome scholar of theirs. Frederick did not wish to clear himself from this suspicion. By comparing various circumstances, we find, on the contrary, that he encouraged the spreading it wide abroad, with all the power of royalty, not only by honoring with particular favors, young men, who, by their beauty and daily intercourse with the king, raised such a suspicion, but chiefly, and above all, by granting leave to the bookseller Bourdeaux, at Berlin, almost under the windows of his palace, to print the *Pucelle d'Orléans,* adulterated by *La Beaumelle.* In this publication, printed at Berlin, with the king's approbation, we find that most impudent and satiric passage, which, with the highest cynic perspicuity and clearness, charges the king with the Grecian taste in love. Had it not been Frederick's wish, that all Europe should believe this charge to be true, he would not have permitted such an impudent libel to be printed in the very place of his residence.** When we further consider how cautious, even in his last illness, Frederick was to conceal that part, which was quite unfit for such Socratic or Jesuitic love, and that it was his will and express order, after his death, not to be undressed, but only to be covered with his military mantle, we may take it, I suppose, to be sufficiently proved, that Frederick, for the sole purpose of concealing the small mutilation, mentioned before, was fond of being charged with a vicious failing of so many Grecians and Romans, of which he never was guilty.

FREDERICK'S DESPERATE CALL FOR MEDICAL HELP, 1786

The physicians of this country . . . tend only to render my disorder worse.

By early June 1786, Frederick's health had deteriorated so much that fears were expressed for his life. The seventy-four-year-old monarch was violently afflicted with a host of ills. In despera-

* *Oeuvres posthumes de Frédéric le Grand,* Vol. IV, pp. 90, 91, 92.

** For the sake of argument, I'll subjoin this passage, leaving out, however, one horrid line. The father confessor of King Charles VII relates a prophetic vision, discovering to him futurity, recites, in what strange positions he saw the kings of future ages,—says something about George II, and, at last, mentions the King of Prussia with the following words:

Mais quand au bout l'auguste enfilage,
Il appurçut entre Iris et son page.

* * *

Cet auteur roi, si dur et si bizarre
Que dans le Nord on admire, on compare,
A Salomon, ainsi que les Germains,
Leur empereur au César des Romains.

tion he turned to a "foreign" doctor for help, Dr. J. G. Zimmermann, first physician to the Duke of York, ruler of Hanover. Dr. Zimmermann had a reputation as a skilled physician. Frederick's appeal for help was made in the following exchange of letters recorded by Dr. Zimmermann.[3]

Dr. Zimmermann,

For eight months past I have been violently afflicted with an asthma. The physicians of this country give me medicines of every kind; but, instead of affording me relief, they tend only to render my disorder worse. As the reputation of your skill is well known throughout all the northern parts of Europe, I should be very glad if you would take a jaunt hither, for a fortnight, that I may consult you respecting my health, and the circumstances of my present case.—You may readily believe that I will defray the expenses of your journey, and make you a proper compensation for your trouble:—if you agree, therefore, to this proposal, I shall send you a letter to his Royal Highness the Duke of York, who will readily grant you permission to comply with my request: and, in this hope, I beg that God may take you under his sacred and safe protection.

Potsdam, June 6, 1786

Though alarmed, at first, by the contents of this letter, I soon assumed courage after I had made the following reflections: "I am undoubtedly indebted to Providence," said I, "for this mark of his Majesty's confidence; and, under the divine direction, one may walk with a firm step, and with perfect safety, in the most dangerous paths. Frederick, it is true, never had much faith either in physicians or medicine; and as he has always treated our art as quackery, he will be more tenacious of the opinion he has formed, that no relief can be given him. He is, and must be, incurable, since physicians so skillful as those who have hitherto attended him, have not been able to free him from his malady.

"However, it must be interesting and instructive, to have a near view of so extraordinary a man; and to converse with him in his last moments. How often does it happen, that I can say nothing else at the close of the day, but that I have ascended and descended, so many pairs of stairs! Will it not be better to brave every danger that may threaten me at Sans Souci, than to be always leading so insipid and monotonous a life? Even supposing that the king's incredulity, with regard to physicians, is invincible, as I doubt not it is, I have, however, great faith in Frederick. As a physician, he may esteem me very little,

[3] *Dr. Zimmermann's Conversations with the late King of Prussia* (London, 1791), pp. 2–6. Hereafter cited as Zimmermann, *Conversations.*

and treat me with contempt; but as a man, I am certain, he will not despise me: for with him, people of worth and good sense have always preserved their rights. Besides, I have learned by long experience that it is much easier to live with great men, than men of ordinary rank. There is no occasion, therefore, to be afraid of having intercourse with the king, however peevish and morose he may be. I know also, that some of the most distinguished princes generally display benevolence and goodness of heart upon many occasions, notwithstanding all the reasons which they may have for despising mankind in general."

By reflections such as these I overcame all my uneasiness, and roused my courage so far, as to resolve to pay this terrible visit at Sans Souci. I told no person that I had received a letter from his Prussian Majesty, because at this time all the gazettes announced that he was better; that he rode out on horseback; and that the summer seemed to have revived him. No one would have believed this intelligence, had it been known that I was called to Sans Souci. Having determined to go thither, I wrote to his Majesty as follows:

> Sire,
>
> I should think myself the happiest of men, if my presence should prove useful to your Majesty. For forty years past, I have followed you with the same interest, and the same zeal, as that with which I am about to depart for Potsdam.
>
> The Duke of York, had he known that your Majesty had done me the honor to write to me, would have made me set out immediately: but I thought it my duty to conform to your Majesty's orders, since you have thought proper to wait for my answer before you send a letter to the Duke.
>
> Could wishing make one a good physician, I am convinced that your Majesty would be cured the moment I had the honor of seeing you.
>
> To that moment I look forward with eagerness, enthusiasm, and courage.

I waited with the utmost impatience for the king's answer; but as it had not arrived on the 16th of June, I thought it necessary to communicate my secret to the Duke of York, begging him to make it known to the ministers of his British Majesty, without whose consent I could not be absent from Hanover. Four days after, I received the following answer, which induced me to set out immediately for Potsdam.

> Dr. Zimmermann,
>
> I was extremely happy to learn by your letter, of the 10th instant, which I have received, that you intend to come and stay a few days with me. I expect you, therefore, and have sent, along with this, a letter for the

Duke of York, of which I spoke to you before, and which you will be so kind as [to] deliver to him, in my name; and may God take you under His holy and safe protection.

Potsdam, June 16, 1786

DR. ZIMMERMANN'S ACCOUNT OF THE FINAL ILLNESS, 1786

I kneeled down, examined his legs . . . and held my tongue.

Dr. Zimmermann saw his important patient on June 24, 1786, at a time when Frederick had just seven weeks to live. The physician's account of his first two visits follows.[4]

Having passed privately through Brunswick, Magdeburg, and Brandenburg, under the title of a Russian merchant, I arrived at Potsdam on the night of the 23d. At the gate, I told my name to the officer on guard; but when he asked me, according to custom, whether I had come to that city on my own private affairs, or in a public capacity, I told him that I visited Potsdam merely as a traveler, in order to show it to my spouse.

A little before midnight, the door of my apartment, at the inn where I lodged, was suddenly opened by a young officer belonging to the First Battalion of Guards, who asked me, in a very military tone, *if I were there by the king's order*. This question of the lieutenant I thought rather singular: "Sir," said I, "do you ask that question in the name of the king?" *"Yes,"* replied he,—*"Yes,"* said I also; and immediately the door was shut, a little more gently than it had been opened.

The king, who had ordered information to be brought to him, the moment I arrived, was made acquainted, next morning at four o'clock, with the answers, word for word, which I had given at the gate of the city, and at the inn. This circumstance afforded me great pleasure, as it enabled his Majesty to judge of my discretion, from what I had said to his officers. I had afterwards several opportunities of giving him fresh proofs of my prudence in this respect, with which he appeared to be extremely well satisfied.

June the 24th was the first, and the most terrible of all those days which I passed with his Majesty. I may venture to say, that it was one of the most painful and disagreeable I ever experienced. None of those which I afterwards spent with Frederick had the least resemblance to it: they all flowed on peaceably and without the least uneasiness.

[4] Zimmermann, *Conversations,* pp. 6–7, 10–15, 18–23.

At six in the morning, his Majesty sent to tell me, that he was informed of my arrival at Potsdam, and that he wished to see me in two hours. With some emotion, though cool and collected, I repaired, at half after seven, to Sans Souci. . . .

[A] Mr. Schoening saluted me very politely, but in a grave manner, and with much reserve. Concluding, very justly, that next to his Majesty it was of some importance to be on a good footing with him, after I had recovered myself a little, I did and said everything that my knowledge and the experience I had acquired of mankind, during the course of my life, could dictate, in order to gain over this hussar.

I found Mr. Schoening to be a sensible, prudent man, who spoke well, with much shrewdness and freedom; and who appeared to be perfectly acquainted with Frederick. He did not conceal from me, that he was an intimate friend of Professor Selle, the physician whom the king had dismissed a little before. This confession greatly increased the good opinion I had already formed of him; because such frankness is not usual among courtiers. However, as it could not be very agreeable to him to see a stranger called in to attend his Majesty, in the room of his friend, I thought it necessary to be very cautious in my conversation with him. Having followed Mr. Schoening as far as the last antechamber, I saw there, above a commode, two very large portraits of the Emperor Joseph II which I had remarked in 1771.

The remembrance of those sensations which I experienced when I ascended the little hill, and of the reflections that then occurred to me, dissipated all my fears; and in this situation of mind I entered the apartment of the king, whom I found sitting in a large elbow chair, with his back turned toward that side of the room by which I had entered. He had on his head a large hat, very much worn, ornamented with a plume of feathers equally ancient; and his dress consisted of a surtout of sky blue satin, all bedaubed and tinged of a brownish yellow color before, with Spanish snuff. He wore boots and rested one of his legs, which was very much swollen, upon a stool; while the other hung down to the floor. When he perceived me, he pulled off his hat, in a very polite and affable manner; and in a mild tone of voice said, "I return you many thanks, Sir, for your kindness in coming hither, and for the speed with which you have performed your journey." I was perfectly sensible that my journey had not been performed with very great dispatch; but, reflecting that his Majesty could not be ignorant that, in the dry season, one must be stopped every moment in the sands of Brandenburg, and that post horses are wretched animals, I did not think it necessary to make any apology for my delay. "The Duke of York," said I, "requested me to deliver this letter to your Majesty."

Frederick read the letter, and our conversation began in the following manner:

Frederick: I am much obliged to the Duke of York, for permitting you to come hither.

Zimmermann: The Duke of York wishes, as ardently as I do, that my journey may be serviceable to your Majesty.

Frederick: How does the Duke of York do?

Zimmermann: Very well—He is always active, lively, and full of spirits.

Frederick: I love the Duke of York as tenderly as a father can love a son.

Zimmermann: The Duke of York is fully sensible of the value of the good opinion which your Majesty entertains of him.

Frederick: You see I am very ill.

Zimmermann: Your Majesty's eye is as good as when I had the honor of seeing you here fifteen years ago. I observe not the least diminution in that fire, and vigor, with which your Majesty's eyes were then animated.

Frederick: Oh! I am grown very old, and I find myself extremely ill.

Zimmermann: Germany and Europe are not sensible of your Majesty's age and illness.

Frederick: My occupations go on in their usual train.

Zimmermann: Your Majesty rises at four in the morning, and by that you prolong and double life.

Frederick: I do not rise; for I never go to bed—I pass the whole night in this easy chair, in which you now see me.

Zimmermann: Your Majesty wrote to me, that for seven months you have found great difficulty in breathing.

Frederick: I am asthmatic, but not dropsical.—You see, however, that my legs are much swollen.

Zimmermann: Will your Majesty permit me to examine your legs a little closer?

Mr. Schoening being called to pull off his Majesty's boots, I kneeled down, examined his legs, the swelling of which extended as far as the thighs—and held my tongue.

Frederick: I have no dropsy.

Zimmermann: A swelling of the legs is often joined with an asthma. Will your Majesty permit me to feel your lower belly?

Frederick: My belly is big, because I am troubled with flatulencies. There is certainly no water in it.

Zimmermann: It is indeed distended, but it is not hard. May I take the liberty of feeling your Majesty's pulse?

His pulse, which was full and strong, indicated a considerable degree of fever. He was much oppressed, and coughed almost without remission.

Zimmermann: Your pulse is not weak.

Frederick: It is impossible to cure me.
Zimmermann: But your Majesty may at least be relieved.
Frederick: What would you advise me to do?
Zimmermann: At present nothing. I will go immediately and learn from your *valet de chambre* the whole history of your disorder, and read all that your Majesty's physicians have written on the subject; after which I shall have the honor of telling you my sentiments.
Frederick: That is proper—Schoening knows the whole.

The king then taking off his hat, with much politeness, said, "I thank you once more for your goodness in coming hither. Be so kind as to return tomorrow at three."

Having returned with Mr. Schoening to the private secretary's office, outside the castle, I did not disclose my sentiments respecting the king's disorder; but I had no reason to doubt that his case was decidedly dropsical. The state of his breast appeared also to be very suspicious. . . .

". . . I learned from Mr. Schoening, that, from morning till noon, the king had coughed without interruption; that he had a violent oppression; and that he expectorated a prodigious quantity of blood. On the first view, his Majesty's situation seemed to be highly alarming: he could not speak; coughed very much, and at every fit the blood flowed from his mouth. He could not breathe but after violent and painful efforts. I even thought every moment that my august patient would be stifled: sometimes he could not sit in his easy chair, but was obliged to stand up. All his strength seemed to be exhausted, and his head hung down, resting on his breast. Soon after he suffered himself to drop into his easy chair, where he immediately fell asleep: his face became agitated by convulsive motions; from time to time a rattling noise was heard in his throat; and his pulse was full, quick, and strong, but at the same time regular.

I stood a long time near him, before he could utter a single syllable, and before I could speak to him. Every moment he appeared as if about to be suffocated; and the first words which he said were, "With all this, I have a violent colic." Scarcely had I returned an answer, when he again fell asleep, and when the rattling in his throat and the convulsive motions returned. A violent fit of coughing soon roused him from his sleep, and the blood began to flow from his mouth as before. This melancholy scene continued half an hour, when his Majesty found himself a little better: I asked permission to prescribe something for his relief, which occasioned the following conversation:

Frederick: What do you intend to do?
Zimmermann: To relieve your breast, and stop the spitting of blood.
Frederick: The spitting of blood is nothing; I expectorated fully as much in the Seven Years' War. What must I do for my colic?

Zimmermann: You must take a clyster [*enema*].

Frederick: It will soon go off like a pistol shot; but, however, I will try your remedy. What must be done besides?

Zimmermann: Everything possible must be done, to ease your breast, without irritating the colic. Your Majesty must take sal ammoniac with oxymel.

Frederick: Oxymel is of no service to me. What will the sal ammoniac do?

Zimmermann: It will cool and ease your breast, which is very necessary, and will not irritate the colic.

Frederick: Order some sal ammoniac for me; and afterwards tell me if you are at present well informed respecting my case.

Zimmermann: I am indeed: but I wish your Majesty would be pleased to allow me to send to Berlin for Professor Selle, in order that we may concert a plan for the treatment of your disorder. Selle is better acquainted with your case than anyone: since the beginning of it he has judged well, and always given your Majesty good advice.

With terrible looks, sparkling eyes, his head raised up, and a voice such as I never heard in my life, his Majesty replied, "I expected that plan from you."

Zimmermann: I will afterwards lay this plan before your Majesty. At present I must endeavor, as much as possible, to relieve the symptoms of the moment.

All the king's strength appeared to be exhausted by this conversation. He soon after fell into the same state of profound sleep, his head leaning on his breast, and convulsions appeared in his countenance as before.

His Majesty held in one of his hands a white handkerchief, which appeared as if it had been dipped in blood. It was of considerable importance to know whether there was not some pus mixed with the blood. Seeing, therefore, a white handkerchief on the table near me, I took it up with one hand, and with the other gently drew toward me that which the king held, when he suddenly awoke, raised up his head, and darted a furious look at me; but very luckily he soon dropped his head again, and fell fast asleep. I then put into his hand, with a little more precaution, the handkerchief I had taken from the table; and on examining that which I took in exchange, I found pure blood with a very little phlegm, but no pus at all. The king remained a long time dozing, and always seemed to breathe with much difficulty. While he was in that state, the sal ammoniac was brought; and Frederick having at length awoke, I said, "Here is the sal ammoniac." He shook his head, took the salt which I gave him, had a clyster administered, and again slept for an hour: but the convulsive motions in his face still continued.

During these painful moments, I was the only person with the king, while one or two hussars attended in the antechamber. I considered myself then as in an awkward situation—a stranger, and alone with the King of Prussia, who appeared to be angry with me on the first day of my arrival, before I had time to say or do anything of importance.

COUNT MIRABEAU ON FREDERICK'S LAST DAYS, 1786

The smallest fever—and the curtain must drop.

According to Count de Mirabeau, French ambassador to Prussia, almost everyone in Berlin was hoping for the end of Frederick's reign. People resented the king's imposition of tax burdens as well as his contempt for the masses. In the abstract, Frederick had always shown a concern for the welfare of his subjects, but this did not prevent him from regarding most of them as worthless cannon fodder. His attitude was well known and as a result there appeared to be little sadness when the severity of his illness became common gossip. All this was the opinion of one observer. Mirabeau described Frederick's last days in these passages from Secret Memoirs of the Court of Berlin.[5]

Letter IX

July 31, 1786

. . . The king is in daily danger of death, though he may live some months. I persist in my autumnal prognostics. Prince Henry having sent for me to Rheinsberg by a very formal and friendly letter, it would appear affectation in me not to go; and I shall set off on Wednesday, after the departure of the courier. I shall not remain there longer than a week, where I shall have good opportunities of intelligence concerning the state of the king, and of gaining information on various matters.

Postscript.—The king is sensibly worse; he has had a fever these two days; this may kill him, or prolong his life. Nature has continually done so much for this extraordinary man, that nothing more is wanting to restore him than a hemorrhoidal eruption. The muscular powers are very great. . . .

Letter X

August 2d, 1786

Written before my departure for Rheinsberg

The king is evidently better, at least with respect to pain, when he does not move; he has even left off the use of the *taraxicum,* or dan-

[5] Honoré-Gabriel Requetti, Comte de Mirabeau, *Secret Memoirs of the Court of Berlin* (New York, 1901), pp. 50–55.

delion, the only thing Zimmermann prescribed, who, consequently, is in despair. He simply takes a tincture of rhubarb mixed with diarrhetics, which give him copious evacuations. His appetite is very good, which he indulges without restaint. The most unhealthy dishes are his greatest favorites. If indigestion be the consequence, as it frequently is, he takes a double aperitive dose.

Frese, his physician of Potsdam, still continues in disgrace, for having dared to whisper the word dropsy on the question being asked him, and an appeal made to his conscience, what was the name and character of the disease. The king is exceedingly chilly, and is continually enveloped in furs, and covered by feather beds. He has not entered his bed these six weeks, but is removed from one armchair to another, in which he takes tolerably long sleeps, turned on his right side. Inflation augments; the scrotum is exceedingly tumid. He perceives this, but will not persuade himself, or appear to believe, that it is anything more than the inflation of convalescence, and the result of great feebleness.

This information is minutely exact, and very recent. There is no doubt of his unwillingness to die. The people best informed think that, as soon as as he believes himself really dropsical and at the point of death, he will submit to be tapped, and to the most violent remedies, rather than peaceably resign himself to sleep with his fathers. He even desired, some time since, incisions might be made in his hams and thighs; but the physicians feared to risk them. With respect to his understanding, it is still sound; and he even continues his labors.

Letter XI

August 8th, 1786

The king is dangerously ill; some affirm he has not many hours to live, but this probably partakes of exaggeration. On the fourth, the erysipelas with blisters on the legs made their appearance; this prognosticates bursting, and soon after gangrene. At present there is suffocation, and a most infectious smell. The smallest fever—and the curtain must drop.

Letter XII

August 12th, 1786

The king is apparently much better. The evacuation which was the consequence of the apertures in his legs, has caused the swelling to abate, and gives ease; but has been followed by a dangerous excess of appetite. He cannot continue in this state. You may expect to receive a grand packet at my return from Rheinsberg.

PART THREE

FREDERICK THE GREAT IN HISTORY

12
Obituary from the *Annual Register*, 1786

One of the greatest captains and masters of the art of war that ever lived.

Throughout the world the death of Frederick was regarded as one of the most important events of the year 1786. Before turning to the judgment of scholars, let us look at the British publication Annual Register. *This reputable journal gave an account of "that dead prince," placing emphasis upon how he endowed hospitals for distressed Berlin, how his temper and disposition were rendered more kindly by age, and how he patronized native literature as well as language.*[1]

There was no event that marked the year of which we treat in such striking and indelible colors as the death of the great Frederick, the illustrious King of Prussia. If he was not the founder of an empire, he accomplished a more arduous task than even that, under its usually concurrent circumstances, has generally proved; for, surrounded as he was by great and jealous potentates, possessed of immense standing armies, and at a time when discipline and the art of war were supposed to have been already carried to their ultimate point of perfection, he, merely by the powers of superior genius and ability, raised a scattered, ill-sorted, disjointed dominion, into the first rank of power, glory, and renown and the newly founded kingdom of Prussia soon became, under his auspices, the terror or admiration of mankind.

But though he must always be considered as one of the greatest captains and masters of the art of war that ever lived, and as having

[1] *Annual Register, 1786* (London, 1788), pp. 160–67.

carried military discipline and field evolution to a degree of perfection before unthought of, and which is now the great object of imitation with all martial nations; his mind was too comprehensive, and his genius too vast, to be confined to tactics, or the business of the field; and he shone forth at the same time with no less ambition of fame, in all the different characters of legislator, historian, poet, and philosopher.

In the course of his long and exceedingly hard-fought wars, contending against a combination of power which has seldom been equalled, and with some of the first generals and greatest nations, he sustained with unfailing constancy, and an unconquerable fortitude, the most dismal reverses of fortune that perhaps have ever been experienced and recovered by any commander; he having been repeatedly and suddenly depressed from the highest pinnacle of success to the lowest extreme of distress and adversity; insomuch, that even the continuance of his existence as a sovereign was more than once a question sufficiently dubious. Through a noble perseverance, and the strenuous exertions of his admirable genius, he still surmounted his difficulties and dangers: fortune again smiled, and seemed only to plunge him in adversity, that he might rise with brighter glory.

In estimates of real character we must necessarily take mankind such as they are, compounds of good and of evil, of great and of little; we should in vain look for resemblances to those imaginary heroes who are represented as so bedizened with virtues, that nothing like nature or truth can be perceived about them; and the picture exhibits as the poet happily observes, "those faultless monsters which the world ne'er saw." On the contrary, the shades in Frederick's character were as strongly marked as the bright parts, and we shall perhaps find that his great qualities had even more than their due proportion of alloy. There certainly have been great captains and conquerors, who afforded superior instances of a noble and generous nature to any that he had the fortune of exhibiting; who were happily better calculated to excite the affection as well as the admiration of mankind; and who were free from any of the defects of his character.—To say that his ambition was boundless would be no more than saying that he held the vice common to great situations; but his ambition afforded too much with rapacity to captivate the imagination, as it otherwise might have done; and he looked more to his interest than his fame in the means which he sometimes used for the attainment of his objects. A strict economy, indeed, was indispensably necessary to the peculiarity of his situation, and to the support of such prodigious armies, with means which would have been totally inadequate in any other hands; but he pushed this virtue too far toward the opposite extreme, so as to carry too much the appearance of a degrading parsimony; and it must be acknowledged by those who pay the greatest respect to his eminent qualities, that he was more fond of gold than corresponds with the established ideas of a great man.

Frederick could brook no opposition to his will either in word or in action; was to the last degree implacable in his resentments; and inheriting from nature, as well as deriving from education and example, a disposition extremely harsh, despotic, and occasionally cruel, it could not be expected that it would have been lessened by the horrors and carnage of war, any more than by the continual personal enforcement in peace of that austere military discipline established by himself, which was as unequalled in its rigor and severity, as in all other respects; and by which man, being reduced to the state of a living machine, was considered and treated merely as such. . . .

This great prince departed the present life on the 17th of August, 1786, in the 75th year of his age; a surprising age, whether we consider it with respect to the greatness, number, and splendor of its actions, the dangers to which it had been exposed, or the unequalled exertions of body and mind, by which, through a long reign of more than forty-six years, it had been continually exhausted.

His decline had for some time been so rapid, that the event was easily foreseen; yet, under the joint pressure of an asthma, dropsy, and lethargy, the former of which had for some time rendered him incapable of repose in a bed, he displayed in the intervals his pristine vigor of mind, and all his usual serenity and cheerfulness in conversation; never uttering the least complaint, nor showing the smallest degree either of regret or impatience at his condition; and on the 15th, only two days before his death, he sent for his cabinet secretaries at four o'clock in the morning, and transacted business for three hours with them; but in the evening of that day the somnolency returned, and he continued nearly in a state of insensibility until his death.

It was a curious if not singular circumstance, that as the king began himself personally to feel the infirmities and incommodities of age, it touched his sympathy so strongly for the distresses of the unprovided in that calamitous condition, that he immediately founded two hospitals in Berlin for the reception of helpless old age, in all cases whatever, without regard to nation, religion, or sex.

There were numerous other instances of his temper and disposition being greatly softened by age; a circumstance very unusual in mankind, and almost without example in conquerors; who so generally become more rigid, harsh, and oppressive, and too frequently degenerate into absolute cruelty at that season of life.

The attention of all Europe had been long drawn to the contemplation of this expected event, and of its probable or possible consequences. Many apprehended that it would prove the signal for immediate war, and perhaps lead to great political revolution. The character of his nephew and successor, the present king, was not yet much developed; and it was easily seen that a new kingdom which had risen suddenly to such unexampled power and greatness as served to excite the jealousy or apprehension of all its neighbors, merely through the abilities of one man, would require abilities not much inferior to withstand the shocks, to which it might be liable upon the loss of its tutelary guardian and genius. . . .

No event or act of the late reign was so universally unpopular throughout Germany, as his predilection for the French language, and the decided preference which he upon all occasions gave to the literature of that nation. The numerous German *literati* in particular could not but be grievously affected by it, and indeed every true patriot, from whatever part of that wide empire he derived his existence, must have felt it sensibly, as an insult offered, and a glaring contempt shown to his language and country. This predilection the king derived from his early acquaintance and intercourse with French poets and philosophers of the modern stamp, to whom he was likewise indebted for other prejudices and principles still more injurious and unfortunate; particularly that indifference (to call it by the softest name) with respect to religion, which stuck to him through life, and was the great blemish of his character.

It must, however, be remembered, that the German writers in the late king's earlier days, were of a very different cast and character from those who have since so far advanced literature and science, have done so much honor to their country by their genius and researches, and who by their successful introduction of the poetic muses have used the most effectual means for softening and wearing down the roughness of their native tongue. On the contrary, at and for a considerable time after his accession, laboriousness and fidelity were the chief praises that could be bestowed on the German writers; their works were proverbially verbose and heavy; they had not yet applied with any success to the *belles lettres;* and their poetry, particularly the dramatic, was barbarous. Early prejudices are with difficulty shaken off, and as life advances, the disposition to that endeavor generally lessens. Frederick had early made himself a party in the affair, by criticisms on, and himself writing against, the German studies and literature. Having thus declared himself, he was too proud and too tenacious of his opinion ever to relinquish it, and would neither observe nor examine the wonderful change and improvement which was taking place in both. And so far was he from affording favor or encouragement to the writers who were thus reforming the language and taste of their country, that it is said, he would not even read their productions if in the vernacular tongue.

Nothing then could be more popular, or more generally gratifying, than the new king's declaration in council, that "Germans we are, and Germans I mean we shall continue"; at the same time giving directions that their native language should resume its natural rank and station, from which it had been for near half a century degraded by the usurping French; the latter only having been during that time spoken at court, addressed in letters to the king, used in all public offices and transactions, and even in the academies. Of these, the Royal Academy of Sciences was composed almost entirely of Frenchmen; but the king now ordered three Germans to be received in it, and public discourses to be occasionally delivered in the Teutonic. To show his attention to the native literature, he settled a handsome pension for life upon Mr. Ramler, the celebrated German lyric poet; and received in the most favorable manner the congratulatory verses which were addressed to him by Professor Gleim, and other men of learning, who all made it a point to write them in the native language. The late king had likewise placed the collection of the taxes and duties, particularly those on tobacco, almost exclusively in the hands of Frenchmen; but they were now generally, if not universally, replaced by Germans, and the foreigners humanely allowed pensions.

The new king strictly prohibited all publications tending to excite a contempt or indifference for religion: observing that he had marked with great concern the progress of impiety and profaneness on the one hand, and of enthusiasm on the other, which were making such rapid advances among the people; and which he attributed in a great degree to the multiplicity of these publications. He declared that he would not have his subjects corrupted either by fanatics or atheists; nor madmen to enrich themselves and the booksellers at the expense of religion. He likewise passed a severe law against duelling in all cases whatever; and erected a court or tribunal of honor to take cognizance of these disputes or differences which might lead to that resort.

Upon the whole, everything that has yet appeared serves to indicate a happy and prosperous reign to that kingdom; and as the monarchy is now thoroughly formed and established, if it should not prove so splendid as the foregoing, it will be so much the better for the people.

13
Macaulay's Unfavorable Estimate, 1842

A tyrant of extraordinary military and political talents. . . .

In 1842, Thomas Babington Macaulay wrote an extended essay on the life of Frederick the Great in which he expressed a decidedly unfavorable judgment. The following excerpts indicate a highly critical attitude.[1]

Early in the year 1740 Frederick William met death with a firmness and dignity worthy of a better and wiser man; and Frederick, who had just completed his twenty-eighth year, became King of Prussia. His character was little understood. That he had good abilities, indeed, no person who had talked with him, or corresponded with him, could doubt. But the easy Epicurean life which he had led, his love of good cookery and good wine, of music, of conversation, of light literature, led many to regard him as a sensual and intellectual voluptuary. His habit of canting about moderation, peace, liberty, and the happiness which a good mind derives from the happiness of others, had imposed on some who should have known better. Those who thought best of him, expected a Telemachus after Fanelon's pattern. Others predicted the approach of a Medicean age, an age propitious to learning and art, and not unpropitious to pleasure. Nobody had the least suspicion that a tyrant of extraordinary military and political talents, of industry more extraordinary still, without fear, without faith, and without mercy, had ascended the throne. . . .

[*As for the Archduchess Maria Theresa*] no sovereign had ever taken possession of a throne by a clearer title [*the Pragmatic Sanction*]. . . . Yet the King of Prussia, the Anti-Machiavel, had already fully determined to commit the great crime of violating his plighted faith, of robbing the ally whom he was bound to defend, and of plunging all

[1] Excerpted from Thomas Babington Macaulay, *Frederick the Great* (London, 1842), *passim.*

Europe into a long, bloody, and desolating war; and all this for no end whatever, except that he might extend his dominions, and see his name in the gazettes. He determined to assemble a great army with speed and secrecy, to invade Silesia before Maria Theresa should be apprised of his design, and to add that rich province to his kingdom. . . .

He had, from the commencement of his reign, applied himself to public business after a fashion unknown among kings. Louis the Fourteenth, indeed, had been his own prime minister, and had exercised a general superintendence over all the departments of the government; but this was not sufficient for Frederick. He was not content with being his own prime minister; he would be his own sole minister. Under him there was no room, not merely for a Richelieu or a Mazarin, but for a Colbert, a Louvois, or a Torcy. A love of labor for its own sake, a restless and insatiable longing to dictate, to intermeddle, to make his power felt, a profound scorn and distrust of his fellow creatures, made him unwilling to ask counsel, to confide important secrets, to delegate ample powers. The highest functionaries under his government were mere clerks, and were not so much trusted by him as valuable clerks are often trusted by the heads of departments. He was his own treasurer, his own commander-in-chief, his own intendant of public works, his own minister for trade and justice, for home affairs and foreign affairs, his own master of the horse, steward, and chamberlain. Matters of which no chief of an office in any other government would ever hear, were, in this singular monarchy, decided by the king in person. If a traveller wished for a good place to see a review, he had to write to Frederick and received next day, from a royal messenger, Frederick's answer signed by Frederick's own hand. This was an extravagant, a morbid activity. The public business would assuredly have been better done if each department had been put under a man of talents and integrity, and if the king had contented himself with a general control. In this manner the advantages which belong to unity of design, and the advantages which belong to the division of labor, would have been to a great extent combined. But such a system would not have suited the peculiar temper of Frederick. He could tolerate no will, no reason, in the State, save his own. He wished for no abler assistance than that of penmen who had just understanding enough to translate and transcribe, to make out his scrawls, and to put his concise Yes and No into an official form. Of the higher intellectual faculties, there is as much in a copying machine, or a lithographic press, as he required from a secretary of the cabinet. . . .

Most of the vices of Frederick's administration resolve themselves into one vice, the spirit of meddling. The indefatigable activity of his intellect, his dictatorial temper, his military habits, all inclined him to this great fault. He drilled his people as he drilled his grenadiers. Capital and industry were diverted from their natural direction by a crowd of preposterous regulations. There was a monopoly of coffee, a monopoly of tobacco, a monopoly of refined sugar. The public money, of which the king was generally so sparing, was lavishly spent in ploughing bogs, in planting mulberry trees amidst the sand, in bringing sheep from Spain to improve the Saxon wool, in bestowing prizes for fine yarn, in building manufactories of porcelain, manufactories of carpets, manufactories of hardware, manufactories of lace. Neither the experience of other rulers, nor his own, could ever teach him that something more than an edict and a grant of public money was required to create a Lyons, a Brussels, or a Birmingham.

For his commercial policy, however, there was some excuse. He had on his side illustrious examples and popular prejudice. Grievously as he erred, he erred in company with his age. In other departments his meddling was altogether without apology. He interfered with the course of justice as well as with the course of trade; and set up his own crude notions of equity against the law as expounded by the unanimous voice of the gravest magistrates. It never occurred to him that men whose lives were passed in adjudicating on questions of civil right were more likely to form correct opinions on such questions than a prince whose attention was divided among a thousand objects, and who had never read a law book through. The resistance opposed to him by the tribunals inflamed him to fury. He reviled his chancellor. He kicked the shins of his judges. He did not, it is true, intend to act unjustly. He firmly believed that he was doing right, and defending the cause of the poor against the wealthy. Yet this well-meant meddling probably did far more harm than all the explosions of his evil passions during the whole of his long reign. We could make shift to live under a debauchee or a tyrant; but to be ruled by a busybody is more than human nature can bear.

The same passion for directing and regulating appeared in every part of the king's policy. Every lad of a certain station in life was forced to go to certain schools within the Prussian dominions. If a young Prussian repaired, though but for a few weeks, to Leyden or Göttingen for the purpose of study, the offense was punished with civil disabilities, and sometimes with the confiscation of property. Nobody was to travel without the royal permission. If the permission were granted, the pocket money of the tourist was fixed by royal ordinance. A merchant might take with him two hundred and fifty rix-dollars in gold, a noble was allowed to take four hundred; for it may be observed, in passing, that Frederick studiously kept up the old distinction between the nobles and the community. In speculation, he was a French philosopher, but in action a German prince. He talked and wrote about the privileges of blood in the style of Sieyès;

but in practice no chapter in the empire looked with a keener eye to genealogies and quarterings.

Such was Frederick the Ruler. But there was another Frederick, the Frederick of Rheinsberg, the fiddler and flute player, the poetaster and metaphysician. Amidst the cares of State the king had retained his passion for music, for reading, for writing, for literary society. To these amusements he devoted all the time that he could snatch from the business of war and government; and perhaps more light is thrown on his character by what passed during his hours of relaxation, than by his battles or his laws. . . .

Hating Christianity with a rancor which made him incapable of rational inquiry, unable to see in the harmony and beauty of the universe the traces of divine power and wisdom, he was the slave of dreams and omens, would not sit down to table with thirteen in company, turned pale if the salt fell towards him, begged his guests not to cross their knives and forks on their plates, and would not for the world commence a journey on Friday. His health was a subject of constant anxiety to him. Whenever his head ached, or his pulse beat quickly, his dastardly fears and effeminate precautions were the jest of all Berlin. All this suited the king's purpose admirably. He wanted somebody by whom he might be amused, and whom he might despise. . . .

Absolute kings seldom have friends; and Frederick's faults were such as, even where perfect equality exists, make friendship exceedingly precarious. He had indeed many qualities which, on a first acquaintance, were captivating. His conversation was lively; his manners, to those whom he desired to please, were even caressing. No man could flatter with more delicacy. No man succeeded more completely in inspiring those who approached him with vague hopes of some great advantage from his kindness. But under this fair exterior he was a tyrant, suspicious, disdainful, and malevolent.

14

Thomas Carlyle's Romanticized Portrait, 1852–1865

He is a King every inch of him.

Thomas Carlyle (1795–1881), British essayist, historian, and philosopher, was deeply impressed by the Prussian military genius who had made his small kingdom a powerful state in Europe. Carlyle journeyed to Germany in 1852, visited the scenes of Frederick's battles, and industriously gathered material for what he was certain would be his masterpiece. The first two volumes appeared in 1852, to be followed by succeeding volumes from 1862 to 1865. The biography called by Emerson "the wittiest ever written," brought Carlyle many honors, including election as lord rector of his old University of Edinburgh and award of the Prussian Order of Merit in 1874.

Historians criticize Carlyle severely because of his overromantic attitude toward his subject and his reduction of complicated situations to simple formulae. One critic excoriated his "poor jargon . . . a mere veil to hide from Carlyle himself the essential poverty of his thoughts." The following brief selection is typical of Carlyle's glowing pen portrait.[1]

PROEM: FREDERICK'S HISTORY FROM THE DISTANCE WE ARE AT

About fourscore years ago, there used to be seen sauntering on the terraces of Sans Souci, for a short time in the afternoon, or you might have met him elsewhere at an earlier hour, riding or driving in a rapid business manner on the open roads or through the scraggy woods and avenues of that intricate amphibious Potsdam region, a high interesting lean little old man, of alert though stooping figure; whose name among strangers was King *Friedrich the Second,* or Frederick the Great of Prussia, and at home among the common people, who much loved and esteemed him, was *Vater Fritz,* Father

[1] Thomas Carlyle, *History of Friedrich II of Prussia, called Frederick the Great,* 10 vols. (New York: Scribner, Welford and Company, 1872), I, 1–3.

Fred—a name of familiarity which had not bred contempt in that instance. He is a King every inch of him, though without the trappings of a King. Presents himself in a Spartan simplicity of vesture: no crown but an old military cocked hat—generally old, or trampled and kneaded into absolute *softness,* if new—no scepter but one like Agamemnon's, a walking stick cut from the woods, which serves also as a riding stick (with which he "hits the horse between the ears," say authors); and for royal robes, a mere soldier's blue coat with red facings, coat likely to be old, and sure to have a good deal of Spanish snuff on the breast of it; rest of the apparel dim, unobtrusive in color or cut, ending in high overknee military boots, which may be brushed (and, I hope, kept soft with an underhand suspicion of oil), but are not permitted to be blackened or varnished; Day and Martin with their soot-pots forbidden to approach.

The man is not of godlike physiognomy, any more than of imposing stature or costume: close-shut mouth with thin lips, prominent jaws and nose, receding brow, by no means of Olympian height; head, however, is of long form, and has superlative gray eyes in it. Not what is called a beautiful man; nor yet, by all appearance, what is called a happy one. On the contrary, the face bears evidence of many sorrows, as they are termed, of much hand labor done in this world; and seems to anticipate nothing but more still coming. Quiet stoicism, capable enough of what joys there were, but not expecting any worth mention; great unconscious and some conscious pride, well tempered with a cheery mockery of humor, are written on that old face; which carries its chin well forward, in spite of the slight stoop about the neck; snuffy nose rather flung into the air, under its old cocked hat—like an old snuffy lion on the watch; and such a pair of eyes as no man or lion or lynx of that century bore elsewhere, according to all the testimony we have. "Those eyes," says Mirabeau, "which, at the bidding of his great soul, fascinated you with seduction or with terror (*portaient, au gré de son âme héroïque, la séduction ou la terreur*)!" Most excellent potent brilliant eyes, swift-darting as the stars, steadfast as the sun; gray, we said, of the azure-gray color; large enough, not of glaring size; the habitual expression of them, vigilance and penetrating sense, rapidity resting on depth. Which is an excellent combination; and gives us the notion of a lambent outer radiance sprung from some great inner sea of light and fire in the man. The voice, if he speak to you, is of similar physiognomy; clear, melodious, and sonorous; all tones are in it, from that of ingenuous inquiry, graceful sociality, light-flowing banter (rather prickly for most part), up to definite word of command, up to desolating word of rebuke and reprobation; a voice the clearest and most "agreeable in conversation I ever heard," says witty Dr. Moore. "He speaks a great deal," continues the doctor; "yet those who hear him, regret that he does not speak a good deal more. His observations are always lively, very often just; and few men possess the talent of repartee in greater perfection."

Just about threescore and ten years ago, his speakings and his workings came to finis in this world of time; and he vanished from all eyes into other worlds, leaving much inquiry about him in the minds of men; which, as my readers and I may feel too well, is yet by no means satisfied. As to his speech, indeed, though it had the worth just ascribed to it and more, and though masses of it were deliberately put on paper by himself, in prose and verse, and continue to be printed and kept legible, what he spoke has pretty much vanished into the inane; and except as record or document of what he did, hardly now concerns mankind. But the things he did were extremely remarkable; and cannot be forgotten by mankind. Indeed, they bear such fruit to the present hour as all the newspapers are obliged to be taking note of, sometimes to an unpleasant degree. Editors vaguely account this man the "Creator of the Prussian Monarchy," which has since grown so large in the world and troublesome to the editorial mind in this and other countries. He was indeed the first who, in a highly public manner, notified creation; announced to all men that it was, in very deed, created; standing on its feet there, and would go a great way, on the impulse it had got from him and others. As it has accordingly done; and may still keep doing to lengths little dreamt of by the British editor in our time; whose prophesyings upon Prussia, and insights into Prussia, in its past or present or future, are truly as yet inconsiderable, in proportion to the noise he makes with them! The more is the pity for him—and for myself too in the enterprise now on hand.

15

W. F. Reddaway on Frederick and Three Great Phenomena of History, 1904

By his single will he shaped the course of history.

In 1904, W. F. Reddaway, fellow and lecturer of King's College, Cambridge, published a popular biography of Frederick based on Frederick's own works, Carlyle's "opulent treasure-house," and the more systematic narrative of Reinhold Koser's Geschichte Friedrichs des Grossen. *In his concluding pages, Reddaway presented this estimate of Frederick.*[1]

As a thinker, then, even in politics and administration, Frederick falls very far short of greatness. His powers were, in reality, those of a man of action. The versatility with which he entered into every department of government in turn is no more astounding than the clearness with which he perceived the immediate obstacles to be overcome in each, the courage with which he faced them, and the force, swift, steady, and irresistible, by which he triumphed. The wonderful energy which prompted him to bear on his own shoulders all the burden of the State in war and peace, and to put forth all his strength at every blow, was yet more marvellous because it was susceptible of control. Frederick, as we have seen, ceased from the labors of the Seven Years' War, only to undertake the reconstruction of the economic life of a great kingdom. By mere overflow of force he finished his *History of the War* early in the year after that in which peace was made. Yet, with all his energy, he was able to realize that not seldom force needs the help of time. He was gratified when some of his enterprises began to repay him after twenty years, and he declined to aggrandize Prussia beyond the limit which his statesmanlike instinct taught him that her strength would warrant.

[1] W. F. Reddaway, *Frederick the Great and Rise of Prussia* (New York and London: G. P. Putnam's Sons, 1904), pp. 356–60.

Among Frederick's powers, then, energy alone is truly great, but his energy was such that to him few achievements were impossible. If we turn from his powers to his performance, we find his name associated with three great phenomena of history. Under his guidance Prussia rose at one step from the third to the highest grade among the Powers. He was, moreover, the pattern of the monarchs of his time, the type of the benevolent despots of the later eighteenth century. Finally, in the great series of events by which Germany has become a united military empire his life-work fills a conspicuous place. How far, we may inquire, should his work in any of these three fields compel the admiration of succeeding ages?

That part of the Hohenzollern legend which portrays Frederick as the conscious or semiconscious architect of the modern German Empire finds little support in the record of his life. Sometimes, it is true, he used the language of Teutonic patriotism and posed as the indignant defender of German liberties against the Habsburg. But he posed with equal indignation as the protector of Polish or Swedish "liberties" against a reforming king or as the champion of Protestantism against powers who might be represented as its foes. The whole course of his life witnessed to his preference for French civilization over German, and to his indifference as to the race of his subjects and assistants, if only they were serviceable to the State. His point of view was invariably and exclusively Prussian. It would never have occurred to him to refuse to barter his Rhenish provinces for parts of Bohemia or Poland because the former were inhabited by Germans and the latter by Slavs. He was far from being shocked at the suggestion that he might one day partition the empire with the Habsburgs. He struggled for equality with Austria, never dreaming of the time when his descendants should expel her from Germany and assume the Imperial crown. Thus, though his work was a step toward their triumph, it was unconscious. He must be judged by viewing his achievements in relation to his own designs.

Frederick's influence upon his contemporaries was enormous, and in many respects it cannot be overpraised. He found what has been styled "Sultan-and-harem economy" prevalent among his peers, together with a tendency to regard the income of the State as the pocket money of the ruler. For this he substituted in Europe a measure of his own ideal of royal duty. Fearing nothing and hoping little from any future state, he was yet too proud to flinch from an atom of the lifelong penance that he believed was prescribed for kings by some law of nature. Duty to his House and duty to his State were to him the same, and they dictated a life of incessant labor for his subjects' good, and forbade the appropriation of more than a living wage. Other sovereigns followed the Prussian mode, and "benevolent despotism" came to be regarded as the panacea for the ills of Europe. Though it hardly survived the storm of the Revolution, it was instrumental in removing many abuses and in promoting during several decades the comfort of the common people. Thanks in great part to Frederick, irresponsible monarchy became impossible forever.

Frederick's fame, nonetheless, finds its most solid basis in the achievement to which all else in his life was subordinate—the successful aggrandizement of Prussia. Though it may be true that another and a better way lay open to him, that the path which he marked out led straight to Jena, that he owed much of his success to fortune, and that his work was rescued by forces which he had not prized, in spite of all it is to him that Prussia owes her place among the nations. By his single will he shaped the course of history. His rule completed the fusion of provinces into a State, his victories gave it prestige, and the success of his work of aggrandizement was great enough to consecrate the very arts by which it was accomplished. Two decades after his death a king of Prussia entered his tomb by night, seeking inspiration to confront Napoleon. The architects of modern Germany declare that all that they have built rests upon the foundations that he laid. As long as the German Empire flourishes and the world is swayed by the principles of its founders, so long will the fame of Frederick the Great remain secure.

16

Pierre Gaxotte on Frederick's Personality and Character, 1942

He had extraordinary vivacity, exuberance of speech, transports of anger, and fits of violence.

Many historians have attempted to describe the elusive temperament and character of Frederick. One of the most successful was the French scholar, Pierre Gaxotte, whose account of Frederick's personality and character follows.[1] *It is to be hoped that in the future much more attention will be paid to a psychoanalytical interpretation of Frederick's formative years in much the same approach used by Erik H. Erikson in his superb* Young Man Luther.

Frederick had a sanguine temperament. Ever since his youth he had complained of "very violent," "unbearable" beating of the heart, of feelings of suffocation, and of hemorrhoids. At thirty-four he endured his first attack of gout; nearly every winter both his legs and his left hand were attacked. At thirty-five he had an attack of some form of hemiplegia, mild enough it is true but it left his neck and legs swollen. And on top of this came fever, colics, cramps of the stomach, and "bloody fluxes," which must have been intestinal hemorrhages. "My soul makes my body work," he used often to say. He must indeed have had a prodigious power of endurance to overcome these ills and trials while leading the life of a "fettered galley slave." From 1758 on he believed he was condemned to an early death, but during a reign of forty-six years he made his bodily "machine" work "at any price," by treating it "like a sorry old nag and digging in the spurs with vigor."

He displayed other symptoms of the sanguine type—mental ones. Firstly, habitual gaiety and a slightly whimsical good humor of which

[1] Pierre Gaxotte, *Frederick the Great,* trans. from the French by R. A. Bell (London: G. Bell & Sons, Ltd., 1941; New Haven: Yale University Press, 1942), pp. 275–79. Reprinted by permission of G. Bell & Sons, Ltd.

misfortune never deprived him completely, for sometimes at tragic moments he still spoke of his reverses with a smile and with brilliant flashes of wit at the "raps" he was giving the enemy. Further, he had fickleness of character, impatience, sensitivity to passing impressions—youthful faults which diminished with the passing of years. He possessed brilliant physical courage, which made him, according to his officers, habitually expose himself too much upon the battlefield. He had enthusiasm, the fundamental optimism of a man of action which showed him the profit behind each trial rather than the hazard of it: one of his close friends said that with him a display of confidence was always the prelude to some reverse, and one of fear to some success. Finally, he had extraordinary vivacity, exuberance of speech, transports of anger, and fits of violence. For a man of such a temperament to want and to act were necessities, were instinctive and irresistible natural functions. Decision and action were synonymous to giving way to a nature of irrepressible strength, giving way joyfully as to a delicious and tyrannical passion. "In short," said he one day, "only the founders of empires can properly be described as men."

The man's political imagination was always in labor, for his mind restlessly fathered plans and projects. He had one for every eventuality: some prepared and precise, other roughed out on bits of paper, summarily "sketched" so as to be "digested" afterward by ministers. In the *Political Testament* of 1752 there is one for the conquest of Saxony, a second for the acquisition of Polish Prussia, others again anticipating a civil war in Russia, the succession of a minor in England, and a vacancy on the throne of France by the extinction of the elder line of the Bourbons. Never did he give himself over to the lazy calm of routine, never was he tied down to a system or a formula. He was not even bound by his signature, except under conditions of evident and durable advantage to himself. He was on the watch for the smallest changes so as to adjust his plans to them, but in the course of his reveries he had turned over so many ideas, gone into so many possible combinations, that he could hardly ever be caught napping. He merely remarked, as in 1756, "The old systems are no more, to wish to reestablish them would be like chasing a shadow."

In the details of his work he used an inexhaustible variety of methods. Anything was good enough for him so long as it succeeded: designing provocation, calculated deals, false news, deceitful cordiality, veiled menace, stubborn incomprehension, corruption, espionage, familiar waggery—every mortal thing, noisy movements of bluff included. "Penetrating minds count upon uniform behavior, that is why it is necessary to change one's game as often as possible and to disguise it; to transform oneself into Proteus, sometimes appearing lively, sometimes slow, sometimes warlike, sometimes peaceful. That is the way to make the enemy lose his bearings." This was a mistake, for he overdid it. He provided refinements of perfidy for his adversaries and allies which were quite foreign to them, he sensed treacheries which did not exist, he changed his behavior because of vague impressions, he got in a fever about nothing. He was showered with blessings by Fortune from the very start, so he thought he could take every sort of liberty with the older courts. Thus he would become uselessly haughty, patronizing, and sarcastic, he chaffed and wounded everybody and kicked up "the devil of a row" for a bagatelle. As an ally of France he wanted to get a promise of vigorous action in Germany from Louis XV and he gave Valori a memorandum which bore this significant title—"Project Which the French Should Follow If They Are Reasonable." The ministers were so afraid of his ways that they agreed with the secretary of the cabinet to stop en route such and such a provocative reply to George II and such and such an insulting letter to Louis XV.

However, he knew his faults too well not to keep an eye on his own conduct. One of the most constant features of his life was precisely the ceaseless restoration of an equilibrium between imagination and calculation. First, he was completely frank with himself: in his *Testament* of 1752 he even went so far as to write of Maria Theresa, "I have not a clear conscience in regard to this princess." Besides, like a gambler who is winning, he had a sense of risk, a "secret instinct" which told him the moment to take a risk and the moment to leave the game. "You must know when it's right to stop; forcing luck is the way to lose it, and always wanting more of it is the way never to be lucky." Finally he meditated powerfully and minutely. His system was always to consider things in writing by drawing up comparative tables: *Reasons which I might have for remaining in alliance with France, reasons which I might have for making peace with the Queen of Hungary,* or else, *items which give rise to just apprehensions the king should have at the pernicious designs of the Queen of Hungary and of the King of England; items which should reassure the king upon the designs of the Queen of Hungary and of the King of England.* These are not vague reasons but carefully qualified possibilities which lead up to an induced conclusion by a process of elimination.

He distrusted easy victories. "A lightning stroke, such as the conquest of Silesia, is like a book, the original of which succeeds while the imitations fall flat." He was equally suspicious of the gigantic edifices raised by visionaries. "A village on the frontier is worth more than a principality sixty leagues away." The height of wit was to see the opportunity approaching and seize it as it passed, for "policy consists rather in drawing profit from favorable events than in preparing them." The light of his mind played upon two types of plan: a long-term plan, which he called his metaphysic, concerned with acts of aggrandizement, which might not mature sooner or later, and in the second place, limited but terribly precise applications of this grasping metaphysic applied as chance directed.

When he did not see his way clearly he drew back. He evaded all conversation with ambassadors or else he refused to receive them without being informed of the subjects on which they intended to touch. One day, when England had put an embarrassing question to him, he wrote to Podewils, "I do not want to bother with that. Reply like an Austrian in polite but completely vague terms, which are neither negative nor affirmative but simply incomprehensible." Three times did the minister present a draft of the letter and three times did the king tear it up because it was too clear, until at last he grew tired of the struggle and himself drafted a twenty-line note in German, which contained a single sentence, so cut up into clauses that it was hopeless to expect to find a main verb and a subject in it. On the other hand when he took a decision nothing could stop him. In his faults, as in his failures, what always saved him was suddenness of action, daring, and promptitude which baffled the enemy. Most important was the fact that he had an obedient army which was always on the alert. "I am not rash enough to give you advice," in view of the uncertainty of events, he wrote to instruct his successor, "I am content to repeat what I have told you in greater detail—control your finances wisely so as to have money when you need it; only make alliances with those who have precisely the same interests as your own; never make treaties to guard against far-off events, wait till the situation arises before you make up your mind and act accordingly; beware of placing confidence in the number and good faith of your allies; count only on yourself, then you will never be deceived." The preservation and extension of the power of Prussia—that was the essential task.

17

George Peabody Gooch on Frederick as Benevolent Despot, 1947

Without him there might have been no Bismarck. . . .

Among the best recent critical appraisals of Frederick is this passage by George Peabody Gooch, the eminent British historian. Objective in his approach, Gooch gave his estimate of Frederick as a benevolent despot, sometimes called enlightened autocrat or philosophic despot.[1]

Frederick the Great ranks with Cromwell and Peter the Great, Washington and Napoleon, Cavour and Bismarck, Lenin, Masaryk, and Mustapha Kemal, Mussolini and Hitler among the men of action who have been denounced as arch-destroyers by some and applauded as master-builders by others. Since all of them were housebreakers as well as architects, it depends on our nationality and ideology which aspect we stress. What is not in dispute is the significance of their work, the depth of the furrows as they plowed their way toward their goal, their influence not only in the land of their birth but in neighboring countries and sometimes in more than one continent. No agreed verdict can be pronounced on any one of them, for their judges wear spectacles of various tints.

None of these makers of history has been the object of more conflicting valuations than the man who by almost superhuman efforts hoisted Prussia into the rank of the great powers and unwittingly paved the way for a united Germany under the aegis of Berlin. No foreign historian except Carlyle has found much to admire in the character of the ruler who inaugurated his reign by the rape of Silesia and thereby doomed Europe to a generation of bloody strife. Joseph de Maistre hailed him as a great Prussian but denied him the title of a

[1] G. P. Gooch, *Frederick the Great: The Ruler, the Writer, the Man* (New York: Alfred A. Knopf, Inc.; London: Longman Group, Ltd., 1947), pp. iv–v, 309–11. Reprinted by permission of Longman Group, Ltd.

great man. The part played by Germany in the staging and waging of two World Wars in our own time has increased the general distaste for the father of Prussian militarism. Yet to the majority of his countrymen Old Fritz has been an object of veneration and gratitude, not only during the sunshine of the Hohenzollern Empire, but in the chill gloom of the Weimar Republic and amid the feverish excitements of the Third Reich. Everyone knows the passage in *Dichtung und Wahrheit* in which Goethe describes his victories in the Seven Years' War as the first real inspiration of German poets, and declares that he and his young contemporaries were all "Frederick-minded." Frederick and Bismarck stand side by side in the national Valhalla, the laurels of victory on their brow, incomparable in resolution and resource; but since 1914 inaugurated a second Thirty Years' War, the sorely tried ruler has meant even more to his countrymen than the Iron Chancellor who knew only success. His grim and dynamic figure has stamped itself on the Prussian character too deeply to be ignored in any interpretation of modern Germany. Without him there might have been no Bismarck, who required a preponderant Prussia for his far-reaching aims, and without the Iron Chancellor there could hardly have been a Hitler and a Third Reich. . . .

The political treatises of Frederick the Great are the classic presentation of the doctrine of Enlightened Autocracy as practiced by the so-called Philosophic Despots. Here in all its clarity and resonance is the gospel of work, proclaimed by a man who scorned delights and lived laborious days. The ruling of a state is exhibited as the grandest and most onerous of human responsibilities. The prince must know everything and supervise everything. There is not only no nonsense about divine right, but no exaggerated dynastic pride. In his *History of the House of Brandenburg* he selects the Great Elector and his own father for special praise, but some of his other ancestors, particularly his grandfather, receive very low marks. Homage is paid not to their birth but to their work. Every ruler must justify himself by his acts. . . .

The watchword of the ruler, according to Frederick, must be *L'État c'est moi,* and he must derive inspiration, not complacency, from the thought. His supreme duty is to maintain its vitality by the maximum development of its resources, the most thrifty administration, the maintenance of justice, the increase of its armed strength; for only a virile, disciplined, and so far as possible self-sufficing community can hope to survive in a world where conflict is the law of life. He must be the model citizen, teaching these lessons not by precept but by example. Frederick's system was better than any regime in Europe except where constitutional government prevailed, and it formed a bridge between feudalism and the modern democratic state. His genuine devotion to the welfare of his subjects shines through his pages, and in the conscientious discharge of the duties of administration he towered above his contemporaries. The Frederician monarchy, small though it was, earned something of the prestige that the France of Louis XIV had possessed in the seventeenth century.

The weakness of Enlightened Absolutism, as of all dictatorships dynastic or otherwise, was that its successful operation postulated an unbroken series of supermen; but Frederick II was the first and last of that species in the Hohenzollern family. The bow of Ulysses is useless if no one can stretch it, and what is just practicable in a small state becomes impossible in a large one. He was more of an autocrat than Louis XIV, for he was Commander-in-Chief as well as head of the state and head of the government, and none of his ministers was allowed the power enjoyed by Colbert and Louvois. How rapidly the imposing edifice crumbled away when the hand of the master-builder was withdrawn was revealed on the stricken field of Jena twenty years after his death. . . . That too much depended on the ruler and that the people might be a partner, even a junior partner, were hidden from his gaze, for he lacked the faith in human nature that enables nations to grow in stature. On one occasion in the last year of his life he spoke of the canaille. "Those who welcomed you yesterday on entering Breslau were not canaille," objected Garve. "Put an old monkey on horseback and drive him through the streets," retorted the king, "and they will come crowding to see it in the same way." He had distant glimpses of the *Rechtsstaat,* but he suggests no means of creating it if it does not exist or of preserving it if it does. Rulers come and go, and even a well-meaning monarch may degenerate. Autocracy and the rule of law are incompatible. Everything depends on the prince, and if he fails there is nothing to be done. "If ever a foolish prince ascends this throne," declared Mirabeau, "we shall see the formidable giant suddenly collapse and Prussia will fall like Sweden." Frederick thought as meanly of most rulers as of their subjects and he sensed the fragility of his edifice, yet he refused to draw the necessary conclusions. The supreme exponent of the theory and practice of benevolent despotism was essentially uncreative. The machine state, in outward appearance so strong, proved in unworthy hands as brittle as glass.

18

D. B. Horn on the Transfiguration of Frederick, 1964

From "enlightened Prussian king . . . into the 'patron saint of Germany.'"

D. B. Horn, late Professor of Modern History in the University of Edinburgh, described the creation of a Frederician myth in the following passage.[1] *At the same time Professor Horn gave an excellent account of the attitudes of historians who have been fascinated by the life and deeds of the great monarch.*

The myth of Frederick the Great has become more important than the reality. It is therefore worthwhile to trace briefly the transformation of the hard-headed, if enlightened, Prussian king, who was disliked in his own lifetime by such varied German authors as Wieland, Winckelmann and Lessing into the "patron saint of Germany," in Lord Rosebery's phrase. Goethe's attitude towards Frederick varied, though in connection with the Seven Years' War he wrote of the King of Prussia as "he who stands firm while all around him falter." * A few years after Frederick's death, Schiller refused to undertake what he called the tremendous task of idealizing him.

The German Romantic writers, in their violent reaction against the eighteenth century, criticized the Frederician state because it was not hallowed by the presence of any higher ideals. Arndt denounced Frederick as un-German, if not anti-German, particularly since he entirely lacked the primitive faith and deep mysticism which he and the other Romantics believed to have been characteristic of medieval Germans. Curiously enough, it was the royal disciple of the Romantics, Frederick William IV, who, aided by Ranke and Droysen, transformed

[1] D. B. Horn, *Frederick the Great and the Rise of Prussia* (London: English Universities Press, 1964), pp. 161–68. Reprinted by permission of the English Universities Press, Ltd.

* Quoted by Veit Valentin in *History,* XIX, 121.

the historical Frederick into the prophet of *Kleindeutsche* nationalism. Frederick's lifelong enmity toward Austria was represented as the first stage of a movement designed to exclude Austria altogether from Germany. His League of Princes foreshadowed the North German Confederation of 1866. Ranke and Droysen accomplished the task Schiller had refused to attempt by linking their interpretations of his character and policy with the political controversies of their own day. At the same time they, unlike previous writers on Frederick, made it their business to study and criticize the primary sources for his life and work which were now becoming available.

Ranke thought of him as the exponent of the balance of power who had brought to its highest point the European state system. Droysen saw him in isolation from Europe as the standard-bearer of Prussian ideals and argued that his achievements gave Prussia a legal as well as a moral claim to make a national German state in her own image. While he was too good a historian to think of Frederick as a German nationalist, he argued that Frederick's work had in fact prepared for and contributed to current conceptions of Germany as a national state. In his view there was a clear line of development from Frederick to Bismarck and from the seizure of Silesia to the Hall of Mirrors at Versailles. Austria's interests were non-, if not anti-German. Those of Prussia accorded with those of Germany as had been proved while Droysen was writing his *History of Prussian Policy* by the establishment of the Hohenzollern *Reich* in 1871.

One of Droysen's pupils was Koser whose biography of Frederick is still the standard life. Koser appreciates his hero's achievements in the belief that they contributed to the Second *Reich* which gave the biographer as he wrote feelings of personal satisfaction and national pride. "A great king who was also a great man" summed up his view of Frederick. He did not hesitate to invoke the actual political set-up in Germany as a justification for some of the shabbier deeds which Frederick had done more than a century before.

Carlyle in his labored defence and, even more so, Macaulay in his swashbuckling attack upon Frederick, were both, like their German contemporaries, more interested in the Frederick myth of their own day and its political and moral implications than with the historic Frederick, while the French historians Broglie and Lavisse were largely concerned to find out what manner of man he was who had inspired the Germans to expel French influence from Central Europe and set up an empire which had overwhelmed Napoleon III and destroyed the military reputation of France at Sedan.

Within Germany, Onno Klopp's *Grossdeutsch* predilections and resentment at Austria's defeat by Prussia in 1866 led him to launch a violent attack upon Frederick. Klopp's works have been used as an armor of weapons by later critics: he himself found it wiser after his outburst to accept an appointment at Vienna. Nearly thirty years later Max Lehmann ventured another attack on Frederick, but on a much narrower front. He denounced Frederick's invasion of Saxony in 1756 as the beginning of an offensive war, but hardly dented the orthodox view that Frederick was acting in self-defense.

The collapse in 1918 of the Hohenzollern *Reich,* amid military disasters unparalleled since Jena, actually strengthened the Frederician myth and gave it even wider currency. Kaiser Wilhelm II disappeared into limbo, and there was a slump in the historical stock of Bismarck, the self-proclaimed architect of that empire. Reduced competition raised Frederick's reputation, as was shown by the extraordinary scenes at Berlin in 1920 during the shooting of a film which gave in a new mass medium a biography of the greatest of Prussia's rulers. Serious historical works, polemical studies and impressionistic journalism helped to keep his memory green.

Between the wars the most influential historians of Frederick were Frederick Meinecke and Gerhard Ritter. Meinecke thought the key to an understanding of Frederick lay in the dichotomy between the enlightened ideas which molded his character and intellect and the idea of political necessity which guided his acts. Ritter on the other hand was mainly concerned to make clear what Frederick had actually achieved in the historical circumstances of his own time, and how these achievements had affected history. After the downfall of the Third *Reich,* he asserted that he had also delicately implied a comparison between Frederick and Hitler. Whereas Frederick had limited objectives in foreign policy, Hitler's ambitions were limitless. While the Frederician state had been based on religious toleration and voluntary limitation of state activity to external things, Hitler had avowed his determination to mold the German people by force and propaganda into conformity with the Nazi ideal. While as a front-line soldier in the First World War Ritter had felt that Frederick was fighting by his side, he quoted against the Nazi conception of the state Kant's saying that the state is concerned with law and not at all with morals. Fortunately for himself the comparison was so delicately drawn that it escaped notice at the time and was only made explicit after the Second World War in a new edition of Ritter's biography.

Hitler himself had no doubts about the legitimacy and paternity of the Third *Reich,* which was proclaimed in the garrison church at Potsdam in the vault where lay the coffins of Frederick the Great and his father Frederick William I. Immediately after President Hindenburg had proclaimed the new empire, Chancellor Hitler placed a crown of laurel leaves, worked in gold, on Frederick's coffin. Though Frederick had been dead for a century and a half, political miracles were still being worked at his shrine.

While Hindenburg's political role in post-war Germany was largely based on the idea that he personified Hohenzollern traditions and Hitler's success was at least partly due to his misrepresentation of his regime as the lineal and legitimate successor of Hohenzollern absolutism, they had no monopoly in appealing to Frederick the Great. In 1936, while still in the service of Hitler's government, Carl Goerdeler prepared a state paper in which he claimed that "salvation for Germany and for the world could be obtained only by self-control, by pursuing modest goals, and by practicing strict economy after the manner of Frederick the Great." * The rejection of such ideas by both Hitler and Goering on the ground that they would mean postponement if not reduction of their plans for rearmament cost Goerdeler their confidence and ultimately led to his becoming the acknowledged leader of underground resistance.

Hitler's defeat convinced German historians that at some point or other Germany must have taken the wrong turning. When something has failed, or even seems for a time to have failed, historians are never at a loss to explain why it failed. In the vigorous debate which is still going on in Germany various turning points have been suggested at which Prussia may be said to have deviated with disastrous results from her old ideals and traditions. Although Dehio has suggested that his countrymen might place their memories of Frederick the Great and Bismarck in a display cabinet, as they do the costly silver which they no longer use on their dinner tables, few German historians seem to have looked as far back as the reign of Frederick the Great for this turning point.

There is still a tendency to identify Frederick as the supreme representative of genuine Prussian ideals and to judge later regimes by his basic ideas on state and society. This is to deny or at least ignore that the essence of the Prussian system of government, as developed by Frederick the Great, was the refusal to give the chance of a political education to the middle and lower classes. Frederick's success tended to perpetuate and fossilize an administrative and social system which steadily lost touch with the political realities of nineteenth- and twentieth-century Europe. Yet this system contrived to extend its influence over the rest of Germany, to draw Germany away from contact with west European liberalism and to make her the associate and bulwark of the east European despotic empires ruled by the Habsburgs and the Romanovs. Lack of political experience contributed to the failure of German liberalism in 1848 and left the way clear for Bismarck who, alike in his denial of political education to the mass of the German people and his uncompromising opposition to responsible government, was Frederick's true, and fatal, heir.

Even after the collapse of the Hohenzollern *Reich* and the emer-

* G. Ritter, *The German Resistance*, trans. R. T. Clark (London, 1958), p. 34.

gence of the Weimar Republic, Hitler, though not himself a Prussian, thought it worth-while to invoke the historical myth of Frederick the Great and to represent or rather misrepresent himself as the standard-bearer of Prussian traditions. Once again, as at Frankfurt in 1848, Germany failed to achieve representative and responsible government with the same fatal consequences for herself and for Europe.

Afterword: Dazzling Success or Tainted National Hero?

Historians are divided in their estimates of Frederick II, but all admit that he was an unusual ruler, outstanding in his time. Certainly Frederick made an indelible mark on the eighteenth century. Scholars agree that—judged on the basis of his accomplishments on the battlefield—he was one of the great military leaders, not only of his century but of the entire course of history.

There are some dissenting opinions, but most historians feel that Frederick was an effective administrator. He regulated every conceivable administrative matter in the most minute detail. He filled public offices with faithful servants inspired by his dictum that idleness was akin to death. He is given credit for extending the work of the Academy of Sciences, for promoting elementary education in his realm, for remodeling the judicial system, and for granting toleration to both Catholics and Protestants. Little wonder that some of his contemporaries regarded him as a kind of demigod! But during the late days of his reign, the masses were annoyed by the pressure of Frederick's tax system, and many felt relief at his passing.

Estimates of Frederick's personality and character depend on the attitude of the individual: some are impressed, others committed to denunciation. As time went by, a Frederician myth was fashioned—the ruler was elevated to the plane of a national hero, occupying a place in German tradition alongside Charlemagne and Luther. Germans began to see Frederick's reign as marking a giant step in the development of Brandenburg-Prussia from a weak electorate into a great military power. There is justice in this point of view, as witness these figures showing the extraordinary progress of the state from the end of the Thirty Years' War to the death of Frederick:

	1648	*1740*	*1786*
Population	750,000	2,500,000	5,000,000
Army	8,000	83,000	200,000

Annual revenue, in *thalers*	?	7,000,000	19,000,000
Stored treasure, in *thalers*	0	8,000,000	51,000,000

But Prussia, Sidney B. Fay reminds us, still remained a despotic state, such as was characteristic of the eighteenth century. Unfortunately, Frederick's genius as an enlightened despot was not a quality to be transmitted to his successors.

Indeed, Frederick made Prussia the one important rival of Austria in the Germanies, and virtually forced his nation into the ranks of the Great Powers. He made Prussia great, although in the process he further assured German disunity. "By his cult of military force and by his own example of military success," said Koppel S. Pinson, "he implanted in Prussia, and through Prussia in Germany, that inordinate reliance on military strength which both the Germany of Bismarck and the Germany of Hitler were to follow. He became the supreme example of the amoral national hero who hovered over and above the everyday concepts of good and evil." *

Most historians believe that Bismarck, the Blood-and-Iron Chancellor, building on the framework forged by Frederick, similarly showed little concern for the democratic will of the masses. Both Frederick and Bismarck were *Realpolitiker* dedicated to the preservation of the Hohenzollern dynasty and opposed to any democratic tendencies that might have weakened that dynastic power structure. During his retirement, Bismarck was said to have had some qualms about his career-long refusal to listen to the voice of the people. The aged Frederick had no such idea: he went to his grave convinced that he was the ideal authoritarian patron for his fortunate people. He was certain that he knew what was good for them, and he expected them to do his bidding as a matter of self-interest. Little did he know that the way of life he set for Prussia (and eventually for Germany) would have tragic consequences for both Germany and the world.

Some current writers on Frederick attribute his "failures" to his inability to transcend a monarchical principle served by loyal but subordinate bureaucrats and by a servile people without political acumen. When Frederick died, they say, his Prussia had become an anachronism with its people politically far behind those of other, better-governed European states. Despite his flurry of activity, Frederick, in the view of such critics, really did not introduce innovations in administration and economic life which would have enabled Prussia to keep pace with her rivals.

* Koppel S. Pinson, *Modern Germany: Its History and Civilization* (New York, 1954), p. 6.

Whether Frederick was a success or failure depends upon the convictions of the observer. But all sides must admit that the central focus of his life was the problem of the use of power. In this respect Frederick had a dual approach. He rejected Machiavellianism in internal affairs, but he continued to use it for all it was worth in foreign policy. He thus drew a fine line between internal and external matters. Historians today continue to be fascinated by this careful distinction.

Whatever the judgment, it is clear that Frederick was one of the great men of history.

Bibliographical Note

GENERAL

There is a vast literature on Frederick. The most important source for his biography is to be found in his own works, which, according to German historian Leopold von Ranke, "form an imperishable monument of his life and opinion." A collected edition of his complete works, *Oeuvres de Frédérick le Grand,* edited by Johann D. E. Preuss and others, appeared in Berlin, 1846–1857. Of these thirty volumes, twelve include his correspondence, seven are historical, six are devoted to Frederick's verse, three present military pieces, and two are made up of philosophical writings. There is an edition of Frederick's three major historical works, edited by E. Boutaric and E. Campardon in two volumes (Paris, 1866), in which are recorded the developments of his reign to 1778. Frederick's political and diplomatic correspondence, *Politische Correspondenz Friedrichs des Grossen,* edited by Gustav Droysen and others, appeared in forty-six volumes in Berlin, 1879–1939. This valuable official edition stimulated the study of Frederick's life and reign.

From 1890 to 1913, the historical section of the Great General Staff published in Berlin *Die Kriege Friedrichs des Grossen,* 3 parts in 18 volumes [Part 1, *Der erste schlesische Krieg, 1740–1742,* 3 vols.; Part 2, *Der zweite schlesische Krieg, 1744–1745,* 3 vols.; Part 3, *Der siebenjährige Krieg,* 12 vols. Detailed and thorough, this is an excellent example of first-rate military history.

BIOGRAPHIES IN ENGLISH

The most celebrated biography of Frederick in English is that by Thomas Carlyle, *History of Friedrich II of Prussia, called Frederick the Great,* 6 vols. (London, 1858–1865) and many editions thereafter (abridged edition in one volume, New York, 1916). Thomas Babington Macaulay painted a critical portrait of Frederick in his *Critical and Historical Essays* in many editions, including the edition (London, 1842) used for this book.

Among the many other biographies in English are Duc de Broglie, *Frederick the Great and Maria Theresa* (London, 1883); Pierre Gaxotte, *Frederick the Great,* trans. from the French by R. A. Bell (London, 1941, and New Haven, 1942); George P. Gooch, *Frederick the Great: The Ruler, the Writer, the Man* (London and New York, 1947); B. H. Lidell Hart, *Great Captains Unveiled* (London, 1927); William F. Reddaway, *Frederick the Great and the Rise of Prussia* (London, 1904, 10th impression, 1948); Edith Simon, *The Making of Frederick the Great* (Boston, 1963); Louis L. Snyder and Ida Mae Brown, *Frederick the Great: Prussian Warrior and Statesman,* in *The Immortals of History* series (New York, 1968); Harold W. V. Temperley, *Frederick the Great and Kaiser Joseph* (London, 1915); and Veit Valentin, "Some Interpretations of Frederick the Great," *History* (September, 1934).

BIOGRAPHIES IN GERMAN

The most important biography in German is Reinhold Koser's *Geschichte Friedrichs des Grossen,* 4 vols., originally published in 1912 to 1914 (latest ed. Berlin, 1921). An excellent political biography, sympathetic to Frederick, its value is enhanced by attention to a bibliography to the date of publication. More than a biography, Koser's work gives equal or more attention to the history of Prussia during Frederick's life. Johann D. E. Preuss, *Friedrich der Grosse, eine Lebensgeschichte,* 10 vols. (Berlin, 1832–1834), is especially valuable for its large number of original documents.

Other biographies in German include Arnold Berney, *Friedrich der Grosse, Entwicklungsgeschichte eines Staatsmannes* (1934); Hilmar Curas, *Anekdoten und Karakterzüge aus dem Leben Friedrichs des Zweiten* (Berlin, 1887); Erwin Dette, *Friedrich der Grosse und sein Heer* (Göttingen, 1914); Walther Elze, *Friedrich der Grosse: Geistige Welt, Schicksal, Taten* (Berlin, 1936); Werner Hegemann, *Fridericus* (Berlin, 1924); Franz Kugler *Geschichte Friedrichs des Grossen* (Leipzig, 1840, trans. London, 1844); D. Nikolai, *Anekdoten von König Friedrich II* (Berlin, 1789); Ernst Siegfried Mittler und Sohn, *Miscellaneen zur Geschichte Königs Friedrich des Grossen* (Berlin, 1878); Gerhard Ritter, *Friedrich der Grosse: ein historisches Profil* (Leipzig, 1936; 3rd ed. Heidelberg, 1954); G. B. Voltz, *Aus der Welt Friedrichs des Grossen* (Dresden, 1922); and W. Wiegand, *Friedrich der Grosse* (Leipzig, 1922).

BIOGRAPHIES IN FRENCH

As early as 1788 Mirabeau published his *De la monarchie prussienne sous Frédéric le Grand,* which spoke admiringly of the Prussian monarch but criticized his economic policies.

Other biographies of Frederick in French include E. H. Bourdeau, *Le Grand Frédéric* (Paris, 1900–1902); L. Paul-Dubois, *Frédéric le Grand d'après sa correspondance politique* (Paris, 1902); Ernst Lavisse, *La jeunesse du Grand Frédéric* (Paris, 1891); and Léonce Rousset, *Les maîtres de la guerre: Frédéric II, Napoléon, Moltke* (Paris, 1899).

MISCELLANEOUS

Among the overwhelming literature on every conceivable phase of Frederick's career as warrior, diplomat, and statesman, the following represents a cross section of the more important works: Walther Mediger, *Moskaus Weg nach Europa: der Aufstieg Russlands zum europäischen Machtstaat im Zeitalter Friedrichs des Grossen* (Brunswick, 1952); Gordon A.

Craig, *The Politics of the Prussian Army, 1640–1945* (Oxford, 1955); W. L. Dorn, *Competition for Empire* (New York, 1940); Chester V. Easum, *Prince Henry of Prussia, Brother of Frederick the Great* (Madison, Wisconsin, 1942); W. O. Henderson, *Studies in the Economic Policy of Frederick the Great* (Frank Cass and Co., Ltd., 1963); Otto Hinze, *Die Hohenzollern und ihr Werk* (2nd ed. Berlin, 1915); Herbert R. Kaplan, *The First Partition of Poland* (New York, 1962); Wladyslaw Konopczyński, *Fryderyk Wielki a Polska [Frederick the Great and Poland]* (Posnań, 1947); Richard Lodge, *Great Britain and Prussia in the Eighteenth Century* (Oxford, 1923); Burkhard Meier, *Potsdam* (Berlin, 1937); T. R. Phillips, trans., *Frederick the Great's Instructions for His Generals* (Harrisburg, Pa., 1944); Hans Rosenberg, *Bureaucracy, Aristocracy and Autocracy, The Prussian Experience, 1660–1815* (Cambridge, Mass., 1958); Stephen Skalweit, *Frankreich und Friedrich der Grosse* (Bonn, 1952); and G. B. Voltz, *Friedrich der Grosse und der Bayrische Erbfolgskrieg* (Berlin, 1932).

Index

A

Alembert, Jean Le Rond d', 57, 97–99
Algarotti, Conte Francesco, 71, 104, 111, 115
Alzire (Voltaire), 44
Amelia (sister of Frederick the Great), 71
Anna Ivanova (of Russia), 59, 62
Annual Register, 146–50
Anspach, Margrave of, 71, 82
Anspach, Margravine of, 69, 70
Anti-Machiavel (Frederick the Great), 8
Argens, Marquis Jean Baptiste d', 54, 100, 104, 123
Arnold, Miller, 125–28
Augustus William, Prince of Prussia (brother of Frederick the Great), 92–94
Austria, 2, 3–4, 8, 17–21, 22, 32–33, 45–48, 48–51, 53–54, 59–62, 89–91, 92, 94, 159, 169

B

La Barberina, 88–89, 135
Bavaria, 3, 21–22, 48, 90
Bismarck, 171
Bohemia, 13, 15, 45, 48, 49, 59, 62, 91, 159
Brandenburg, 1, 2, 20, 59, 89, 122
Britain, see England
Brunswick, Duchess of (sister of Frederick the Great), 57–58, 70, 106
Brunswick, Prince of, 71

C

Candide (Voltaire), 52
Carlyle, Thomas, 51, 63, 79, 155–57, 158, 165, 169
Catherine II (of Russia), 9
Catt, Henri de, 20–21, 92–96, 96–99, 129–31
César (Voltaire), 44
Charles, Prince of Lorraine, 90–91, 100
Charles VI (Holy Roman Emperor), 59, 60, 61
Charles VII (Holy Roman Emperor), 89
Chatelet, Madame Gabrielle Emilie du, 112–14
Chotusitz, battle of, 8
Cocceji, Samuel von, 29, 88–89
Conrad of Hohenzollern, 1
Convention of Westminster, 8
Conway, Field Marshal Henry Seymour, 105–6
Corneille, Pierre, 44
Cosel, battle of, 14
Cossacks, 21
Cumberland, Duke of, 49
Czaslau, battle of, 12

D

De la littérature allemande (Frederick the Great), 67
Dickins, 101–2
Doctor Akakia (Voltaire), 116–20
Dutch Republic, see Holland

E

Elizabeth (of Russia), 4, 9
Elizabeth Christina of Brunswick-Bevern (wife of Frederick the Great), 8
England, 3, 8, 24, 46, 49–50, 53, 62, 78, 90–91, 101–2, 162, 163, 164
Essay on the Forms of Government and on the Duties of Sovereigns (Frederick the Great), 23
Eugene, Prince, 14, 84

F

Ferdinand, Prince (brother of Frederick the Great), 69, 71, 92
Ferdinand, Prince of Brunswick, 72
Finckenstein, Lieutenant-General Finck von, 75, 128
First Partition of Poland, 9
First Silesian War, 8
First Treaty of Versailles, 8
Fontenoy, battle of, 8

France, 3–4, 8, 9, 12, 17–18, 24, 46, 48–51, 84, 101, 162, 163
Francis, Prince of Brunswick, 95
Frankfurt, 34–35
Frederick Barbarossa, 1
Frederick of Brandenburg-Kulmbach (Margrave of Bayreuth), 81–82
Frederick, Prince of Brunswick, 71
Frederick II (the Great):
as administrator, 4–5, 23–40, 125–28, 146–47, 152–54, 173
attitude toward German culture, 6, 63–65, 67–68, 96–100, 102–3, 149–50, 159
death of, 5, 9, 148
early life of, 2, 41–42, 74–83, 151
illnesses of, 5, 57–58, 111, 129–45, 148, 161
last will of, 69–73
as letter writer, 41–58
marriage of, 8, 84, 132–34
as military leader, 17–22, 30, 32–34, 37–38, 145–46, 173
military tactics of, 3, 4, 11–17, 48–51
observed by contemporaries, 84–108
philosophy of government of, 5, 6, 23–28, 144, 159–60, 166–67, 174
religious beliefs of, 6, 38, 154
in retrospect, 6–7, 146–75
and Voltaire, 5, 6, 42–45, 55–57, 65–67, 109–24
Frederick III (of Prussia), 2
Frederick William (the Great Elector), 1–2, 17
Frederick William, Margrave of Schwedt, 81
Frederick William I (father of Frederick the Great), 2, 8, 29, 41–42, 74–83, 86–87, 96, 170
Frederick William II (of Prussia), 69, 70
Frederick William IV (of Prussia), 168
Freytag, Herr, 121–22

G

Gaxotte, Pierre, 161–64
Gellert, Professor, 63–65
George II (of England), 101, 163
Germany, 1, 22, 24, 36
influence of Prussia on, 1, 2, 6–7, 159–60, 165–66, 170–72, 174
Goerdeler, Carl, 171
Goethe, 166, 168
Gooch, George Peabody, 165–67
Grossjägerndorf, battle of, 49
Grumbkow, Field Marshal von, 81–83

H

Habsburgs, 1, 3, 59, 159, 171
Hanover, 46, 48, 57, 58, 101–2, 132, 137, 138
Henriade (Voltaire), 44
Henry, Prince of Bayreuth, 82–83
Henry, Prince of Prussia (brother of Frederick the Great), 69, 71, 92, 144
Henry, Prince of Schwedt, 133
Hertford, Marquis of, 105
Heuking, Colonel, 126–27
Hindenburg, Paul von, 170–71
History of My Times (Frederick the Great), 46–47, 61–62
History of the House of Brandenburg (Frederick the Great), 166
History of the War (Frederick the Great), 158
Hitler, Adolph, 170–72
Hochkirch, battle of, 94–96
Hohenfriedberg, battle of, 8, 12, 13, 89–91
Hohenstaufens, 1
Hohenzollerns, 1, 2, 6, 48, 159, 166, 167, 169, 170, 171
Holland, 62, 90, 119, 129
Holy Roman Empire, 2, 89
Horn, D. B., 168–72
Horst, Baron, 134–35
Hubertusburg, 33–34
Hungary, 62, 163

I

Ireni (Voltaire), 66
Ivan, Grand Duke of Russia, 62

J

Jandun, Jacques Egi du Duhan de, 75–76
Joseph II (of Austria), 9, 22, 140
Joseph Frederick William, Duke of Hildburghausen, 17

K

Karl, Prince of Lorraine, 18
Katte, Lieutenant Hans Hermann von, 8, 36, 77–81
Keith, Karl von, 77, 95
Keller, Major-General Baron von, 38
Kesseldorf, battle of, 12
Klopp, Onno, 169–70
Koenig, 115, 116
Kolin, 49
battle of, 13

Koser, Reinhold, 158, 169
Kunersdorf, battle of, 3, 9, 20–21
Küstrin, 8, 79–82, 126, 128

L

Landshut, battle of, 54
League of German Princes, 9, 169
Leczinski, Stanislaus, 53
Lehmann, Max, 170
Leopold I (Holy Roman Emperor), 2
Lepel, General, 80
Lessing, Gotthold Ephraim, 168
Leuthen, battle of, 3, 4, 9, 17, 18–19
Liegnitz (Pfaffendorf), battle of, 9, 54
Louis XIV (of France), 1, 100, 167
Louis XV (of France), 45–48, 51, 163

M

Macaulay, Thomas Babington, 151–54, 169
Maistre, Joseph de, 165–66
Maria Theresa (of Austria), 3, 8, 46, 59, 62, 89–90, 151, 163
Maximilian Joseph (Holy Roman Emperor), 22, 89
Maupertuis, Pierre Louis Moreau de, 100, 104, 111, 114–21
Meinecke, Frederick, 170
Mirabeau, Count Honoré Gabriel de, 144–45, 156, 167
Mollwitz, battle of, 8, 12
Moore, Dr., 107–8, 156

N

Noltenius, 75–76
North German Confederation, 169

O

Olmütz, siege of, 19–20
Orange, Princess of (niece of Frederick the Great), 71, 115, 116

P

Palatinate, 17
Palladion (Frederick the Great), 135
Peace of Aix-la-Chapelle, 3, 8
Peace of Hubertusburg, 4, 9
Peter III (of Russia), 4, 9
Philippine, Princess of Schwedt (niece of Frederick the Great), 71
Philippsburg, 84–85
Pizner, Father Francis, 38–39
Poland, 2, 6, 9, 21, 24, 33–34, 37, 53–54, 59, 159, 162
Political Testament (Frederick the Great), 23, 162, 163
Pomerania, 49, 50
Potsdam, 5, 24, 55, 74, 77, 78, 96, 97, 100, 101–8, 110, 112, 113, 120, 124, 132, 135, 138, 139–40, 145, 155, 170
Praeceptor Germaniae, 6
Pragmatic Sanction, 62, 151
Prague, 48
  siege of, 13, 48, 49
Prussia, 1–4, 8–9, 17–22, 23, 32–33, 45–51, 53, 59–62, 89–91, 96, 101, 120, 128, 146, 159, 165, 167, 173–74

R

Rambonet, Privy-Counsellor, 111–12
Ranke, Leopold von, 168–69
Raucouz, battle of, 13
Reddaway, W. F., 158–60
Rheinsberg, 8, 61, 134, 144, 145, 154
Ritter, Gerhard, 170
Rossbach, battle of, 3, 4, 9, 17–18, 133
Rousseau, Jean-Jacques, 96, 99
Royal Academy of Berlin, 96, 99, 114, 115, 119, 150, 173
Russia, 3–4, 9, 20–21, 32–33, 47, 49, 53–54, 62, 162

S

Saldern, General, 33–34
Saltykov, Count Peter Semyonovich, 20
Sans Souci, 8, 70, 71, 101, 106, 115, 120, 137, 138, 140, 155
Saxony, 3–4, 8, 13, 17, 20, 22, 33–34, 46–48, 50, 62, 90–91, 162, 170
Schiller, Johann Christoph Friedrich von, 168–69
Second Silesian War, 8, 45
Second Treaty of Versailles, 9, 48
Selle, Professor, 140, 143
Senef, battle of, 13
Seven Years' War, 3–4, 8, 9, 17, 20, 32, 48–51, 53, 92, 129, 132, 135, 158, 166, 168
Silesia, 3–4, 6, 8–9, 13, 19, 31, 32–33, 46, 50, 59–62, 90–91, 94, 112, 152, 163, 165, 169
Soor, battle of, 8, 12, 45
Soubise, Prince Rohan de, 17
Spain, 3, 24, 46
Sweden, 3–4, 49–50, 167
  queen of, 69, 71

T

Thiebault, Dieudonné, 96–99
Third Silesian War, see Seven Years' War
Thirty Years' War, 3, 173
Torgau, battle of, 9
Treaty of Dresden, 8, 46
Treaty of Hubertusburg, see Peace of Hubertusburg
Treaty of Teschen, 22
Turkey, 24

U

Union of Frankfurt, 8
Union of Warsaw, 8, 90

V

Voltaire, 6, 23, 65–67, 100, 104, 132, 134, 135
  correspondence with Frederick the Great, 5, 42–45, 51–53, 55–57
  at Frederick's court, 8, 109–24

W

War of the Austrian Succession, 3, 8, 48
War of the Bavarian Succession, 21–22
War of the Polish Succession, 84
War of the Spanish Succession, 2, 101
Weissenfels, Duke of, 81, 90–91
Welfs, 48
West Prussia, 2
Wettins, 48
Wieland, Christoph Martin, 168
Wilhelmina (sister of Frederick the Great), 9, 49–51, 71, 74, 76–88, 92
William, Prince of Brunswick, 71
William III (of England), 2
Winckelmann, Johann Joachim, 168
Wittelsbachs, 48
Wolff, Christian, 43
Württemberg, Prince of, 21, 71

Y

York, Duke of, 137–41

Z

Zadig (Voltaire), 52
Zedliz, Baron Joseph Christian von, 36, 128
Zimmermann, Doctor Johann Georg von, 57–58, 88–89, 125–28, 132–44, 145
Zorndorf, battle of, 9, 94

ST. MARY'S COLLEGE OF MARYLAND
ST. MARY'S CITY, MARYLAND

42394